CALGARY AQUINAS STUDIES

CALGARY AQUINAS STUDIES

EDITED BY

ANTHONY PAREL

PONTIFICAL INSTITUTE OF MEDIAEVAL STUDIES
TORONTO, 1978

ACKNOWLEDGMENT

This book has been published with the help of a grant
from the Humanities Research Council of Canada,
using funds provided by the Canada Council

CANADIAN CATALOGUING IN PUBLICATION DATA

Aquinas Septicentennial Conference, University of Calgary, 1974.
    Calgary Aquinas studies

Papers originally presented at the Aquinas Septicentennial Conference, held at the
University of Calgary in October 1974.

Bibliography: p.
Includes index.
ISBN 0-88844-407-9

1. Thomas Aquinas, Saint, 1225?-1274 — Congresses. I. Parel, Anthony, 1926-
II. Pontifical Institute of Mediaeval Studies.   III. Title.

B765.T54A218 1974   189'.4   C78-001028-0

PRINTED BY UNIVERSA, WETTEREN, BELGIUM

Contents

Rev. Avery Dulles, s.j. is a professor of theology in the School of Religious Studies at The Catholic University of America.

Dr. Dante Germino is professor of government and foreign affairs, and director of the Political and Social Thought Program at the University of Virginia at Charlottesville.

Prof. Anthony Parel is chairman of the Department of Political Science at The University of Calgary.

Dr. Anton C. Pegis is Professor Emeritus of philosophy at the University of Toronto, and Fellow of the Pontifical Institute of Mediaeval Studies.

Dr. Jaroslav Pelikan is Sterling Professor of History and Religious Studies and chairman of Medieval Studies at Yale University.

Prof. Paul E. Sigmund teaches the history of political theory in the Department of Politics at Princeton Univeristy.

Rev. Edward A. Synan is professor of philosophy, and Fellow and President of the Pontifical Institute of Mediaeval Studies.

Preface

The Studies contained in this volume were originally presented at the Aquinas Septicentennial Conference held at the University of Calgary in October, 1974. They deal with three main issues of contemporary interest on which Aquinas' views are still considered illuminating — the nature and destiny of man, the nature of his relationship to fellow men and the nature of his relationship to God. The style of philosophizing on these matters, like style in many other things, has of course changed since the time of Aquinas. In the last quarter of the twentieth century we have our own, if diverse, approaches to these issues. Yet surprisingly enough, the substance of Aquinas' thought and the spirit of his approach remain an important and, I think, an indispensable element in any serious appraisal of man's secular and religious activities.

No conscious effort is being made in these pages to be obsessively critical or dogmatically apologetic about the "common doctor." While some authors represented in this volume are ranked among the leading Thomists of our times, others are not even Thomists. Aquinas is not treated as an oracle, as a sort of court philosopher of the Curia, a task from which, happily for Thomas and for the Church, Vatican II seems to have freed even the most dedicated Thomists. Rather our effort has been to look upon Aquinas as a thinker of universal, not confessional, significance, one who cannot reasonably be ignored in any consideration of human affairs which assumes that existence has more than a purely empirical significance.

The papers follow diverse methodologies depending on the subject matter and the specialty of the authors. This is to be expected in a common inter-disciplinary venture, undertaken by social scientists and theologians. This diversity of approach, it seems to me, is especially fitting when one is dealing with a many-sided genius like Thomas Aquinas. It is also in keeping with the chief purpose of this volume, which is to assess Aquinas' contributions to our understanding of man's secular and religious existence, or, if you prefer, man's natural and supernatural destinies.

The editor wishes to acknowledge with thanks the assistance for publication received from the following donors: The Faculty of Social Sciences and the University Research Policy and Grants Committee of The University of Calgary; The Canada Council and the HRCC.

Calgary   Anthony PAREL
1st May 1976

1

Aquinas and his Age

Edward A. Synan
Pontifical Institute of Mediaeval Studies

The most probable date for the birth of Thomas Aquinas at Roccasecca is 1225 and it is certain that 1274 is the year in which he died at Fossanova. With all but mathematical precision, these dates limit his life to the second and third quarters of the thirteenth century. To the extent that the calendar calibrates a man's wayfaring through the world, to define the "age" of Aquinas poses no problems. Still, one need not be a Thomist of the strict observance to acknowledge that the mathematical is abstract and that the abstract—useful, not to say indispensable, though it may be—buys precision at the price of "putting into brackets" our untidy real world.

Needless to insist, the medieval experience as a whole, and the thirteenth century in particular, has evoked opposed responses in dialectical alternation. Romanticist glorification displaces and is displaced by contemptuous dismissal. This tiresome and futile antiphony was already beginning as the Middle Ages were ending. Humanist, reformer, Cartesian, encyclopedist, classicist, rationalist—each in turn was to find new and different reasons to denigrate the medieval fact, yet each category of critics harbored fifth columnists to weaken the common front. For some humanists respected some medievals (and this is true of no one more than of Saint Thomas),[1]

---

[1] See, for instance, John W. O'Malley, "Some Renaissance Panegyrics of Aquinas," *Renaissance Quarterly*, 27 (1974), 174-192, in which the author adds thirteen panegyrics to that of Valla, this last discussed in P. O. Kristeller, *Le Thomisme et la pensée italienne de la Renaissance* (Montréal: Institut d'Études Médiévales, Paris: J. Vrin, 1967), pp. 76-80.

sixteenth-century reformers could feel kinship with some medieval heretics, here or there could identify a "morning star" to presage their own dawn; Gilson followed up a suggestion of Lévy-Bruhl and uncovered for us the unexpectedly "medieval" sources of Descartes;[2] as men of the Enlightenment moved up the social ladder they cultivated the history, institutions, letters, and architecture of the medieval past.[3]

At one moment hailed as "the greatest of centuries,"[4] the century of Saint Thomas somehow has lost rank in our time. A renaissance has been discovered, not in the thirteenth, but in the twelfth century;[5] a respectable part of modern logic, De Morgan Laws included, has been discerned in the texts of fourteenth-century logicians.[6] Wedged, as it is seen to have been, between twelfth-century humanism and fourteenth-century achievements in logic, mathematics, and kinetics, what can be done with the age of Aquinas, presumably less elegant than the era it succeeded and less precise than the era to come?

I THE AGE

Chenu on the Two Worlds of Aquinas

Thomistic studies can never be in future what they were before the interventions of M.-D. Chenu, o.p. His intimate control of what Saint Thomas has written permits him to surprise us continuously; in 1925 he did so with an exposition of the profound meaning and value of those scholastic enigmas, the *authentica* and *magistralia*,[7] those "authorities" whose noses, as Alan of Lille remarked, can be turned in any direction because they are made of wax.[8] He has done so once more in this very year with a vision of the Thomistic man as creator of a moral cosmos in his surging back to the

---

[2] E. Gilson, *The Philosopher and Theology* (New York: Random House, 1962), p. 87.

[3] L. Gossman, *Medievalism and the Ideologies of the Enlightenment: The World and Work of LaCurne de Sainte-Palaye* (Baltimore: John Hopkins Press, 1968).

[4] J. J. Walsh, *The Thirteenth, Greatest of Centuries* (New York: Catholic Summer School Press, 1907).

[5] C. H. Haskins, *The Renaissance of the Twelfth Century* (Cambridge, Mass.: Harvard University Press, 1927).

[6] I. M. Bochénski, *A History of Formal Logic*, trans. and rev. by I. Thomas (Notre Dame, Ind.: University of Notre Dame Press, 1961), nos. 31.35 and 31.36, p. 207; see also pp. 236, 250.

[7] M.-D. Chenu, "'Authentica' et 'magistralia'. Deux lieux théologiques aux xiie-xiiie siècles," *Divus Thomas* (Piacenza), 28 (1925), 257-285.

[8] Auctoritas cereum habet nasum, id est, in diversum potest flecti sensum. Alan of Lille, *De fide catholica* 1.30; PL 210, 333 A.

One from Whom, thanks to a sovereignly free creative act, the Many, that is our world, burgeons into being.[9]

If Chenu's doctrinal interpretations are of the first quality, he has not been alone in taking the rest of us to the heart of the Thomistic matter; Gilson and Maritain, Grabmann and Pieper, Leo XIII and Bañez and Peter of Bergamo—how long the lists would become should we balance the books of seven hundred years of Christian reflection under the sign of the Common Doctor!

Where Chenu stands alone is in his perspectives on the human matrix within which Saint Thomas lived and worked and died.[10] He has seen that the Age of Aquinas was an epoch in which one world was ending and another was coming to birth. An old world, typified by the castle and its dependent manors, was visibly receding before the pressures of a new world. That new world was incarnate in turbulent cities where the townsmen, a new sociological formation, were forcing charters of liberties from their feudal overlords. This transition in the temporal order matched a transformation in the way the Church proposed her trans-temporal ideals to our earthbound society. The Church had felt most herself in the monastery, on its mountaintop or in its valley, an ecclesiastical analogue of the lord's castle; now the new mendicant orders leavened the city populations. Abbots had been appointed to rule their monasteries for life; priors of the begging friars rotated through short terms of office. In the monastery, peace and silence were held to be the indispensable conditions of contemplation, whereas the friars, no less convinced that contemplation is the end of man, sought their evangelical goals in the markets, in the shops, the universities, on the docks, aboard ships.

Begging friars met with a mixed reception in the universities and in the streets. Since the friars captured dramatically the imagination of large segments of the population, including university youth, they disrupted the vested clerical interests. "Secular" masters were not slow to produce theological demonstrations that begging friars had no right to administer sacraments, to preach, to hold university chairs, to bypass the network of bishops on the plea that they had papal approbation. Above all the friars

[9] M.-D. Chenu, "Création et histoire," in *St. Thomas Aquinas, 1274-1974: Commemorative Studies* (Toronto: Pontifical Institute of Mediaeval Studies, 1974), 2: 391-399.

[10] M.-D. Chenu, *Introduction à l'étude de saint Thomas d'Aquin*, Publications de l'Institut d'Études Médiévales, 9 (Montréal, Paris: Université de Montréal, 1950); an English version of this work has appeared under the title: *Toward Understanding Saint Thomas*, trans. and rev. by A.-M. Landry and D. Hughes (Chicago: Henry Regnery Co., 1964). Also M.-D. Chenu, *Saint Thomas d'Aquin et la théologie*, Maîtres spirituels (Paris: Éditions du Seuil, 1959).

4   E. A. SYNAN

tended to break the solid front of university professors when, for good
reasons, the latter had gone on strike. Mendicants, in fact, offered useful
referents for the horrors of the Last Times as these had been foreseen by
Abbot Joachim; the *Perils of these Last Times*[11] were the consequence of
giving beggars status in Church and School.

European men had for centuries hardly adverted to what lay beyond the
frontiers of the old empire, but now successive waves of fugitives from the
fierce cavalry of the Tartars pressed into Christendom and after the hunted
came the hunters. Pope and khan exchanged letters, but no correspondents
could have understood each other less. Pope Innocent iv invited the khan to
conversion and to peace; Guyuk Khan summoned the pope to vassalage:
"...That I might find a good entry into baptism ... this prayer of yours I
have not understood," wrote the khan; "You, at the head of all the princes," he added, "come at once to serve and to wait upon us. ... If you do
otherwise, God knows what I know."[12]

Before Marco Polo the friars, Franciscans and Dominicans, travelled as
far as China under papal warrant and returned to persuade Europeans that
they held but a corner of the inhabited world. Thus has Chenu juxtaposed
the two worlds that this age presented to the young Aquinas. Aquinas lived
in a variegated religious world as well. A believer of the Latin Church, he
thought and prayed and taught in the presence, direct or indirect, of the
Oriental Church, of Judaism, of Islam. To those must be added pagan
Greek thought to which his contemporaries were adopting ambivalent attitudes.

Latin Christendom

Despite a turbulence inseparable from life, Latin Christians were achieving a sense of security in more directions than one. When the thirteenth
century opened, Latin learning was felt by the Latins themselves to be inferior to Graeco-Arab erudition. By mid-century a massive effort in trans-
lating non-Christian texts in order to learn from them permitted Latin doctors to sit in judgment on their teachers, not only in the name of Christian
faith, but on the philosophical and scientific planes as well. William of
Auvergne, a Parisian professor of theology who became the bishop of Paris,

---

[11] William of Saint-Amour, *Opera omnia ... de periculis novissimorum temporum agitur*,
ed. Valérie de Flavigny (Constance: Alitophilos, 1632); the title evokes 2 Tim. 3:1, "Hoc
autem scito, quod in novissimis diebus instabunt tempora periculosa...."
[12] See J. A. Brundage, *The Crusades. A Documentary Survey* (Milwaukee: Marquette
University Press, 1962), pp. 259, 260.

could exhort his students to acquaint themselves with Averröes if they
aspired to be philosophers:

> You ought to be circumspect in debating with men who want to be con-
> sidered philosophers, even though they have not so much as learned the
> rudiments of philosophy. As for the rudiments of philosophy, without a doubt
> there is involved both the notion of matter and the notion of form. Since the
> notion of the material has been laid down by Averröes, most noble of philo-
> sophers, it would be a good thing if men of this stripe, who have the presump-
> tion to speak on philosophical issues so inconsiderately, would first learn with
> certitude and clarity his intentions and those of other men who are to be
> followed and imitated as leaders in philosophy.[13]

Yet as bishop, the same man would twice convoke the university in order to
excoriate professors who failed to see that the Agent Intellect of the Philosopher and the Commentator is in fact the God of the Bible, or at least one
of His angels. No less a witness than Roger Bacon, o.f.m. assures us that he
did so:

> The "Agent Intellect" is primarily God and secondarily the angels who
> illumine us.... I twice heard the venerable bishop of the Church of Paris, the
> Lord William of Auvergne, having convoked the university in his presence,
> scold them and debate with them, and he proved they were all in error.... The
> Lord Robert, too, bishop of Lincoln, and Brother Adam of Marsh, the greatest
> clerks in the world and perfect in their wisdom, both human and divine, estab-
> lished this same point. "What is the Agent Intellect?" some presumptuous
> Friars Minor asked Brother Adam in order to try him and to deride him; "The
> raven of Elijah," he answered, meaning to say by this that it was God, or an
> angel.[14]

---

[13] Debes autem circumspectus esse in disputando cum hominibus qui philosophi haberi
volunt et nec ipsa rudimenta philosophiae ad hoc apprehenderunt. De rudimentis enim
philosophiae est procul dubio ratio materiae et ratio formae: et cum ipsa ratio materiae
posita sit ab Averroe, philosopho nobilissimo, expediret ut intentiones ejus et aliorum, qui
tanquam duces philosophiae sequendi et imitandi sunt hujusmodi homines qui de rebus
philosophicis tam inconsiderate loqui praesumunt, apprehendissent prius ad certum et
liquidum. William of Auvergne, *Opera omnia* (Paris: A. Pralard, 1674), 1: 851 C.

[14] Intellectus agens est Deus principaliter, et secundario Angeli, qui illuminant nos....
Unde ego bis audivi venerabilem antistitem Parisiensis ecclesiae, dominum Guillielmum
Alvernensem, congregata universitate coram eo, reprobare eos, et disputare cum eis; et
probavit ... quod omnes erraverunt. Dominus vero Robertus episcopus Lincolniensis, et
frater Adam de Marisco, majores clerici de mundo, et perfecti in sapientia divina et humana,
hoc idem firmaverunt. Unde quando per tentationem et derisionem aliqui Minores prae-
sumptuosi quaesiverunt a fratre Adam, "Quid est intellectus agens?" respondit, "Corvus
Eliae"; volens per hoc dicere quod fuit Deus vel angelus. Roger Bacon, *Opera quaedam hactenus inedita*, 1: *Opus tertium*, cap. 23, ed. J. S. Brewer (London: Longman, Green,
Longman, and Roberts, 1859), pp. 74-75.

The age of Aquinas was a papal age. As the century opened, the imperial Innocent III was pope; as it closed, the even more imperial Boniface VIII had succeeded to the Chair of Peter. The confidence of the popes was such that Innocent IV did not fail to excommunicate the formidable Emperor Frederick II and a council, unjustly dominated by the same pope, if Frederick's defenders were right, deposed him. Popes continued, and more then once succeeded in, their efforts to raise crusades, not always directed toward the traditional objective of the Holy Sepulchre. As a consequence Latin bishops, who followed the armies, ruled in what had been Byzantine territory; William of Moerbeke, for instance, was archbishop of Corinth. This gave Latin Christendom a presence beyond that of the "Frankish" kings and barons who ruled their counties and kingdoms in the Territory of Warfare that bordered the Territory of Islam, this last the zone of Surrender to Allah as He was believed by Muslims to have spoken through Mohammed.

Greek Christendom

It is not easy to recapture the precise atmosphere of the division between Latin and Greek Christendom in the thirteenth century. If Latin Christians had outgrown their inferiority complex with regard to pagan Greek and Arabic erudition, the Eastern Empire still felt culturally superior to the "Franks" and not without reason. The ecclesial schism, to be sure, weighed on the Christian conscience and although the mutual excommunications of pope and patriarch in 1054 would not be taken off the books until our own day, the occasion, if not the cause, of the First Crusade in 1095 seems to have been an appeal by the Greek emperor for Latin soldiers to assist him in repelling the Seljuk Turks.[15]

Crusading, as might have been expected, was a fragile foundation for east-west friendship. From the beginning, Latin crusaders were met regularly by a kind of military police, charged by the Byzantine emperor with escorting them as quickly and as quietly as possible to the frontiers of his own territory where their disconcerting pugnacity could find victims other than the Greeks who were in theory their allies. At times the Byzantine police overpowered unruly crusaders, at times crusaders massacred the police.[16] Worst of all, in 1204 a crusading army captured and sacked Constantinople. The western knights then established a Latin empire that endured precariouly until 1261 when Byzantine government was restored; the

---

[15] Brundage, *The Crusades*, pp. 14-16; H. E. Mayer, *The Crusades*, trans. J. Gillingham (London: Oxford University Press, 1972), pp. 9ff.
[16] See Mayer, ibid., pp. 43, 47, 48-49, 138, 190, 191.

experience deepened beyond measure the enmity that divided Latin from Greek Christians.

A more promising approach to this permanent crisis in the Church marked the ecumenical councils held at Lyons in 1245 (Lyons I) and 1274 (Lyons II). The first was convoked to heal the "five wounds of the Church," one of which was the east-west schism, but attendance by bishops was minimal and its sole accomplishment was the deposition of the Emperor Frederick II. For a moment the second Council of Lyons might have seemed successful: legates of the eastern emperor, by this date one of the restored Byzantine line, subscribed to the primacy of the Roman pontiff and to the *filioque*; but by 1289 the union of the Churches was at an end.

Judaism

Judaism in the age of Saint Thomas was incarnate in the fragmented and repressed remnant that had survived the disasters of the ancient Diaspora and the two Revolts. Jewish life was circumscribed, not only by Christian statutes, but also, as Abelard had noted acutely in the twelfth century, by Torah and by rabbinic precepts. Abelard makes a Jew say:

> We are afflicted as intolerably by the yoke of the Law as by the oppression of men! ... Who would not abhor or fear, whether out of shame or pain, our sacrament of circumcision? ... What bitterness is as great as that of the boorish herbs we take as the condiment of the Paschal sacrifice? Who does not see that almost all delightful foods are forbidden to us? ... Who would not be horrified, not only to suffer, but even to inflict upon the guilty, the severe penalties of the Law—"tooth for tooth, eye for eye, life for life"? ... Everyone obeying our Law has the right to cry forth to God that line of the Psalmist: "Because of the words of Your lips, I have kept to harsh paths" (Ps. 16 (17):4).[17]

Thirteenth-century Jews lived precariously between pogroms, for persecution of them could wear an aspect of pious zeal. On this too Abelard provided a striking formulation of the Jewish plight:

> We commit our lives to our greatest enemies. ... Sleep that especially fosters and restores run-down nature, disturbs us with so great disquiet that not even when asleep do we have the right to take thought of anything but the danger that looms over our throats; only to heaven is our going secure. ... When we travel forth, we engage at no small fee a hireling guard in whom we put small

---

[17] My translation; for the Latin text, see Peter Abelard, *Dialogus inter philosophum, iudaeum et christianum*, ed. R. Thomas (Stuttgart-Bad Cannstaat: F. Frommann Verlag, 1970), pp. 51-52, ll. 295-321.

faith. The princes themselves, for whose patronage we pay dearly, desire our death exactly to the point that they can then the more freely seize whatever we possess. ... We are permitted possession of neither fields nor vines. ... The principal gain left for us is that we sustain this miserable life by making loans to those of other races, a thing that renders us particularly invidious to them.[18]

Meanwhile, the intervals of peace and toleration were grounded on motives obnoxious in principle to a People Chosen for so dolorous a destiny: they were held, by Christian speculation, to be guardians of Scriptures that they themselves failed to understand; those Scriptures were thought to announce the "conversion" of the Jews to Christianity at the end of time, a conversion that Jews could see only as apostasy.[19]

Islam

In Spain the Christian counterattack against Islam was succeeding slowly but relentlessly; Saint Thomas was born more than a decade after the Christian victory at Las Navas de Tolosa in 1212, the year, incidentally of the tragic "Children's Crusade." But in another dimension, Christians felt threatened by Islam and on their home ground. This was the ground of philosophical and theological speculation. The difficult text of Aristotle cried out for clarification and the Spanish Muslim commentator, Ibn Rushd (Averroës) earned the antonomastic title of "the Commentator." Now Averroës had held, and set out with considerable cogency, a whole series of positions that are incompatible with biblical faith. His Christian readers responded in a variety of ways: for some, both the Philosopher and his Commentator were adjudged to be impossible of assimilation by Christian thought;[20] some held that the solution was to restrict the notion and the name of "truth" to dogmas of the Creed, but to concede simultaneously that the reasoning of Averroës to conclusions that oppose the truth of faith is "necessary," that is, logically unassailable.[21] Still others claimed that on those issues the Commentator had misread the Philosopher and that his

---

[18] Ibid., p. 51, ll. 274-291.

[19] See E. A. Synan, *The Popes and the Jews in the Middle Ages* (New York: Macmillan, 1965) p. 2 and passim.

[20] Bonaventure held a nuanced version of this; see E. A. Synan, "Cardinal Virtues in the Cosmos of Saint Bonaventure," in *S. Bonaventura 1274-1974* (Grottaferrata, Rome: Collegio S. Bonaventura, 1973), 3: 27.

[21] Siger of Brabant and Boethius of Dacia have been attacked on this ground, but they are not without defenders among the historians of those events; see the judicious evaluation by A. A. Maurer, "Boethius of Dacia and the Double Truth," *Mediaeval Studies*, 17 (1955), 233-239.

purported demonstrations were in fact sophistical.[22] Condemnations by Church authorities at Paris in 1270 and 1277, at Oxford in 1277 and 1284,[23] bore on the Averroistic claim that the world is eternal, that there is a single intellect for all men, that human life ends with the experience of death, and with these were linked other teachings some few of which are theses of Saint Thomas.[24] Hence a crisis of faith among Christians who wanted to think about what they believed.

Classical Philosophy

Aristotle was present to the thirteenth century in his texts, by then available in Latin translations, but it would be a mistake to think his the only voice of pagan Greek philosophizing that was heard in the age of Aquinas. Plato was known through a handful of his dialogues but even more through indirect transmission; what the nineteenth century would name "Neoplatonism" contaminated the Aristotelian corpus with treatises that derive from Proclus and from other representatives of the later Platonism. Titles unknown to the Stagirite circulated under his name and loaned the prestige of that name to their second-hand Neoplatonism: *On Death*, *On the Apple*, and above all, *The Book of Causes* were eagerly copied and read as Aristotelian essays. A Latin version of the *Enneads* by Plotinus rejoiced in the title, *The Theology of Aristotle*. Still, it is a serious accomplishment of the Latin thirteenth-century scholars that they collected an Aristotelian corpus which lacks no major work of his that we possess today. If they did not know the *Constitution of Athens*, not every "good graduate student" (our analogue to Macaulay's erudite schoolboy) knows it now.

[22] This is the position of Aquinas for whom the "unity of intellect," for instance, is in contradiction to Christian faith—"repugnat veritati fidei Christianae"—to the principles of philosophy—"non minus contra philosophiae principia esse, quam contra fidei documenta"—but also to the teaching of Aristotle himself—"ostendemus primo positionem praedictam eius verbis et sententiae repugnare omnino"; see *Sancti Thomae Aquinatis tractatus de unitate intellectus contra Averroistas*, ed. L. W. Keeler, Textus et documenta, series philosophica, 12 (Rome: Pontificia universitas Gregoriana, 1936), pp. 2-3, ll. 18-31.

[23] See *Chartularium universitatis Parisiensis*, ed. H. Denifle, E. Chatelain (Paris: Delalain, 1889), 1: 486-487 (Paris 1270), pp. 543-558 (Paris 1277), and pp. 558-560 (Oxford 1277; the Oxford 1284 condemnation simply restated that of 1277).

[24] Instances that might be cited are numbers 81 and 96 of the 1277 Parisian condemned propositions, to the effect that immaterial beings cannot be multiplied within the same species, a position defended by Aquinas, sт 1.50.4; number 215 formulates the Thomist doctrine of sт 1.2.2 ad 3 and 1.3.4 ad 2, that we know the statement "God is" to be true, but that we cannot know Him according to His essence.

II THE MAN

Aquinas has given some readers the impression of a man who thought
and wrote in a supra-temporal dimension. A simplistic formulation of this
view asserts bluntly:

> His thought is entirely concerned with universal truth, whether natural or
> supernatural, and truth of this sort is not conditioned by time or culture.[25]

This impression, however wrongheaded, is not without causes to explain it.
First, the life of Saint Thomas was relatively placid and orderly; no shat-
tering conversion in the style of say, Augustine, interrupted his calm advance from high promise to fulfilment. Second, his disposition seems to
have been mild;[26] he was thoughtful and reflective, designed by nature for
quiet contemplation;[27] his religious ideals made him resist the most ex-
cusable irritation.[28] Third, as friar and priest he was necessarily exempted
from bearing arms, the normal destiny of his class in a bellicose century.
Precisely because he was laborious—the best authorized modern expert accepts as a possibility the claim made by the chronicler William of Tocco
that he kept a team of scribes busy as he dictated different writings simultaneously[29]—the life of Brother Thomas could be full even though it was
not marked by striking "events." Last and even more to the point, since it
is our impression rather than his truth that we must unravel, the wide
dissemination of at least a superficial acquaintance with the *Summa theologiae* is matched, outside specialist circles, by an unawareness of nearly all
his other work.

Now in the intention of its author the *Summa* was an effort to avoid the
disorder and repetition that is inseparable from the real life of every human
mind, the theological mind included:

> For we have considered that novices in this discipline have been much im-
> peded by what different people have written; partly because useless questions,

---

[25] Carol Jackson Robinson, "Dis-Honoring St. Thomas," *The Wanderer*, 23 May 1974,
in a feature story attacking a colloquium of mine on the "Innovations of Aquinas."

[26] See William of Tocco, *Hystoria* c. 38 in *Fontes vitae sancti Thomae*, edd. D. Prümmer
and H. Laurent, Supplements to *Revue thomiste* (Toulouse), 1911-1934, pp. 111-112.

[27] Tocco, ibid., c. 43 (*Fontes*, pp. 116-117).

[28] Tocco, ibid., cc. 25, 26 (*Fontes*, pp. 98-100).

[29] ...Dicter dans le même temps à plusieurs secrétaires sur des sujets distincts est propre
aux plus grands génies ... César ... Napoléon.... Il n'est pas invraisemblable qu'un saint
Thomas d'Aquin ait été doué d'une même faculté. A. Dondaine, *Les secrétaires de s.
Thomas* (Rome: Commissio Leonina, 1956), p. 18; see Tocco, *Hystoria*, c. 17 (*Fontes*, p.
89).

articles, and arguments are multiplied; partly too because those points which are necessary for this sort of student are not presented in accord with the order of the discipline, but rather in accord with what the order of books required, or according as the happenstance of debating suggested; partly because their frequent repetition generated both distaste and confusion in the minds of those who are the auditors.[30]

The *Summa theologiae* is a manual designed for beginners in the discipline and it adopts what seemed to Aquinas most useful in the Neoplatonic schema. This schematization derives the Many from the One and then traces the ascent of that Many back to the One, along with what has been termed the "'Christian' conditions" of that return.[31] Hence, the *First Part* sets out the eternal divine Unity and the eternal processions of the Persons. It then presents the temporal procession of the created Many from the One God of Genesis, along with a sophisticated analysis of the metaphysically stated constitution of angels, of men, and of their powers. Since the eternal destiny of the angels has been fixed, the two parts of the *Second Part* are devoted to the end that God has set for man, man's virtues and his vices, law and grace. The "historical" *Third Part* deals with the Redeeming Messiah, Church, and sacraments; not a single article is devoted to any event of "sacred history" after the resurrection of Jesus.

Despite a unique importance it would be fatuous to deny, the *Summa theologiae* is but one of about ninety authentic writings by the Common Doctor,[32] many of which lead us straight into the turbulence within which he maintained so admirable, but so deceptive, a calm. Behind the Master of the Sacred Page is the human person, bound by affection for which we possess an abundance of testimony to that most sinewy of social formations, the extended south Italian family. In becoming a Dominican, Brother

[30] Consideravimus namque huius doctrinae novitios in his quae a diversis conscripta sunt plurimum impediri; partim quidem propter multiplicationem inutilium quaestionum, articulorum et argumentorum; partim etiam quia quae sunt necessaria talibus ad sciendum non traduntur secundum ordinem disciplinae, sec secundum quod requirebat librorum expositio, vel secundum quod se praebebat occasio disputandi; partim quidem quia eorundem frequens repetitio et fastidium et confusionem generabat in animis auditorum. sᴛ 1, prologus.

[31] Chenu, *Toward Understanding Saint Thomas*, p. 305; Chenu's context, especially pp. 297-322, is preoccupied with the Thomistic achievement in locating the free and contingent episodes of salvation history within the heavily Neoplatonic schema of a scientific theology, a theology that meets abundantly the demands of Aristotle who, it may be remarked, thought history "less philosophical" than poetry precisely because history has the singular, contingent fact as content (Poetics 9; 1451b5-11).

[32] See "A Catalogue of St. Thomas's Works" by I. T. Eschman, an appendix to E. Gilson, *The Christian Philosophy of St. Thomas Aquinas*, trans. by L. K. Shook (New York: Random House, 1956), pp. 381-439.

Thomas renounced the roles of troubador and crusader; he could not, and
did not wish to, rupture the ties with his brothers who played those roles,
with his sister the abbess or with his sisters who married local nobles.

For Thomas Aquinas was born into the feudal world which, as Chenu
has seen, was giving way before a new world. The Aquinas family was by
no means on the lowest social plane although, to be sure, the branch to
which the saint belonged was not quite so grand as the older chroniclers
would have us believe. Landulph, the father of Saint Thomas, was not a
count but a knight[33] and his mother, Theodora, was not "sister to the
queens of Sicily and Aragon"; she was a noblewoman of Norman antecedents.[34] Chesterton was correct to say that Thomas had thrown away his
shield for, in the normal course of events, he might well have become a
knight like his brothers and his father, but the master of paradox was taken
in by amiable "saint's-life" exaggerations when he asserted that Thomas
"could have quartered half the kingdoms of Europe" on the discarded
shield.[35] As Aristotle long ago observed "we all tell a story with additions,
in the belief that we are doing our hearers a pleasure."[36]

Chenu's sure instinct led him to see the castle—in the thirteenth-century
Regnum Siciliae much more a fortress than a palace—as symbol of the
world into which Thomas Aquinas had been born, but which he would
renounce. If Bossuet was to give the impression that he was always climbing
into the king's coach, Brother Thomas was frequently to be found at a
castle, usually one held by a relative, and what is more, the saint would
come to suffer a twinge of conscience on the point. For he was born at the
family stronghold of Roccasecca[37] where the *Regnum* bordered on papal
territory; the family takes its name from the castle at Aquino (with which,
however, his branch of the clan had no direct connection).[38] His mother and
brothers could arrange for his detention at the castle of Montesangiovanni
within the papal states[39] as well as at Roccasecca[40] when there seemed still

[33] "Kal. ianuarii obiit ... Landulphus de Aquino miles..." (Fragment du nécrologe de
l'abbaye du Mont-Cassin), *Fontes, Documenta* (fasc. 6; St. Maximin: *Revue thomiste*,
1937), p. 541. This text has been dated "before 1245."
[34] A. Walz, P. Novarina, *Saint Thomas d'Aquin*, Philosophes médiévaux 5 (Louvain:
Publications universitaires, Paris: Béatrice-Nauwelaerts, 1962), p. 13.
[35] G. K. Chesterton, *St. Thomas Aquinas* (New York: Sheed and Ward, 1933), p. 43.
[36] *Poetics* 24; 1460a17.
[37] Despite overwhelming evidence, this location has been contested; see Walz and
Novarina, *Saint Thomas d'Aquin*, pp. 16-17.
[38] F. Scandone, "La vita, la famiglia e la patria dei S. Tommaso," in *S. Tommaso
d'Aquino. Miscellanea storico-artistica* (Rome: Manuzio, 1924), p. 42.
[39] Tocco, c. 8 (*Fontes*, p. 73).
[40] Calo, c. 4 (*Fontes*, p. 22).

to be hope that, though already a young Dominican, Thomas might be persuaded not to leave the ambience of castles.

One sister of Saint Thomas, Theodora, was wife of the count of Marisco, who held a castle called San Severino;[41] the saint's last journey included a visit there as well as a stop at the castle of Maenza where his niece, the Lady Frances, countess of Ceccano,[42] was his hostess. We have testimony that he had visited the castle of Maenza frequently[43] and it was there that he fell into his last illness.[44] His sister Adelesia was wife to Roger of Aquila, count of Traiecto (or Traetto, now Minturno) and Fondi; Brother Thomas acted as executor of Count Roger's will and this at the dead count's castle of Minturno.[45] Richard degli Annibaldi, cardinal of Sant'Angelo was a close friend of Aquinas and there is evidence that the saint visited the cardinal's castle of Molaria (or Molara) near Rome several times.[46] If we do not know at which castle he wrote his penultimate work (the letter on divine foreknowledge addressed to the abbot of Monte Cassino) it is all but certain that he did so either at the castle of Roccasecca, or at Aquino, or at Maenza.[47] When Brother Thomas realized that the illness into which he had fallen at Maenza might well be his last, he evidently felt a scruple:

> If the Lord should wish to visit me, it is better that I be found in a house of religious than in the houses of seculars.

For this devout reason, Thomas arranged to be carried to the monastery of Fossanova.[48]

After having been put into the Benedictine abbey of Monte Cassino to be educated by the monks when he was about five years old,[49] Thomas showed an inclination for the religious life. His family, if we can so interpret the

---

[41] Calo, c. 24 (*Fontes*, p. 43); Tocco, c. 44 (*Fontes*, p. 118); *Proc. canoniz.* no. 49 (*Fontes*, p. 330); no. 79 (*Fontes*, p. 377).

[42] Calo, c. 26 (*Fontes*, p. 47); Tocco, c. 56 (*Fontes*, p. 129).

[43] *Proc. canoniz.*, no. 15 (*Fontes*, p. 286); cf. no. 79 (*Fontes*, p. 377).

[44] *Proc. canoniz.*, no. 8 (*Fontes*, p. 276).

[45] *Proc. canoniz. Fossae Novae*, no. 26 (*Fontes*, p. 576).

[46] Calo, c. 14 (*Fontes*, p. 33); Tocco, c. 22 (*Fontes*, p. 96).

[47] A. Dondaine, "La lettre de saint Thomas à l'abbé du Mont-Cassin," in *St. Thomas Aquinas, 1274-1974: Commemorative Studies* (Toronto: Pontifical Institute of Mediaeval Studies, 1974), 1: 100.

[48] See the testimony of the Abbot of Fossanova at the canonization process, no. 8: "...dixit, ut audivi a pluribus: 'Si Dominus voluerit me visitare, melius est quod reperiar in domo religiosorum quam in domibus secularium'. Et ex tunc causa devotionis fecit se portari ad monasterium Fosse-Nove, quod distat a dicto castro per miliaria sex vel circa" (*Fontes*, p. 277).

[49] Calo, c. 3 (*Fontes*, p. 19); Tocco, cc. 4, 5 (*Fontes*, pp. 69-70); Gui, c. 3 (*Fontes*, p. 169).

"prophecies" ascribed to a local hermit before the birth of Thomas, were ready to accept the role of abbot for him:

> You and your husband will think to make him a monk in the monastery of Monte Cassino (in which the body of Saint Benedict rests) entertaining the hope that you will reach out to the great revenues of that monastery thanks to his promotion to the summit of prelacy: but God will ordain otherwise in his regard.[50]

Brother Thomas persisted stubbornly in his Dominican vocation, as the hermit had predicted; a papal dispensation that would have permitted him to rule the Benedictine abbey of Monte Cassino while wearing his Dominican habit was an offer he managed to refuse.[51] That this promising son of a family so deeply enmeshed in the feudal arrangments of their district should have opted for a mendicant vocation, was, as Chenu has pointed out, an authentic parallel to the renunciation made by Saint Francis of Assisi a generation earlier.[52] Yet even in his detachment from material ambitions Brother Thomas avoided fanatical extremes. William of Tocco has noted, as modern biographers sometimes fail to do, that when the Aquinas clan was in straitened circumstances, owing to their opposition to the Emperor Frederick II, Thomas was able to assist them from unspecified Church funds to which he somehow had access and for which he had the approbation of the pope, who must have been Innocent IV. Immediately before his account of this, Tocco mentioned offers made to Aquinas by the later pope, Clement IV:

> And therefore, as for those dignities and revenues offered to him by the pope, Clement IV[53] of happy memory, who held the aforesaid doctor very dear, why, he renounced revenues and honors together. ... Nevertheless, when that aforesaid doctor had all his noble close relatives on the run in Campania

---

[50] Et tu et vir tuus cogitabitis eum facere monachum in monasterio montis Casini, in quo corpus B. Benedicti quiescit, habentes spem ad magnos ipsius monasterii reditus pervenire, per ipsius promotionem ad apicem prelaturae: sed Deus de ipso aliter ordinabit. Tocco, c. 1 (*Fontes*, pp. 66-67); cf. Calo, c. 1 (*Fontes*, p. 18); Gui, c. 1 (*Fontes*, p. 168).

[51] Authors cite in this connection Tolomeo (Bartholomew) of Lucca, *Historia ecclesiastica*, lib. 22, c. 17 and lib. 23, c. 16, texts available in L. A. Muratori, *Rerum Italicarum Scriptores* 11 (Milan: Societas palatina, 1724), and Thomas de Cantimpré, *Bonum universale de apibus* (Douai: B. Belleri, 1627), 1: 20.

[52] "Le refus du Mont-Cassin est, chez Thomas d'Aquin, l'exacte réplique du geste de François d'Assise" (Chenu, *St. Thomas et la théologie*, p. 11).

[53] On the identification of this pope, see the reservations of K. Foster, trans., ed., *The Life of Saint Thomas Aquinas. Biographical Documents* (London: Longmans, Green, 1950), p. 67 n. 28; cf. ibid., p. 76 n. 82; the difficulty noted assumes that chronological order is respected in the two paragraphs.

for the cause of the Church (owing to persecution by Emperor Frederick), affection based on birth and the charitable gratitude due towards men so noble, exiles as they were in the cause of the Church, had been able to move him to subsidize them even—with permission from the Pope—out of the goods of the Church: just as he sustained his own necessities, yet loving God the while, so could he sustain the necessities of others.[54]

Latin Culture

A first class primary and secondary education at Monte Cassino and in the imperial university at Naples rooted Thomas Aquinas squarely in the soil of Latin, and indeed, of Italian letters. As for the second, we have the formal testimony of Bernard Gui on the effectiveness with which he preached in the vernacular[55] and perhaps also the sonnet written in the dialect of his time and place ascribed to him, although, it must be conceded, the attribution cannot be made without grave reservations.[56] As to the first, there is the overwhelming evidence of his capacity to express himself in correct and lucid Latin; that the Latin prose of Aquinas is not "Ciceronian" is no more than evidence that Latin had lived through many a century between the end of the Republic and the age of Aquinas. To his Latin prose must be added the accomplishment of his Latin metres in the Office of Corpus Christi, judiciously evaluated by Chenu, who reminds us of the appropriate criteria to be applied and who concedes that the qualification of "poet" somewhat outruns the evidence.[57]

Aquinas was inevitably a "Latin" as distinguished from a "Greek" theologian, yet we shall not fall into the vice of provincialism by emphasizing his openness to the wealth of the Christian orient. Apart from any other achievement, Saint Thomas would have left his mark on Latin theologizing by his introduction of Greek conciliar and patristic materials.

[54] Et ideo oblatas sibi dignitates et redditus a B. M. Clemente IV, Summo Pontifice, qui dictum doctorem nimis carum habebat, ipse simul renuit redditus et honores. ... Cum tamen praedictus Doctor omnes sui generis propinquos et nobiles, sub persecutione Frederici imperatoris pro causa Ecclesiae haberet in Campania profugos: quibus ad subveniendum de bonis etiam ecclesiasticis de licentia Summi Pontificis movere eum poterat naturalis affectio, et ad tam nobiles pro causa Ecclesiae exules caritatis debita gratitudo: Qui sicut amore Dei necessitates sustinuit proprias, sic sustinere potuit alienas." Tocco, c. 42 (*Fontes*, pp. 115-116).

[55] Gui, c. 29 (*Fontes*, pp. 195-196).

[56] K. Foster, *Life of St. Thomas*, Appendix 2, pp. 165-167.

[57] "IX. SAINT THOMAS THE POET. ... A versified short work ... the sequence entitled *Lauda Sion*, commonly presents him to us under this somewhat exaggerated designation..." (Chenu, *Toward Understanding*, p. 344).

The gesture was returned: key works by Augustine and by Aquinas were translated into Greek.[58]

Greek Christendom

It is impossible to find a work by Saint Thomas that has been more seriously misunderstood than his manual, *Against the Errors of the Greeks*.[59] For the inflammatory title expresses precisely the opposite of what it ought to do; the book purports to show that Greek authorities, far from endorsing what Latins hold to be theological errors, can be interpreted in harmony with the Latin Catholic tradition. In substance it is a study, commissioned by Pope Urban IV, of a collection of allegedly patristic texts from the Eastern Church; this collection that underlies the study by Aquinas disappeared and was completely forgotten until discovered in 1869 by Uccelli;[60] once found, it poses new enigmas. For this anthology seems to have been assembled by a south Italian Latin bishop of Greek antecedents, Nicholas of Durazzo (or of Cotrone), between 1231 and 1256; it is marked by a high incidence of forgeries and mal-attributions.

Aquinas did not question the status of the excerpted texts that he had been asked to evaluate, nor did he supplement them with others from Greek tradition that he most certainly knew. After a preface in which he adverted to the norms of adequate translation and to the temporally conditioned status of dogmatic formulations,[61] he proceeded to do what he had been asked to do. This was to show that citations, purportedly from Greek Fathers, in fact support what east-west polemic had represented as peculiarly "Latin" positions, notably, the term *filioque* introduced into the Nicene Creed, the primacy of the Roman bishop, the legitimacy of using unleavened bread in confecting the eucharist, and the reality of purgatory. When Aquinas was summoned by Pope Gregory X to the council at Lyons,

---

[58] See M. Rackl, "Demetrios Kydones als Verteidiger und Uebersetzer des heiligen Thomas von Aquin," *Der Katholik*, 1 (1915), 21-40; idem, "Die ungedruckte Verteidigungsschrift des Demetrios Kydones für Thomas von Aquin gegen Neilos Kabasilas," *Divus Thomas* (Wien-Berlin), 7 (1920), 303-317; and the study by Stylianos G. Papadopoulos, Ἑλληνικαὶ μεταφράσεις Θωμιστικῶν ἔργων, φιλοθωμισταὶ καὶ ἀντιθωμισταὶ ἐν Βυζαντίῳ (Βιβλιοθήκη τῆς ἐν Ἀθήναις Φιλεκπαιδευτικῆς Ἑταιρείας, 47; Ἀθῆναι, 1967).

[59] Eschmann, "Catalogue," accurately lists this work under "Expert Opinions," p. 415, rather than under "Polemical Writings."

[60] The Leonine text of the *Contra errores Graecorum* is to be found in volume 40 (Rome, 1967) of that series; there, pp. A 109 - A 151 is the Greek collection that occasioned the response by Aquinas: *Liber de fide trinitatis ex diversis auctoritatibus sanctorum grecorum confectus contra grecos*; for a discussion of the response by the editors, see the preface, ch. 2, no. 4, p. A 7.

[61] *Ibid.*, p. 71, ll. 16-44.

he was asked to bring with him this evaluation of Greek texts;[62] since the council was intended to reconcile the Greek and Latin Churches, the treatise by Aquinas must have been adjudged irenic.

But more important than an apologetic intervention of this sort is the creative and innovating use Aquinas made of Greek materials in his general theological work. He is the first Latin who is known to have used *verbatim* the acts of the first five ecumenical councils in his Trinitarian and Christological reflections;[63] he ferreted out Greek patristic texts not commonly available in the schools for his *Golden Chain*, a "continuous exposition" on the four Gospel accounts; indeed, he cited fifty-seven Greek Fathers in this work as against twenty-two Latin Fathers.[64] We possess in his wretched handwriting the commentaries he heard Albert pronounce at Cologne on the Pseudo-Dionysian theological masterpiece of Greek Christendom entitled *On the Divine Names*.[65] At a date before 1268 when a Latin version of Proclus, *Theological Elements*, began to circulate, Aquinas produced his own *Exposition on the Divine Names*, its composition before 1268 guaranteed by the negative fact that in it there is no visible influence of Proclus.[66]

Judaism

We have evidence of contact between Judaism and Brother Thomas on three planes. The first of these planes is that of the statutory situation of the Jews and the implications this had for Christians who were charged with governing a Christendom where those statutes ran. In a letter to the duchess of Brabant, whose identity is not certain,[67] Brother Thomas dealt with two themes as a theological expert; these are financial problems (by no means confined to the Jews) and the regulations set down by the Fourth Lateran

---

[62] Quarto errorem illum antiquum grecorum scismaticorum in multis errancium sed signanter in hoc, quod romano pontifici obedire recusant, contra quos de mandato Urbani pape specialem libellum edidit, in quo per doctores grecos ipsos convincit. Calo, c. 12 (*Fontes*, p. 32); cf. Calo, c. 27 (*Fontes*, pp. 46-47).

[63] Profecto nonnisi opere ac merito S. Thomae et post an. 1260 Acta primorum Conciliorum generalium scriptaque S. Cyrilli Alexandrini prima vice scholasticis innotuerunt, scilicet in *Catena aurea* (1262-1267) Aquinatis et in eius *Summa theologica* (1267-1273). Alexander de Hales, *Summa theologica seu ... "Summa fratris Alexandri"* (Quaracchi: Collegium S. Bonaventurae, 1948) 4: (Prolegomena), p. xc.

[64] See J. A. Weisheipl, *Friar Thomas d'Aquino. His Life, Thought and Work* (New York: Doubleday, 1974), p. 173; he cites G. Geenen, *Dictionnaire de théologie catholique*, vol. 15, part 1, col. 743; cf. Eschmann, "Catalogue," pp. 396, 397.

[65] Dondaine, *Les secrétaires*, p. 20.

[66] Eschmann, "Catalogue," p. 407.

[67] Formerly thought to have been Aleyde (Alix) of Brabant, "a plausible bid for Marguerite of France" has been made; see Eschmann, "Catalogue," p. 422.

Council in 1215 governing the dress of Jews (and Muslims) who lived within Christendom.[68] A justifiably famous passage in the *Summa theologiae* defends the right of Jewish parents to refuse the forced baptism of their children. Faithful to his principle that nature is prior to grace, Brother Thomas read out of court any plea based on patristic tradition that might be urged to infringe upon parental rights based on nature, and, he was careful to add, the custom of the Church had always defended those rights against Christian zealots.[69]

Despite some conspicuous instances to the contrary, the conversion of Jews was notoriously difficult. Chroniclers recount as evidence of the tact and acumen of Aquinas an anecdote according to which two Jews conferred with him on certain points of faith at Molaria, the castle of the cardinal of Sant'Angelo and, thanks to the impression made by his personal qualities and by the cogency of his responses, the two "learned and wealthy" Jews asked for baptism the next day.[70]

But Aquinas was first and last a theologian and the most significant plane on which he encountered Judaism remains his properly theological speculation. J. Guttmann[71] was right to adduce Solomon Ibn Gebirol, "Avicebron" according to the Latins, as a Jewish thinker whose work was taken with the utmost seriousness by Aquinas. That Brother Thomas gave Ibn Gebirol's *Fountain of Life* considerable weight is evident in his painstaking refutation of its exposition of what came to be known as the *binarium famosissimum*, "the famous pair" of doctrines: universal hylomorphism and plurality of substantial forms. Where William of Auvergne erroneously had made Avicebron both a Christian and singularly "noble philosopher,"[72] Giordano Bruno in the sixteenth century would identify him as an "Arab" or a "Moor,"[73] Thomas Aquinas habitually cited him as simply the author

---

[68] Giovanni D. Mansi, *Sacrorum conciliorum nova et amplissima collectio* ... (Venice: A. Zatta, 1776), 22: 1055; the canon at issue is no. 68; for an English translation, see Synan, *Popes and Jews*, p. 235.

[69] ST 2-2.10.12.

[70] Calo, c. 14 (*Fontes*, p. 33); Tocco, c. 22 (*Fontes*, pp. 96-97); Gui, c. 14 (*Fontes*, pp. 181-182).

[71] J. Guttmann, *Das Verhältniss des Thomas von Aquino zum Judentum und zur jüdischen Literatur* (Göttingen: Vandenhoeck u. Ruprecht's Verlag, 1891).

[72] "Manifestum est quod et unicus omnium philosphantium nobilissimus vidit: dixit enim quod indicium largitatis datoris bonitatis est obedientia universorum ad ipsum" (*De trinitate*, c. 12—*Opera omnia*, 2: 16); for identification of this singularly noble philosopher, see *Avencebrolis (Ibn Gebirol) Fons Vitae*, ed. C. Baeumker, Beiträge zur Geschichte der Philosophie des Mittelalters, Band 1, Heft 2-4 (Munster: Aschendorff, 1892-95), pp. 318-330; on his alleged Christianity: "Avicembron autem Theologus nomine, stylo, ut videtur Arabs ... puto ipsum fuisse Christianum" (*De universo*, 1.1.26—*Opera omnia*, 1: 621ʙ).

[73] "As an Arab has stated in a book entitled *The Spring of Life*...." Giordano Bruno,

of the *Fons vitae*; there is, to my knowledge, no evidence that Brother Thomas was aware that he was dealing with a Jewish sage in the *auctor libri Fontis vitae*.

On the other hand, Aquinas, with all his world, knew the identity of the author of *The Guide of the Perplexed*. "Rabbi Moyses Aegypticus," as the Latins habitually styled Rabbi Moses ben Maimon, functions for Brother Thomas as a source of theological considerations—for instance, that what can be known by human reason is appropriately the theme of revelation. Most men, no metaphysicians, would fail to reach it and even those who might succeed in arriving at such truth would do so with a deplorable admixture of error, nor would all of those with adequate capacity have the necessary leisure for reflection; these are intolerable hazards on issues that pertain to salvation.[74] Although Aquinas appealed to analogical predication of positive attributes to God against the Rambam's reduction of predication to meaningless equivocation or to what, in this context, would be blasphemous univocity,[75] his insistence on the negative quality of our knowledge of God evokes the Rambam's pronouncement that the "true attributes of God are the negative ones."[76] Nor does he seem far from the conviction of Moses ben Maimon that the angels of Scripture are identical with Aristotle's forces of Nature.[77]

Islam

Aquinas encountered the influence of Islam in two modes. One was the concrete and living presence of Muslims in his world. His brother Aimone went on the fifth crusade and was held for ransom on Cyprus;[78] King Louis IX of France, at whose table Aquinas was welcome,[79] died on a crusade against Islam and Dominican missionaries who faced Islamic apologists must have summoned the theologians to their assistance. In another mode,

---

Cause, Principle and Unity: Five Dialogues, trans. by J. Lindsay (Castle Hedingham: Daimon Press, 1962), Third Dialogue, p. 99.

[74] Thus Aquinas, ST 1.1.1; cf. Moses ben Maimon, *The Guide of the Perplexed*, trans. by Shlomo Pines (Chicago: University of Chicago Press, 1963), 1.34 (pp. 72-79).

[75] ST 1.13.2 resp. and 1.13.5 where Aquinas names Rabbi Moses as one of those whom he opposes, without, however, espousing univocal prediction of God and of creatures.

[76] "We have no way of describing Him unless it be through negations and not otherwise" (*Guide*, 1.58 passim—trans. Pines, p. 134).

[77] "For every force charged by God, may He be exalted, with some business is an angel put in charge of that thing" (*Guide*, 2.6—trans. Pines, p. 264); see Aquinas, *Opera Omnia* [Leonine edition] 26: *Expositio super Iob ad litteram* (Rome, 1965), p. 13, ll. 705-715.

[78] Documentum, 5 (*Fontes, Documenta*, pp. 536-537).

[79] Calo, c. 24 (*Fontes*, p. 42); Tocco, c. 43 (*Fontes*, p. 116); Gui, c. 25 (*Fontes*, p. 191).

Islam was present in the speculation of the great Muslim intellectuals who had preceded by centuries the Christian intelligensia in their assimilation and expansion of the philosophical heritage of antiquity. Now Aquinas was a man of the schools and his first concern was with the literary texts current in the universities: with Alfarabi, Avicenna, Averroës, and the rest. The suggestion has been made that his *Summa contra gentiles*, literally taken, a "Summary in opposition to the Nations," is in fact a handbook for the use of Dominican missionaries in Spain who faced a sophisticated Islamic population. Against this we ought to weigh the fact that an internal criticism easily demonstrates that Aquinas had in mind not Muslims exclusively, but any one who was not convinced by Catholic faith. In a memorable passage he noted the common ground on which a Christian controversialist might meet each of his possible opponents: with a Jew, he could appeal to the Hebrew Scriptures, but not to those of the New Law; with a Muslim, or a pagan (medieval authors habitually put both categories together)[80] no Scripture will serve; against Christian heretics and schismatics, the New Law is appropriate; against any and all we may adduce the resources of natural reason "to which," he asserted with some optimism, "all are bound to assent."[81] This *Summa*, therefore, is directed against the "Gentiles" in the sense the term carries in the Hebrew Scriptures, that is, against all those who do not now accept the authentic revelation of the Holy One. For the Jews, all non-Jews were and are "gentiles," *goyim*; in the lexicon of the Latin Vulgate Bible, *nationes, gentiles*. For Thomas Aquinas, an equally rigorous dichotomy divides our race: there are Catholics and all others. The People of God face the "gentiles," whether these be schismatics, heretics, Jews, Muslims, or men of no identifiable religious orientation. These last are accessible simply as men, only by appeal to their capacity to reason and this always with the Thomist caution that a matter of faith is not susceptible of rational demonstration.[82]

If Aquinas has provided no direct discussion of the morality of crusading, one reference in the *Summa theologiae* argues for the legitimacy of the military monastic orders in adducing without reservation the practice of enjoining that penitents campaign "in aid of the Holy Land."[83] Still, it is a

---

[80] See, for instance, C. Baronio, O. Rinaldi, J. Laderchi, *Annales ecclesiastici* (Bar-le-Duc, Paris, 1869), 16: 434.

[81] Unde necesse est ad naturalem rationem recurrere, cui omnes assentire coguntur. *Summa contra gentiles*, ed. manualis (Rome: Commissio Leonina, 1934), 1.2 (p. 2).

[82] SCG 1.1-9 (ed. manualis, pp. 1-8) on the relationship between demonstrative reasoning and the truths of faith.

[83] ST 2-2.188.3 ad 3.

fact that he has devoted not one article of his great *Summa theologiae* to what must have been a topic of unending debate among thirteenth-century men. To say the least, his treatise *On Kingship, to the King of Cyprus* assumes the Crusades for, without them, no Latin king of Cyprus could have been the recipient of a treatise in political theology composed by a begging friar, which is precisely the way Aquinas styled this gift:

> As I was turning over in my mind what I might present to Your Majesty as a gift at once worthy of Your Royal Highness and befitting my profession and office....[84]

Greek Philosophy

Nothing could be more awkward than to be obliged to speak out against what "everybody knows" and everybody thinks he "knows," that Aquinas was but Aristotle baptised. Nothing could be less precise. Aristotle's world was small and neat and orderly, eternal and cyclic and pagan. In his *Physics* the Philosopher spoke of Prime Mover in the singular,[85] but in the *Metaphysics* he was ready to acknowledge between fifty-five and forty-seven, depending upon the as yet undetermined actual number of absolute planetary motions.[86] Pascal was right to have said that the god of the philosophers is not the God of Abraham, Isaac and Jacob.[87] Aristotle's god or gods moved as "loved and desired," not as loving and still less as having any desires with regard to the sublunary world; for indeed, the god for Aristotle is a "thought that thinks itself" and in so thinking actualizes, without any margin left over, all its capacity to think.[88] What is more, Aristotle was obviously confident that his physics and biology and cosmology were secure sciences. In his view, they were instances of that *epistēmē*, universal and necessary conclusions, deduced with logical rigor from premises of equal necessity, that had been engendered by discriminating experience.[89] Aquinas did not think so. In the midst of a careful exposition of the Aristotelian astronomy he made the casual observation

---

[84] Thomas Aquinas, *On Kingship to the King of Cyprus*, trans. by G. B. Phelan, rev. intro., notes by I. Th. Eschmann (Toronto: Pontifical Institute of Mediaeval Studies, 1949), p. 2.

[85] *Physics* 8.6; 259a7-13.

[86] *Metaphysics* 12.8; 1074a6-13; on Aristotle's diffidence, since the ground of his reasoning provided by the astronomers was not certain, see the lines immediately following, 14-17.

[87] Blaise Pascal, *Pensées*, trans., notes by H. F. Stewart (New York: Pantheon, 1950), pp. 6-9.

[88] *Metaphysics* 12.7; 1074b13-29.

[89] *Posterior analytics* 1.2; 71b8ff.

that men may contrive other ways to save the appearances[90]—"casual"
perhaps, but devastating to the Aristotelian claim that this was "science,"
epistēmē. The remark seems slight and innocent, but it is the "cloud, no
larger than a man's hand" (3 Kings 18:44), between Aristotle's conviction
and the reserve of Aquinas. Like so much that "everybody knows," the
alleged identity between Aristotelian thought and that of Aquinas is
illusory.

Still, Aquinas remains one of the great Aristotelian interpreters. Not only
did he master and use both the lexicon and the conceptual scheme of
Aristotle, he enriched the Arts Faculty at Paris with urbane commentaries
on an immense range of the Stagirite's difficult and extensive works,[91]
purified the canon of inauthentic works as his own information on Greek
philosophizing widened and put to work the medieval technique of the
"pious interpretation" to make the text of Aristotle carry as much truth as
his words can bear.

*   *   *

Because Aquinas was a professional theologian, it is on his theological
accomplishment that he must be judged. Scriptural exegesis, as it came to
the thirteenth century, was dominated by the conviction that the Bible is a
polyvalent text, the sense of which can be subsumed under three "spiritual"
and one "literal" or "historical" meanings. The least fruitful of these
meanings, it was agreed, is the "literal" sense.[92] Saint Thomas thought the

---

[90] Illorum tamen suppositiones quas adinvenerunt, non est necessarium esse veras: licet
enim, talibus suppositionibus factis, apparentia salvarentur, non tamen oportet dicere has
suppositiones esse veras; quia forte secundum aliquem alium modum, nondum ab hominibus
comprehensum, apparentia circa stellas salvantur. Aristoteles tamen utitur huiusmodi suppositionibus quantum ad qualitatem motuum, tanquam veris." *Opera omnia* [Leonine
edition] 3: *De caelo et mundo* (Rome, 1886), pp. 186-187. To this somwhat banal, if important text, may be added the reservation Aquinas expressed in his exposition of Aristotle's
Meteorologicorum 1.1.1.9, *Opera omnia* [Leonine edition] 3 (Rome, 1886), p. 327: "Dicit
[Aristoteles] autem *fere*, quia non omnia naturalia ab homine cognosci possunt," and ibid.,
1.7.11.1, p. 354: "...de talibus, quae sunt immanifesta sensui, non est exquirenda certa
demonstratio et necessaria, sicut in mathematicis et in his quae subiacent sensui."

[91] Eschmann, "Catalogue," nos. 28-39 (pp. 400-405).

[92] A striking formulation of this view is to be found in Godfrey of Saint-Victor, *Fons
philosophiae*, ed. P. Michaud-Quantin, Analecta mediaevalia namurcensis, 8 (Namur:
Godenne, 1956), ll. 540-544:

> Qui cum, sicut diximus, sit quadripartitus,
> Veteris istoria plus informat ritus
> Et ob hoc ad alterum magis vertit litus;
> Nobis est uicinior modus tripartitus.

This is to say that the Jews, who cultivate the literal sense, lose the struggle with Christian
exegetes, who favor the threefold "spiritual" sense.

opposite. For him the literal rather than the "allegorical," "anagogic," or "moral" senses must ground the reflections of the theologian. Without pretending that Aquinas effected the revolution, the scholarship of our day ascribes to him the credit for turning the direction of exegesis from an excessive and sterile concern with the "spiritual" senses to the more pedestrian, but also more secure, literal understanding.[93] One conspicuous instance of this is his *Expositio super Iob* and nothing can surpass the discretion with which he intimated that the moment had arrived to go beyond the exegetical tradition that Pope Gregory the Great had made the classic approach to Job:

> In accordance with what capacity we have, for we have confidence in divine assistance, we intend to explain in a compendious way this book entitled *The Book of Job* according to the literal sense. Blessed Pope Gregory has set out its mystical aspects so subtly and learnedly that it seems to us unnecessary to add anything to his work.[94]

The success of this move is incontestable. His own former master, Albert the German, was the first to follow the trail Brother Thomas blazed and the greatest of medieval exegetes, Nicholas of Lyra (ca. 1270-1340), a long generation later would accept unequivocally the priority attributed to the literal sense. Some traditionalists would regret the shift and see in Nicholas an embryo Luther:

> Si Nicholas non lyrasset,
> Lutherus non saltasset.

they chanted, punning on the "Lyra" of his name:

> Had Nicholas his lyre not played,
> Luther in no dance had swayed.

The founder of modern exegesis, Richard Simon (1638-1712) would name Nicholas of Lyra as the most significant contributor to an understanding of the Bible since Jerome (ca. 342-420); without the intervention of Aquinas, the contribution of Nicholas might well have been other than it was.

Biblical revelation retains an ineluctable priority for the teacher of sacred doctrine and men of the Middle Ages willingly acknowledged this: they

---

[93] See remarks by the Leonine editors under the heading, "Succès de l'interprétation selon le sens littéral," *Opera omnia* 26: *Expositio super Iob* (Rome, 1965), pp. 41*-43*.

[94] Intendimus enim compendiose secundum nostram possibilitatem, de divino auxilio fiduciam habentes, librum istum qui intitulatur *Beati Iob* secundum litteralem sensum exponere; eius enim mysteria tam subtiliter et diserte beatus papa Gregorius nobis aperuit ut his nihil ultra addendum videatur. *Opera omnia* 26: *Expositio super Iob* (Rome, 1965), p. 4, ll. 96-102.

named theologians "masters of the Sacred Page." The work of a theologian, however, is not finished when he has arrived at the meaning of a biblical text. It is his function to understand and to clarify, against the broadest conceivable background, the innermost meaning of what his text says. For Augustine and for his thirteenth-century followers, any understanding of truth argued a divine illumination of the human mind. Aquinas did not deny this necessity for an illumination that comes from God, but he identified it with what Aristotle had termed the "intellect that makes everything" as well as the "intellect that becomes everything." When Brother Thomas commented on the text of Aristotle, his concern was to combat the cosmic separate and single intellect which, he felt, Averroës had read mistakenly into the text of the Philosopher:

> The aforesaid position is against the intention of Aristotle who said expressly that these two different powers, namely, the agent intellect and the possible intellect, are *in* the soul, from which he gives us to understand explicitly that they are parts or powers *of* the soul and not some separated substances.[95]

When on the contrary, Aquinas was addressing the theological community, heavily indebted as it was to the Augustinian noetic, he acknowledged the truth of the Augustinian proposition that we do know "in the eternal reasons," but he hastened to explain what this means:

> The intellectual light which is in us is nothing other than a certain participated resemblance of the Uncreated Light in which the eternal reasons are contained.[96]

We need read no farther than the next article to recognize that as Augustine had been "imbued with the teachings of the Platonists," so Aquinas was squarely in the Aristotelian tradition as he transformed the water of philosophy into the wine of theology. It is by our possession of intellect that we share, in our measure, the eternal light of the Creator.

Is it necessary to insist that to be "in the Aristotelian tradition" is by no means to be a carbon copy of Aristotle? Aquinas brought to his theological vocation a competence in philosophy that makes him an indispensable participant in the ongoing work of theology from his day to our own. We shall

[95] Est etiam praedicta positio contra Aristotelis intentionem: qui expresse dixit, has differentias duas, scilicet intellectum agentem et intellectum possibilem, esse in anima: ex quo expresse dat intelligere, quod sint partes animae, vel potentiae, et non aliquae substantiae separatae. Thomas Aquinas, *In Aristotelis librum de anima commentarium*, ed. A. M. Pirotta (Turin: Marietti, 1925), no. 736, p. 241 (on *De anima* 3.5; 430a17).
[96] Ipsum enim lumen intellectuale quod est in nobis, nihil est aliud quam quaedam participata similitudo luminis increati, in quo continentur rationes aeternae. ST 1.84.6 resp.

hardly depend upon him for guidance on the literary genre of the Book of Job—he was persuaded that Job was a historical person[97]—but we should be the poorer for ignoring his views on how Being and the Good and the One are verified of God, on how creatures may "participate" and "imitate," *pace Aristotele*,[98] the Being and the Goodness and the Unity of the Bible's God, on how our human discourse, verbal or conceptual, can stammer out its inadequate, but precious, conclusions from the data of faith.

No doubt it is true that the wisdom of Aquinas has allowed him to transcend his age. If he speaks to us across an abyss of seven centuries—and he does—Brother Thomas was nonetheless firmly established in his own time and place and social class. An offhand remark on falcons[99] and his expansions on what Job had to say about war-horses[100] are in the very idiom of chivalry. To read the advice he sent to the king of Cyprus is to know with immediacy the far-off realities of a crusading age when "Franks" marched east, not always with unmixed motives, and sometimes remained to carve out principalities for themselves at the expense of Saracens or of their own Greek allies.

By a paradox, this archetypal thirteenth-century theologian vindicates a place for himself in the great conversation that the sapiential disciplines prolong into our time. Precisely because Thomas Aquinas was so fully a man of his own age, his work can speak to every age. The Common Doctor has something to say to all of us universally; no reader of Aristotle will be perplexed to find universality incarnate in one so straitly defined by "where" and "when" and "of such a sort."

---

[97] Fuerunt autem aliqui quibus visum est quod iste Iob non fuerit aliquid in rerum natura, sed quod fuerit quaedam parabola conficta.... Et quamvis ad intentionem libri non multum differat ... refert tamen quantum ad ipsam veritatem. Videtur enim praedicta opinio auctoritati sacrae Scripturae obviare. *Opera omnia* 26: *Expositio super Iob* (Rome, 1965), p. 4, ll. 72-81.

[98] *Metaphysics* 1.6; 987b10ff. and 1.9; 991a19ff.

[99] ...Unde dicit *Penna struthionis similis est pennis herodii*, idest nobilissimi falconis qui girfalcus dicitur, et *accipitris*, qui est avis nota, et ambae sunt aves boni volatus. *Opera omnia* 26: *Expositio super Iob* (Rome, 1965), p. 210, ll. 163-166.

[100] Equus habet quasdam proprietates ad nobilitatem pertinentes ... fortitudinem, scilicet non solum corporis prout est potens ad onus ferendum, sed etiam animi prout audacter ad pericula vadit.... Alia proprietas est ... audacia ipsius in bellis ... nobilis et admiranda.... Odoratu percipit bellum imminere et quasi videtur sentire belli praeparationem, dum scilicet duces suis exhortationibus animant milites. Ibid., pp. 210-211, ll. 215-281.

2

Imago Dei
An Explication of *Summa theologiae,*
Part 1, Question 93

Jaroslav PELIKAN

Yale University

Of all the doctrines of Thomas Aquinas, there is perhaps none whose present-day significance is greater than that of his teaching that man was made after the image of God. As the late John Courtney Murray put it, "the Basic Issues of our time concern the spiritual substance of a free society, as it has historically derived from the central Christian concept, *res sacra homo*."[1] And *res sacra homo* is another Latin term for *imago Dei.* Although the doctrine had occupied the attention of Christian thinkers since the days of the Church Fathers, there was by no means a consensus about its meaning. Probably the most extensive theological debate over "image" had dealt not with man as *imago Dei*, but with the legitimacy of the use of images in Christian worship; yet even in this iconoclastic controversy the problem of the *imago Dei* in man had played an important role.[2] Thomas' doctrine of the image, like all of his theology, was an effort to interpret the tradition of the Church Fathers faithfully and yet critically, and it is therefore a useful index of his theological method in this respect. It also illustrates his method in an even more basic way, for the doctrine of *imago Dei* belongs simultaneously to natural theology and to revelation. In this

---

[1] John Courtney Murray, *We Hold These Truths: Catholic Reflections on the American Proposition* (New York: Sheed and Ward, 1964), p. 198.
[2] Cf., for example, Theodore of Studios, *Epistolae* 1.13.

paper I want to examine it under these two rubrics, basing my analysis on Part 1, Question 93 of the *Summa theologiae*, as illuminated by other parts of Thomas' work, especially by his comments on the *Sentences* and by Question 10 of *On Truth* [*De veritate*].

I

The doctrine of the image of God was an important element of the natural theology of Thomas. In fact, it formed the fundamental presupposition for natural theology in his thought. It did not appear in Thomas' celebrated presentation of the "five ways" by which he argued that it was possible for the mind of man to know and to demonstrate the existence of God; here the classic text about the natural knowledge of God from the creation, Romans 1:19-20, and the "towering text"[3] on Christian ontology, Exodus 3:14, provided the biblical justification for Thomas' argument, while man's having been created in the image of God played no direct role.[4] Even where a consideration of the objection that "the soul does not understand anything by natural reason without an image, [and] we cannot have an image of God, who is incorporeal"[5] seemed to be an open invitation to refer to the image of God in man as a refutation of this ground for opposition to the idea of the natural knowledge of God, Thomas did not make use of this resource, contenting himself with the reply that "God is known by natural knowledge through the images of his effects." Curiously, he did use the theologoumenon of the image of God in angels to substantiate the natural knowledge of God in angels,[6] but did not do so in considering the natural knowledge of God in man. But the exposition of the proofs for the existence of God and of the natural knowledge of God at the beginning of Part 1 of the *Summa theologiae* was supplemented in later questions, and here in Question 93 of Part 1 Thomas made explicit the anthropological—and, if one may use the term, psychological—basis for the proofs.

With a cross-reference to these earlier considerations of natural theology, Thomas first reiterated his frequent distinction between the natural knowledge of God and the kind of knowledge and love that was "meritorious";[7] this latter was not by nature, but only by grace. But it was also

---

[3] John Courtney Murray, *The Problem of God Yesterday and Today* (New Haven: Yale University Press, 1964), p. 5.

[4] ST 1.2.2-3.

[5] ST 1.12.12 obj. 2.

[6] ST 1.56.3 resp.

[7] ST 1.93.8 ad 3.

by nature that the mind could have "knowledge and love of God in some sense [*aliqua Dei cognitio et dilectio naturalis*]." Such knowledge of God, as was evident in the five ways, was attainable by the use of human reason, which was present in man also after the fall of Adam. Because reason continued to be an attribute even of fallen man and therefore a "natural" quality and power, it followed that the image of God had remained in the human mind. The converse of this would be that it was the permanence of the image of God in man that assured the continuing power of reason and therefore the very possibility of the natural knowledge of God. From Augustine's insistence that the human soul was rational and intellectual even when reason appeared to be quite "torpid" in a particular individual,[8] Thomas drew the conclusion that reason was never absent from the human mind, and that therefore none was utterly devoid of the divine image. Thus it properly belonged also to natural theology to consider the image of God in man. Nor was it valid to maintain that because the doctrine of the Trinity was a matter of revelation and was not accessible to natural knowledge, there could not be an image of the three persons of the Trinity in man;[9] for, again paraphrasing Augustine,[10] the trinity in man was something that could be seen, while the Trinity in God was something that had to be believed.

It would be both "natural" and "reasonable" to suppose that, as an article of the natural theology of Thomas, the image of God would find substantiation in the writings of classical antiquity, especially in the works of the ancient philosophers. The Neoplatonic doctrine of archetypes contained elements that could have been developed—and indeed were by some early Christian writers, including Pseudo-Dionysius—into an anticipation and a counterpart of the biblical metaphor of the image of God. One would expect, therefore, that Thomas, too, in his endeavor to give nature its due, would have drawn upon philosophical sources for the content of the image of God in natural man. One of the most widely read theological treatises on the doctrine of man in this century confirms this expectation: "In Thomas Aquinas," it says, "intellectualistic and Biblical conceptions of the 'image of God' are compounded, with the Aristotelian elements achieving predominance."[11] Similar statements occur in other theological literature. When we turn from the secondary accounts to the *Summa theologiae*, it is

---

[8] Augustine, *De trinitate* 14.4.6.
[9] ST 1.93.5 obj. 3.
[10] Augustine, *De trinitate* 15.6.10.
[11] Reinhold Niebuhr, *The Nature and Destiny of Man*, 1: *Human Nature* (New York, 1941), p. 153 n. 4.

almost a shock to discover how insignificant a part is played there by these
so-called "Aristotelian elements" or, for that matter, by any elements
drawn from the thought of pre-Christian philosophers. There are, it seems,
only two specific citations of Aristotle in all of Question 93 on the image of
God: the first is a reference to the *Categories*,[12] introduced with the formula
dicitur, where it is said that "substance" is not liable to an increase or a
decrease;[13] the second, with the formula *ut dicitur in Meta[physica]*,[14] asserts
that "oneness in quality [*unum in qualitate*] causes likeness,"[15] the latter
term being, of course, the second member of the pair of terms used in the
creation story in Genesis, "image" and "likeness." In neither passage was
Aristotle referred to either by name or as *ille philosophus*. There were not,
as nearly as I can determine, any other references to philosophical or pagan
sources, although there are, as I shall point out, some parallels in such
sources to some of the statements being made; the very absence of citations
from such sources, some of which were certainly known to Thomas, is itself
deserving of notice in a doctrine where "Aristotelian elements" are supposed to have "achieved predominance."

As all the specific facts adduced in the "five ways" proving the existence
of God indicate, consideration of the natural knowledge of God in man is
obliged to pay attention not only to God and to man, but also to "nature"
in the sense in which Thomas occasionally used the word, that is, to
nonrational creatures. One issue in the doctrine of the image of God as a
part of natural theology, therefore, was the implication of the doctrine for
nonrational creatures. This issue was addressed in article 2 of Question 93.
As I noted earlier, the nearest pagan counterpart to the doctrine of the
image of God was probably to be found in such Neoplatonic notions as type
and archetype, which could not be confined to the nature of man. From
these Neoplatonic sources they had come into Christian thought through
such channels as the speculations of Pseudo-Dionysius the Areopagite and
the religiously neutral *Consolation of Philosophy* of Boethius. It is upon
these two bodies of writing that Thomas drew for his examination of the
question whether there was an image of God also in nonrational creatures.
Dionysius had used the term "images [εἰχόνες]" in his treatise *On the Divine
Names*[16] to identify links in what he called the "chain"[17] that bound

---

[12] Aristotle, *Categories* 5.3b33.
[13] ST 1.93.3 ad 3.
[14] Aristotle, *Metaphysics* 4.15; 1021a11.
[15] ST 1.93.9 resp.
[16] Dionysius the Areopagite, *De divinis nominibus* 2.8.
[17] Ibid., 3.1.

together various levels of reality. "Things that are caused," he said in the translation used by Thomas, "have the contingent images of the things that cause them." He had also identified the radiance of the sun as the most accurate created likeness of the goodness of God;[18] in this he was drawing upon the Greek patristic tradition, most notably articulated by Athanasius,[19] and ultimately upon the New Testament (Hebrews 1:3), where the term "radiance [ἀπαύγασμα]" was employed to specify the relation of Christ as Son of God to the Father. Boethius' *Consolation*, which performed some of the same function in the West that the Dionysian corpus performed in the East, had likewise found in the term "image" a way of describing the reality of "the created world [*mundus*]" as it was formed and carried by the mind of the Maker.[20] It would be plausible to conclude from this statement of Boethius that the quality of being "after the image of God" was not restricted to rational creatures, but should be attributed to the entire world.[21]

For his response to these two eminent patristic authorities, Thomas took up the specification of the terms appearing in the quotations. Thus Dionysius had not simply called effects "images" of their causes, but had made clear that they were "contingent [ἐνδεχόμεναι] images." This qualification meant, according to Thomas, that such realities were not "images" in the strict sense of the word, but only to the extent that—not by necessity but by contingency[22]—they happened to participate in the notion of the image, because, and to the extent that, even in their imperfection, they participated in that which was perfect; for they did have "some sort of likeness to God [*aliqualem similitudinem Dei*]."[23] Now this explanation of the language of Dionysius might suffice for some of the many images he applied to the relation between the Creator and the entire creation—images such as the "chain," referred to earlier—but something more was needed to make sense of the "metaphysics of light" underlying the second reference from Dionysius; for this was not merely one concept among others, but the decisive metaphor in the ontology of Dionysius and of much of the Greek patristic tradition before and after him, climaxing in the doctrine of "uncreated light" in the Hesychastic theology of Gregory Palamas. When Thomas had come, in an earlier question in Part 1 of the *Summa*,[24] to

---

[18] Ibid., 4.4.
[19] See, for example, Athanasius, *Orationes contra Arianos* 1.9.
[20] Boethius, *De consolatione philosophiae* 3.9.8.
[21] ST 1.93.2 obj. 4.
[22] ST 1.22.4 ad 3.
[23] ST 1.93.2 ad 1.
[24] ST 1.67.1.

study the relation between "light" and other figurative ways of speaking about God, he cited a statement from Dionysius[25] as an authority for the important place of this term among the names for God and an even more unequivocal one from Augustine,[26] who had said that "Christ is not called 'light' in the same sense as he is called 'stone'; the former is to be taken strictly [*proprie*], and the latter metaphorically." Yet he put all of this aside, drawing upon a statement of Ambrose, who had included the term "radiance [*splendor*]" from Hebrews 1:3 among the many metaphorical names for God and Christ with which he opened the second book of his opus *De fide*, written for the emperor Gratian.[27] In much the same way Thomas proceeded here in Question 93, article 2 to base Dionysius' statement about the light of the sun as bearing the greatest similitude to the goodness of God upon the analogy between the "causality" attributable to the sun and that which belonged to God, rather than upon "the intrinsic worth of its nature, which is required for the idea of image."[28] This satisfied the immediate purpose, but did not address the larger issue. Thomas' way of coping with the passage from Boethius was more apt. Acknowledging that the term "image" could be used in more than one sense, he gave the following definition for the term as it had been employed by Boethius: "the likeness by which a work of art imitates the exemplar of the art that is in the mind of the artist [*similitudo qua artificiatum imitatur speciem artis quae est in mente artificis*]." But here in the doctrine of the image of God the term "image" referred more particularly to a "likeness of nature." In this specific sense, then, all things could be said to have such a likeness to God as "first being" insofar as they themselves were beings, and in the Boethian sense every creature could be said to be "the image of the exemplar which it has in the mind of God." And so, as Thomas said a little later, "there is in all creatures some sort of likeness to God."[29]

But he immediately went on to say that although this was true, yet "it is only in the rational creature that a likeness to God in the form of an image [*per modum imaginis*] is to be found." Yet if "image of God" was not an accurate term for the created world as a whole or for the nonrational creatures in it, except in the broader sense of the term employed for example by Boethius, was it, strictly speaking, an accurate term even for all the human species? Did the term apply to the female of the species as well as to

[25] Dionysius the Areopagite, *De divinis nominibus* 4.5.
[26] Augustine, *De Genesi ad litteram* 4.28.
[27] Ambrose, *De fide* 2.pr.
[28] ST 1.67.1 ad 2.
[29] ST 1.93.6 resp.

the male? To make this question as urgent as possible before he brushed it aside, Thomas—it seems deliberately—misquoted the words of the apostle Paul in 1 Corinthians 11:7 to read, "The man is the image of God, but woman is the image of man." (The passage actually reads, also in Thomas' Latin version, "He [the man] is the image and glory of God; but woman is the glory of man.") In his refutation of this objection,[30] Thomas did not make a point of correcting the misquotation, but countered it with the words of the creation story in Genesis: "After the image of God He [God] created *him* [man]; male and female He created *them*." This verse did not, of course, assert in so many words that woman, too, was created after the image of God; and even Augustine's reference to the biblical rejection of the androgynous myth did not entirely resolve the matter.[31] Thomas added, moreover, that the female found her "origin and goal [*principium et finis*]" in the male, just as God was the origin and goal of all creatures; and for this he quoted 1 Corinthians 11:7 again, adding the next two verses for amplification of the argument. The discussion of the status of woman and of the relation between man and woman in the divine creation had occupied Thomas in the question immediately preceding this one on the image of God. Therefore he was able to dispose rather quickly of this objection, and even more quickly of a notion, labeled by Augustine as "not probable" and as "erroneous"[32] but by Thomas as "prima facie absurd," that the male represented the Father in the Trinity, the female represented the Holy Spirit, and their child represented the Son.[33]

A more serious obstacle to the claim that all members of the human race had the divine image was derived from the tendency of some passages of the New Testament and of some statements in the fathers to connect the image of God directly with Jesus Christ and hence to confine it as an anthropological term to those who could be said to be "in Christ." Although the christological bearing of the image of God will occupy us a little later in this paper, when we discuss the image as a datum of revelation in Thomas, the tendency to which I refer also pertains to the matter of natural theology. For if, as it seemed to say, there was no image of God in those who were apart from Christ and his revelation, then the universality of the image of God would have to be surrendered; indeed, as we have seen, Thomas would then be obliged to forfeit his entire scheme of demonstrations of the existence of God, since the presupposition for their probative force was the

---

[30] ST 1.93.4 ad 1.
[31] Augustine, *De Genesi ad litteram* 3.22.
[32] Augustine, *De trinitate* 12.5.5.
[33] ST 1.93.6 ad 2.

universality and the persistence of the image. At issue now was not chiefly
the finiteness of man and his consequent incapacity to grasp the infinity of
God, but the sin of man and his alienation from the holiness of God. An
irreducible minimum in the content of the term "image of God" seemed
certainly to be some sort of likeness between the image and the original.
"But as a result of sin," Thomas said, "man becomes unlike God." Did this
mean that "therefore he loses the image of God"?[34] From among sinners,
moreover, God had, according to Romans 8:29, foreknown some to be conformed to the image of his Son, and these he had predestined; since not all
were predestined, did this mean that "not all human beings have a conformity to the image"?[35] To deal with these objections, it was necessary to
distinguish between the image of God according to nature and the image according to grace and glory: according to nature man had never lost the
image of God and hence did not need to have it restored, while according to
grace it was restored, albeit imperfectly, and according to glory it was to be
restored perfectly and completely.[36] Considered according to nature,
therefore, all men still had the image of God.

Such an affirmation would, however, carry more sound than meaning
unless the content of the image were specified. One conceivable specification of it would be to locate it in the body of man, since, after all, the
primary connotation of the term "image" was that of a figure or shape,
which pertained directly to the body.[37] This suggestion that the locus of the
image of God was in the body had very little support even in the aberrant
literature of Christian theology, and Thomas had rejected it earlier in the
Summa.[38] But there was considerable support in Christian literature for the
correctness of the pagan insight that the erect posture of the human body
was a mark of the special standing of the human species among creatures.
Of Roman writers, for instance, both Cicero and Ovid had advanced this
argument. Thomas' source for it was the Augustinian treatise *On Eighty-
Three Questions*, which declared that the distinctive stance of the human
body by contrast with that of the other animals was evidence that "it may
properly be taken to have been made more after the image of God than
other bodies."[39] Despite this prestigious endorsement, Thomas would not
concede that the locus of the image of God, in the precise sense of the word,

[34] ST 1.93.4 obj. 3.
[35] ST 1.93.4 obj. 2.
[36] ST 1.93.4 resp.
[37] ST 1.93.6 obj. 3.
[38] ST 1.3.1 ad 2.
[39] Augustine, *De diversis quaestionibus* LXXXIII 51.

could be the human body. At most he was willing to grant that the human body, by its figure and shape, "represented" the image of God, which was properly in the soul. This "representing" it did, moreover, "after the fashion of a vestige [*per modum vestigii*]."[40] From his use of this term earlier in this same article it is evident that it implied for him a contrast with "image," so that he could describe the "likeness [*similitudo*]" of the human mind to God as a likeness "after the fashion of an image" and that of all the other parts of a human being as a likeness "after the fashion of a vestige."

If the image of God was not to be located in the body of man, then, since Thomas was a dichotomist, it had to be in the soul. But it needs to be emphasized that Thomas' doctrine of the soul was in large part an element of his natural theology, even though there were important aspects of it, notably such ideas as the beatific vision, that were derived from revelation. Thus one cannot understand the Thomistic doctrine of man and the soul without examining the subtle interrelations of its Augustinian and Aristotelian components. As part of the natural theology of Thomas, more specifically as part of his doctrine of the image of God, the concept of the soul needed to be clarified. This required him to define the capacity of the soul, by nature and not only by grace, for moral virtues, so as to give nature its due—neither more than its due (which would be the Pelagian heresy) nor less than its due (which would be the Manichean heresy). In drawing this fine line, which was of course central to his whole enterprise, Thomas denied to nature as now constituted any capacity for innocence and for righteousness, which had been lost through the fall of Adam and could now be restored to the soul only by grace.[41] On the other hand, he did not permit his recognition of this basic limitation upon the capacity of the soul for virtue to negate the reality of "those virtues [that] are indwelling naturally in the soul." On the basis of these virtues it was possible to attribute to the soul a "natural likeness" to God, even though Thomas was also obliged to qualify his affirmation of these natural virtues by adding that they were indwelling in the soul "at least in some way seminally [*ad minus secundum quaedam earum semina*]."[42] In order to articulate his doctrine of the soul as part of the idea of the image of God, Thomas also had to reassert, here as elsewhere, the patristic insistence, over against some strains of classical philosophy, on the unbridgeable ontological difference between the soul and God, as between creature and Creator. Image of God though it was, the soul

---

[40] ST 1.93.6 ad 3.
[41] ST 1.93.9 obj. 2.
[42] ST 1.93.9 ad 2.

was not an emanation from God, nor a part of God, but part of "the order
of rational creatures, lower than God and higher than the other
creatures."[43]

It was, then, the image of God in the soul of man that set him apart from
the other terrestrial creatures. The very "being [*esse*]" of man, that which
made him human, was to be found in the image, marking the distinction between him and the other animals; but it did so "inasmuch as we possess a
mind [*inquantum mentem habemus*]."[44] This argument had served Thomas
earlier in his consideration of the simplicity of God, where the reason and
intellect of man, as that by which he excelled other animals, were sub-
stantiating evidence for the incorporeality of God, since man was said to
have been created in the image of God.[45] Here in the question devoted to
the image itself, the exclusively mental and intellectual definition of the
image was stated even more unequivocally. A comparison between rational
and nonrational creatures would show that the difference between them was
the presence of reason in the former: this seeming tautology, formulated in
article 6 of the question on the image of God, actually was intended to
identify not so much the differentia between man and beast as the differentia between soul and body in man; for Thomas went on from it to the
thesis "that not even in the rational creature itself is the image of God
found except according to the mind."[46] Similarly, a comparison between
rational creatures and their Creator would show that, despite the unbridgeable ontological difference mentioned earlier, the being of God the
Creator and the being of man the creature had in common "the distinctive
characteristics of an intellectual nature [*ea quae sunt propria intellectualis
naturae*]."[47] Both these comparisons, that between Creator and creature and
that between rational creature and nonrational creature, were intended to
locate the "ultimate difference,"[48] which, as Thomas had said in an earlier
question, was "determinate" since it made a specific being what it was.[49]
Now some creatures were considered to be similar to God simply by virtue
of their having being, others by virtue of their having life in addition to
being, and yet others by virtue of their having intelligence in addition to
being and life. Beings of this third category were, in the words of an Augus-

---

[43] ST 2-2.19.11.
[44] ST 1.93.7 ad 1.
[45] ST 1.3.1 ad 2.
[46] ST 1.93.6 resp.
[47] ST 1.93.9 ad 2.
[48] ST 1.93.2 resp.
[49] ST 1.75.7 ad 2.

tinian formula[50] quoted by Thomas, "so close in their likeness to God that nothing among all creatures is any closer."[51]

There is an interesting parenthesis in Thomas' rejection of the suggestion that the image of God in man applied in any direct sense to his body. After asserting that "not even in the rational creature itself is the image of God found except according to the mind," he added that "in its others parts (if the rational creature has any)" there was not the likeness after the fashion of an image.[52] This *obiter dictum*, "if the rational creature has any," was, of course, intended to refer to the other group of rational creatures, the angels. For if the image of God in man was to be identified with his rational soul, which was joined with a body to make a composite being in whom the intellect was the "form of the human body,"[53] then an order of creatures in whom there was only intellect and no body must likewise be "after the image of God." There was, to be sure, no explicit biblical testimony to support the extension of the term "image of God" to the angels. Nevertheless, there was patristic support for the idea. Thomas[54] quoted Gregory the Great to the effect that "the likeness of the divine image" had been imprinted on the angels more distinctly than on human beings.[55] Dionysius the Areopagite had ascribed an image of God to angels also,[56] although Thomas did not quote him here. Athanasius, by contrast, had expressly distinguished between the human and the angelic creature by restricting the image to man, so that Christ, as the image of God in person, could be seen as the one who, through his incarnation in human form, had achieved the new creation of mankind after the image of God.[57] Apparently it was not only the predominant weight of the quotations from the fathers, on which he had also commented in his exposition of the *Sentences*,[58] that moved Thomas to teach that the angels were made after the image of God; it was a necessary inference to be drawn from his formulations of the two doctrines involved, namely, the intellectual nature of the angels and the identification of the image with intellect. In its own way this inference served to reinforce what was also for Thomas the primary content of the doctrine of the image of God, namely, the creation of man after the image.

---

[50] Augustine, *De diversis quaestionibus* LXXXIII 51.
[51] ST 1.93.2 resp.
[52] ST 1.93.6 resp.
[53] ST 1.76.1 resp.
[54] ST 1.93.3 s.c.
[55] Gregory the Great, *In evangelia homiliae* 2.34.
[56] Dionysius the Areopagite, *De divinis nominibus* 4.22.
[57] Athanasius, *De incarnatione Verbi* 13.7.
[58] *In I Sent.* D 3.3.

It would, however, be a mistake—and a mistake often made by interpreters of Thomas, both friendly and hostile—to emphasize the intellectual content of the image of God in man in such a way that the place of love in his doctrine of the image is overlooked or understated. Especially when it is set into the context of the earlier probing of the manner and the extent of knowledge and intellection among the angels, the doctrine of the image as mind may seem to have a chilling effect on Thomas' interpretation of the relation between God and man. But a more careful *explication de texte*, applied specifically to Question 93, discloses his recurring stress on love of God rather than knowledge about God as the goal and fulfillment of the image of God in man. Such a stress on love was obligatory in the doctrine of the image of God because it was integral to the doctrine of God itself. Thus Thomas could declare: "Since it is on the basis of his intellectual nature that man is said to be after the image of God, he is after the image of God to the greatest degree at the point at which an intellectual nature is able to imitate God to the greatest degree. Now an intellectual nature imitates God to the greatest degree inasmuch as it imitates this, that God understands *and loves* himself."[59] Again in a later article: "The image of the Trinity in the mind is perceived first and foremost on the basis of action, namely, to the extent that, on the basis of the knowledge that we have, we form an inner word through thought, and from this we break out into love [*ex hoc in amorem prorumpimus*]."[60] And in still a later article, by way of summary: "The divine image is perceived in man on the basis of the word conceived out of the knowledge of God and of the love that is derived from this."[61] The centrality of love in Thomas' doctrine of the image of God, and for that matter in his very definition of knowledge, may also be gauged from the place occupied by these three quotations in their respective articles: each of them belongs to the *responsio*, "in which," as Chenu reminds us, "are expounded at least the principles from which the author would solve the problem if not always the organically structured doctrine he holds."[62] It would seem safe to conclude from this that, far from being the "rationalism" that it is often said to have been, Thomas' doctrine of the image of God pointed, through reason but beyond reason, to what a much younger contemporary of his was to call "the love that moves the sun and the other stars [*l'amor che move il sole e l'altre stelle*]."[63]

[59] ST 1.93.4 resp.

[60] ST 1.93.7 resp.

[61] ST 1.93.8 resp.

[62] M.-D. Chenu, *Toward Understanding Saint Thomas*, trans. and rev. by A.-M. Landry and D. Hughes (Chicago: Henry Regnery, 1964), p. 95.

[63] Dante Alighieri, *Paradiso* 33.145.

II

The realization that Thomas' doctrine of the image of God included not only reason, but also a love that transcended reason, indicates that this doctrine was for him not only an element of natural theology, but also a datum of divine revelation. Indeed, both his anthropology and his epistemology required that the image of God belong to nature and to grace. Thus in his disquisition on the universality of the image in all men Thomas outlined a threefold distinction.[64] The image of God was to be seen, first, in the natural aptitude for understanding and loving God. This was not acquired from the outside, but belonged to the structure of the mind itself and therefore was common to all men, believers or not. But it was necessary to look at the image from the perspective of grace as well as from that of nature. Seen in this way, the image referred not merely to an "aptitude [*aptitudo*]," but to a "habitude [*habitus*]," whereby one had passed from potentially knowing and loving God to knowing and loving him "actually [*actu*], albeit imperfectly." The source of this habitude was the grace of God, by which nature was re-created to be, as the apostle said in Romans 8:29, "conformed to the image of [God's] Son." Yet this "conformity of grace" was not complete until it attained the actuality of a perfect knowledge and love of God in the beatific glory of eternal life. Despite the tripartite division of this formulation, it does need to be pointed out that the fundamental distinction was that between grace and nature,[65] which was a distinction of kind, while the distinction between grace and glory was a distinction of degree (even though one must add that in Thomas' usage the distinction between "imperfect" and "perfect" was, in a way, qualitative rather than quantitative). It was an application of this distinction between nature and grace to the Augustinian idea of the image of the Trinity when Thomas summarized this idea in the dictum from Augustine's *De trinitate*:[66] "The trinity that is within ourselves we see rather than believe, but that God is Trinity we believe rather than see."[67]

As a datum of revelation, the doctrine of the image of God was contained in the Bible and had been made explicit in the tradition of the Church. Although two passages from the Psalms and two passages from the prophets appeared in his examination of the biblical and patristic evidence, Thomas relied chiefly on the *locus classicus* of the doctrine of the image of God in

---

[64] st 1.93.4 resp.
[65] st 1.93.9 ad 3.
[66] Augustine, *De trinitate* 15.6.
[67] st 1.93.5 ad 3.

the Old Testament, Genesis 1:26-27, and on the New Testament passages, all of them from the apostle Paul, in which this text from the creation story had been given its distinctively Christian interpretation. In the very first article of Question 93, Thomas used the words of Genesis 1:26, "Let us make man after our image and likeness," as the *sed contra* on the question, "Whether there is an image of God in man."[68] In article 4, the text from Genesis, when quoted as a commentary on itself, enabled Thomas to extract from the creation story what it had not said in so many words, namely, that woman as well as man had been created after the image. For "when Genesis had said, 'after the image of God He created him,' namely, the human being, it went on to say: 'Male and female He created them.'" Taken as a whole, then, the passage meant that "the image of God is found both in the man and in the woman as far as that is concerned in which the concept of the image chiefly consists, namely, the intellectual nature."[69] A little later, this extension of the image to both male and the female served as a foil for the consideration of the suggestion that the body, not only the mind, was the place of the image, since the difference between male and female was in their bodies;[70] but this interpretation was rejected with the counterargument that the intent of the words, "Male and female He created them," in the Genesis account was not to involve the physical distinction between the sexes in the definition of the image of God, but, on the contrary, to assign the image to the mind, where there was no such distinction because the mind, and therefore the image, was common to both sexes.[71]

In Thomas' Latin Bible, the proof text from Genesis reads: "Et ait: 'Faciamus hominem *ad* imaginem et similitudinem nostram'. Et creavit Deus hominem *ad* imaginem suam, ad imaginem Dei creavit illum, masculum et feminam creavit eos." The preposition, *ad*, rendered the Hebrew prepositional prefix, *Beth*, which the Septuagint had translated as κατά. In Latin it usually carried some connotation of direction; and even in Christian Latin, where its meaning often tended to have, as we read in Blaise-Chirat, "a more extended sense than in classical Latin,"[72] this connotation was not lost. Thomas used *ad aliquid* to mean "related," as, for example, in an important discussion of the relation between the persons of the Trinity.[73] Some of that significance was also carried over into the inter-

---

[68] ST 1.93.1 s.c.
[69] ST 1.93.4 ad 1.
[70] ST 1.93.6 obj. 2.
[71] ST 1.93.6 ad 2.
[72] Albert Blaise and Henri Chirat, *Dictionnaire latin-français des auteurs chrétiens* (Strasbourg: Le Latin Chrétien, 1954), p. 46.
[73] ST 1.28.1 s.c.

pretation of *ad imaginem*; for that reason we have followed earlier English usage in speaking of creation "after the image of God." The preposition provided the biblical warrant for treating of the image of God as "of the end or term of the creation of man [*de fine sive termino productionis hominis*]," as Thomas stated in the opening sentence of Question 93.[74] This meaning of *ad* was elaborated later in the body of the question, in article 5.[75] Here Thomas pointed out, with great care and precision, that *ad* could refer either to the "term [*terminus*]" and aim of an action or to the "exemplary cause [*causa exemplaris*]" and pattern according to which an action was fashioned, as when God had been called earlier "the prime exemplary cause of all things."[76] At the same time, however, *ad* was useful as a means of stressing the immanence represented by the idea of "image" while preserving the transcendence required by the qualification that it was the image "of God"; "for the preposition *ad*," Thomas asserted, "signifies that sort of nearness [*accessus*] which lies within the competence of a thing that is at a distance."[77] It was important to safeguard the doctrine of divine transcendence when speaking about the image of God not only because the dogma of God the Creator required it, but also because christology (to which I shall be returning a little later) had to be kept distinct from anthropology. The formula "*ad imaginem*" was a convenient means for preserving that distinction: Christ, as "the first-born of all creation" (Col. 1:15), was "the perfect image of God" and was therefore never said to be "*ad imaginem*," while man, though sometimes called "image" because of his likeness to God, was, strictly speaking, only "after the image" because he did not share in the "identity of nature" or ὁμοουσία between the Father and the Son in the Trinity.[78]

The *locus classicus* in the first chapter of Genesis was likewise the source for the distinction between "image [*imago*]" and "likeness [*similitudo*]." For our purposes here it is irrelevant to inquire whether any such distinction was in fact implied by the original text, as the Church Fathers taught, or whether this was simply an instance of the familiar Hebrew *parallelismus membrorum*, as modern exegetes maintain. To Thomas, quoting from Augustine,[79] it seemed evident that some sort of distinction between the two had been intended, "since, if they were one and the same, one noun could

---

[74] ST 1.93.
[75] ST 1.95.5 ad 4.
[76] ST 1.44.3 resp.
[77] ST 1.93.1 resp.
[78] ST 1.93.1 ad 2.
[79] Augustine, *De diversis quaestionibus* LXXXIII 51.

have sufficed."[80] Once they were taken as distinct, the two terms had to be specified in relation to each other. To begin with, Thomas stated the difference and the reciprocal relation between them in the formula, "Likeness belongs to the definition of image [*est de ratione imaginis*], and image adds something over and above the definition of likeness."[81] Refining this formula somewhat, he went on to make clear that "not just any likeness," but only "a likeness with respect to species [*similitudo secundum speciem*]" was necessary for an image.[82] The analysis of the interrelation between image and likeness produced a composite term, "likeness of God in the form of an image [*per modum imaginis*]," which was peculiar to rational creatures and stood in contrast with "likeness in the form of a vestige [*per modum vestigii*]," which could be predicated also of nonrational creatures.[83] Then in the final article of the question, Thomas contrasted image and likeness at greater length, showing that "likeness" could be seen as prior to "image" in the sense that it acted as its "presupposition [*praeambulum*]" but also as subsequent to "image" as its "expression and perfection."[84] He acknowledged, moreover, that in this clarification of biblical terminology he was going beyond ordinary language, where "likeness is included in the very definition of image."[85] In the same article he also cited two other distinctions between image and likeness from the history of Christian thought: the opinion of "some theologians [*aliqui*]" that the "spirit, that is, the mind" was made after the image of God, while other parts of man, including even his body, were made after His likeness;[86] and the opinion of John of Damascus, and of much of the Greek patristic tradition, that "image" referred to rationality, which remained after the fall of Adam, but that "likeness" referred to "the likeness of virtue [*similitudo virtutis*; ὁμοίωσις τῆς ἀρετῆς]," which was not fully possible without grace.[87]

Neither the explication of the preposition *ad* nor the contrast between "image" and "likeness" represented the most characteristically Western exegesis of Genesis 1:26-27. Ever since Augustine, Latin interpreters had taken these words to mean that the human mind was made after the image of the Trinity—a speculative idea of far-reaching "historical importance."[88]

---

[80] ST 1.93.9 s.c.
[81] ST 1.93.1 resp.
[82] ST 1.93.2 resp.
[83] ST 1.93.6 resp.
[84] ST 1.93.9 resp.
[85] ST 1.93.9 ad 1.
[86] Augustine, *De diversis quaestionibus LXXXIII* 51.
[87] John of Damascus, *De fide orthodoxa* 2.12.
[88] Etienne Gilson, *Introduction à l'étude de Saint Augustin*, 4th ed. (Paris: J. Vrin, 1969), p. 291.

It was, of course, a universal patristic consensus among both Latins and Greeks that the plural in "Let us make" was a reference to the Trinity, but Alfred Schindler has recently pointed out again "that among Greek Christian writers there is no model for the trinitarian analogies of Augustine to be found."[89] Therefore when Thomas came to the question whether the image of God in man was the image of the persons of the Trinity,[90] he quoted two Greek Church Fathers who appeared to be teaching that the image was the image of the divine essence rather than that of the Trinity: John of Damascus, who had found the image in τὸ νοερὸν καὶ αὐτ-εξούσιον,[91] and Gregory of Nyssa, who had specifically referred the image to the Godhead, but not to the Trinity of hypostases.[92] The reply to this objection, interestingly, did not deal with the two quotations, as Thomas usually did, but showed what was implied by the teaching that the image of God in man was the image of the Trinity and then disposed of the objections with the terse verdict, "From this the response to the first two [objections] is obvious."[93] Nor were the Greek Fathers the only ones whose authority might be cited against the trinitarian interpretation of the image. Hilary, who had provided the oft-repeated axiom that the image was of the same species as that which it represented,[94] stated that man had been created "after their common image,"[95] namely, the image of that which was common to Father, Son, and Holy Spirit, which was single, rather than after the image of their distinctness, which was trine.[96] Although Thomas attempted to rescue Hilary a little later by attributing to him the argument that man's creation after the image of God proved the plurality of divine persons,[97] Hilary was in fact doing nothing more in the passage cited than repeating the stock argument for the Trinity on the basis of the plural "Let us make."[98]

For the trinitarian interpretation of the image of God, as distinct from the trinitarian interpretation of the creation narrative itself, it was necessary to turn to Augustine, who had almost single-handedly turned western the-

---

[89] Alfred Schindler, *Wort und Analogie in Augustins Trinitätslehre* (Tübingen: J. C. B. Mohr, 1965), p. 44.

[90] ST 1.93.5 obj. 2.

[91] John of Damascus, *De fide orthodoxa* 2.12.

[92] Gregory of Nyssa, *De hominis opificio* 16.

[93] ST 1.93.5 resp.

[94] Hilary of Poitiers, *De synodis* 13.

[95] Ibid., 5.8.

[96] ST 1.93.5 obj. 1.

[97] ST 1.93.5 s.c.

[98] Hilary of Poitiers, *De synodis* 4.17-20.

ology in this direction. There were, to be sure, many other passages from Augustine to be considered, more, in fact, from him than from all other Christian writers combined. These dealt with almost all the various aspects of the image of God, as a simple statistical tabulation will suggest: there were two quotations from Augustine in article 1, two in article 2, two in article 3, one in article 4, four in article 5, four in article 6, ten in article 7, four in article 8, and four in article 9. Thomas gave little or no attention to the place of the doctrine of creation after the image of God as an issue between Augustine and his Pelagian opponents, but he did comment on several familiar excerpts from Augustine's exposition of the creation story, the *De Genesi ad litteram*.[99] There was only one reference to Augustine's *City of God*, not the well-known passage in Book 12 in which Augustine summarized the general teaching of the church on creation after the image of God,[100] but the less common passage in Book 11, in which Augustine made explicit his characteristic idea that "we recognize in ourselves the image of God, that is, of the supreme Trinity,"[101] and that therefore there was a trinity in the image, one of being what we are, of knowing what we are, and of loving what we are.[102] And this idea was, of course, developed much more fully in Augustine's theological masterwork, *On the Trinity*, than anywhere else in his entire œuvre.

An examination of the many quotations from Augustine's *On the Trinity* in Question 93 of the *Summa*—some, though by no means all, of them having appeared in the *Sentences* of Peter Lombard[103] and Thomas' commentary on the *Sentences*—suggests that he put his reading from this treatise to several uses. The most typically Augustinian of the quotations were those in which what Michael Schmaus has called his "psychological doctrine of the Trinity" was rehearsed.[104] Thus there was the trinity of "mind, knowledge, and love"[105] and the trinity of "memory, understanding, and will";[106] both of these were endowments of man which depended neither upon grace for their presence nor upon revelation for their visibility, but were "natural faculties of the soul," as Peter Lombard had said.[107] Having

---

[99] ST 1.93.2 s.c.; 1.93.4 ad 1; 1.93.6 obj. 4.

[100] Augustine, *De civitate Dei* 12.23.

[101] Ibid., 11.26.

[102] ST 1.93.7 obj. 1.

[103] Peter Lombard, *Sententiarum libri* IV 1.3.7.

[104] Michael Schmaus, *Die psychologische Trinitätslehre des heiligen Augustinus* (Münster: Aschendorff, 1927).

[105] Augustine, *De trinitate* 9.12.

[106] Ibid., 10.12.

[107] Peter Lombard, *Sententiarum libri* IV 1.3.2.

referred to both of these in his objections,[108] Thomas went on in his responses to show that Augustine's statements were not to be understood as con-
tradicting each other or the Augustinian doctrine generally. This he proved
by appealing from Augustine to Augustine,[109] as further consideration had
shown the Church Fathers that an earlier formulation was "somehow or
other inadequate [*quodammodo deficiens*]."[110] Students of Thomas will
recognize here his customary style of handling patristic objections, one of
"exposition [*exponere*]" rather than of "extension [*extendere*]."[111] By this
means Thomas incorporated into his tract on the image of God, as into his
tracts on the Trinity, the results of Augustine's speculations on the image of
the Trinity in man. But in doing so, he also drew upon the same source to
protect these speculations from various distortions to which they could all
too easily be subject. From the admission that the images of the Trinity in
the mind were "natural faculties" it might seem possible to conclude "that
man is able to know the Trinity of divine persons by natural knowledge,"
which had been rejected earlier. In replying to this objection, Thomas made
a point of citing Augustine *On the Trinity* again, and that in two quotations
in quick succession: first, to reiterate that there was "the greatest possible
difference" between God as Trinity and any image of Him in man;[112]
second, to distinguish between faith as the means by which man perceived
the transcendent divine Trinity and sight as the means by which he perceived the immanent human trinity.[113] These emphases were in keeping with
the revelatory status of the words of Genesis on the image of God.

In most of the history of the Christian doctrine of the image of God outside the Augustinian tradition, the trinitarian exegesis of the words "Let us
make man" was accompanied not by a trinitarian definition of the image,
but by a christological one. The identification of Jesus Christ as "the image
of God" in a special sense was the explicit and repeated teaching of the
apostle Paul, and on the basis of this identification the Church Fathers had
filled the Old Testament concept of the image with more specific content
than it had possessed in the creation story itself. Thomas noted this predominant tendency of the tradition and even found a quotation from
Augustine that seemed to prefer it to the trinitarian interpretation. From the

[108] ST 1.93.7 obj. 2-3.

[109] ST 1.93.7 ad 2-3.

[110] Cf. Etienne Gilson, "Pourquoi saint Thomas a critiqué saint Augustin," *Archives d'histoire doctrinale et littéraire du moyen âge*, 1 (1926-27), 5-127.

[111] ST 1.39.5 ad 1.

[112] Augustine, *De trinitate* 15.20.

[113] Ibid., 15.6.

very pages of Augustine's *On the Trinity* came the statement:[114] "He [the Son of God] is the Word in the same way that he is the image, but the Father and the Son are not the image together, but the Son alone is the image of the Father."[115] Did this mean that the creation of man after the image of God was after the image of the second person of the Trinity rather than after that of the entire Trinity? The answer to this version of Augustine came from Augustine, who "rejects this":[116] it was not necessary to restrict the content of the image of God to christology. But it did not follow from this vindication of the Augustinian theory that a specifically christocentric account of the image was ruled out altogether. On the contrary, Thomas had devoted an entire earlier question to the metaphor of the second person of the Trinity as image,[117] and he continued his examination of the metaphor here. In fact, he had even taken the occasion of the earlier examination to note that there was a difference between the Greek East and the Latin West on the matter, with the Greeks calling the Holy Spirit "image" and the Latins reserving the term for the Son.[118] He did not repeat that point here, but he did make use of the cognate issue of the *filioque* doctrine to clarify other aspects of the image.[119]

Of the several passages from the Pauline epistles cited in Thomas' examination of the image of God, two referred to the Son as image and directly connected that reference to the creation and salvation of man in the image; both of them were quoted in objections and then dealt with in responses. One was Romans 8:29, which read in the Latin, as it does in the Greek and in the English, "Those whom [God] foreknew he also predestined to be conformed to the image of his Son," but which for some reason Thomas quoted in a different form: "Those whom he foreknew to be conformed to the image of his Son, these he predestined." This appeared to exclude those who had not been conformed and predestined to the image of the Son from the image of God altogether.[120] The other passage was Colossians 1:15, where the Son of God was called "the image of the invisible God, the first-born of all creation." If this assignment of the image were to be taken in an exclusive sense, it would preclude an image of God in anyone except the Son.[121] Committed though he was to the Augustinian

---

[114] Ibid., 6.2.
[115] sᴛ 1.93.5 obj. 4.
[116] sᴛ 1.93.5 ad 4.
[117] sᴛ 1.35.
[118] sᴛ 1.35.2 resp.
[119] sᴛ 1.93.6 resp.; 1.93.7 resp.
[120] sᴛ 1.93.4 obj. 2.
[121] sᴛ 1.93.1 obj. 2.

view that the soul of man bore the image of God the Trinity, Thomas was also intent on being faithful to biblical language and doctrine. The Pauline doctrine of the Son of God as the image of God made a signal contribution to Thomas' doctrine of creation—not only the creation of man after the image of God, but the creation of all things. In the rather unlikely context of the doctrine of the beatific vision, Thomas described it as including the vision of all temporal creatures "in God himself." The ontological ground for such a comprehensive doctrine of the vision of God was supplied by the thesis: "In the uncreated Word are the ideas [*rationes*] of all creatures."[122] In an earlier question[123] he had defined ideas, on the basis of Augustine,[124] as "exemplars existing in the divine mind," and, on the basis of Plato, as "the principles of the knowledge of things and of their generation."[125] Here he carried the doctrine of ideas an important step further by locating them in the eternal reality of the Logos, the image of the Father.

The most substantial contribution of the christological definition of the image to Thomas' doctrine of man as created after the image of God came by way of the contrast between the perfect and the imperfect image. In a passage to which we have referred earlier, Thomas argued on the basis of the consistent pattern of biblical language that the Son of God was always called "the image" and was never said to be "after the image." Strictly speaking, only the Son could be called "the image," because only he had an "identity of nature" or ὁμοουσία with God and therefore formed a perfect image of the Father. When man was called "image" and not merely "after the image," this did not imply a perfect image but only an authentic likeness, yet one that was present in "an alien nature,"[126] what the Greek Fathers had called a ἑτεροουσία. The same distinction served as a key to the words of Hilary, defining an identity of "species" as essential to a true image; as I mentioned earlier, Thomas quoted these words twice in this question and also in the discussion of the Son as "image" in Question 35.[127] Thomas was able to explain Hilary's insistence on an identity of "species" as a reference to "the idea of the perfect image," by which the Son of God did have such an identity with the Father, rather than as a reference to the "imperfect image" present in man, who was not identical in "species" with that of which he was the image. This basic contrast between

[122] st 1.93.8 ad 4.
[123] st 1.15.3 s.c.
[124] Augustine, *De diversis quaestionibus* LXXXIII 46.
[125] st 1.15.3 resp.
[126] st 1.93.1 ad 2.
[127] st 1.35.1 obj. 2.

the perfect image in the Son and the imperfect image in the creature must not, however, be permitted to obscure the validity of the doctrine of creation after the image of God. Indeed, even in the case of the nonrational creatures one had to insist that "everything that is imperfect is [nevertheless] some sort of participation in that which is perfect [*omne imperfectum est quaedam participatio perfecti*]."[128] This insistence applied *a fortiori* to rational creatures, made after the image of God in the distinctive sense taught by Scripture. Thus Christ, the revelation of God to man, was also the revelation of man to man, showing in his divine and human natures what it meant to be the image of God.

Although we have distinguished the image of God as an element of natural theology from the image of God as a datum of divine revelation, Thomas himself did not divide his presentation according to this schema. But he did divide his larger work this way, and it would appear to be faithful to his intention to look at his doctrine of the image first according to nature and then according to grace. Otherwise one or the other aspect of the doctrine would suffer, and this means, according to his fundamental theological stance, that both aspects would suffer. Only if man, created after the image of God, manifested that image, even though only in vestiges after the fall, could the fullness of the image be recognized as standing in continuity with his humanity; and, conversely, it was only the revelation of the Trinity, as believed and confessed by the Church, that provided the authentic content and deeper meaning of the creation after the image of God, seen and known by natural knowledge. For in the doctrine of creation after the image of God, as in the doctrine of God as such and in the doctrine of creation as such, we can see the working of the fundamental axiom enunciated in the very first question of the *Summa theologiae*: "Grace does not do away with nature, but brings it to perfection [*Gratia non tollit naturam, sed perficit*]."[129]

---

[128] ST 1.93.2 ad 1.
[129] ST 1.1.8 ad 2.

3

Saint Thomas
and the Meaning of Human Existence

Anton C. Pegis

Pontifical Institute of Mediaeval Studies

I

To propose that the man we are honoring at this Calgary Symposium was a theologian would cause no great stir were it not for one complication. Saint Thomas was by profession a theologian and that profession was embodied in what he wrote. In other words, he wrote theology; which means, among other things, that he did not write philosophy as a philosopher would, he rather used philosophy as a theologian. And this is the complication. The complication is not that there is a philosophy at work in Saint Thomas' theology; the issue before us is that this philosophy, living in a state of service to theology, becomes and is theology. Everything in the *Summa theologiae*, for example, is theology, including those questions that it is still fashionable to read as philosophy. This is, clearly enough, a complication. Confronted by such a state of affairs, confronted, that is, by the fact that philosophy enjoys an instrumental role in the theological world of Saint Thomas, serving its mistress and not its own human ends, the modern student is called upon to make some effort to recognize the philosophy of Saint Thomas in the world of its service and yet not to identify it with that service.

Here the difficulties and the disagreements begin. I do not wish to recount on this occasion all the brands of Thomism that are available in the world today. But this is 1974 and I can scarcely avoid asking why we are remembering Saint Thomas. There can be many reasons, and indeed many reasons have already been expressed in congresses around the world—from Rome to Paris to Washington to Ottawa to Louvain, and now Calgary. And surely to remember Saint Thomas the man, the dedicated theologian, the indefatigable Dominican friar, does not need a defense. But what exactly is it that we are remembering in remembering Saint Thomas the philosophical thinker, the man who is said to have Christianized Aristotle in the face of some contemporaries who believed that the task was impossible on religious grounds and other contemporaries who believed that it was indefensible on philosophical grounds? Out of this impossible and indefensible effort was born that maddening reality that is Saint Thomas' Aristotle, and the question is to know what was in Saint Thomas' mind when he created an Aristotle who as a philosopher seemed to be so steadily on the way to the Christian revelation. That the Thomistic Aristotle was a theological creation can scarcely be doubted. That Saint Thomas served a religious purpose in the turmoil of the thirteenth century when he made Aristotle speak for the philosophical reason within the world of theology, is equally not to be doubted. How could any theologian let Aristotle speak for reason unless that same theologian had somehow managed to see in the ancient Stagirite truths that could be made part of a philosophy that was native to the Christian world? When Aristotle became the Philosopher, he also became the congenial philosophical neighbor of Saint Thomas the theologian. For better or for worse, this is what Aristotle has been since the thirteenth century. Hence, if there is a question at this frontier between philosophy and theology, it is this: what did Saint Thomas see in Aristotle that led him to contribute so much of himself in order to Christianize an ancient pagan thinker?

Let me set aside the historical reasons that invited Saint Thomas' Christianization of Aristotle and consider the other side of the coin, namely, the effect of such an effort on Saint Thomas' own Christian teaching. For that effect is, in its own way, not only the evidence of Saint Thomas' purpose but also the ground on which he still stands and speaks to us today. No doctrine, I believe, more forcefully illustrates and tests Saint Thomas' option than the notion of man that he learned from Aristotle and, against centuries of Augustinian Platonism, made part of his theology. I am referring not only to the unity of man in his existence but also to what has been for me a much more difficult and deeper notion, the unity of man in his nature. More specifically, I am here concerned with the totally spiritual meaning of the human composite as Saint Thomas understood it, including the spiritual presence that man exercises in the world around him.

II

Let me begin with what is a moment of crisis for Saint Thomas' account of the unity of man's nature. That moment is death. I have asked myself more than once how Saint Thomas could defend, as indeed he does, the unity of man's nature in the face of death.[1] The point at issue is worth more than a passing notice. If you believe that man is composed of an incorruptible soul and a corruptible body, then it seems quite natural to believe that the soul will not die and that the body will. This is, so to speak, how things are. But Saint Thomas did more than recognize that this is indeed how things are. Unless I am mistaken, for the first time in the history of both theology and philosophy he introduced into the discussion of immortality and death a notion that is as decisive as it is difficult to manage. That notion is the far-reaching idea that, in their union, soul and body not only somehow make up one being, the being we call man, they also constitute and are essential parts of one nature, namely, the nature of man. The unity of human nature is a formidable doctrine in Saint Thomas, and it is formidable whether we look in the direction of the Christian theology of man or in the direction of the philosophers who were Saint Thomas' predecessors. And this is my problem. When you say, in the teaching of Saint Thomas, that a man dies, you mean much more than simply that the soul and the body have been separated from one another. You mean, literally, that in some sense a nature has been sundered, and the question is to know the meaning of a nature which, at the moment of death, dies, but not entirely, and also lives, but not entirely. At this precise and austere point Saint Thomas does not seem to have had any predecessors, whether pagan or Christian.

If we could say that a man dies wholly, then we would be facing no philosophical problem on the score of his unity. A Marcus Aurelius could try to school himself to realize that some day he would be royal dust, and that his dear universe would then have claimed him entirely and pitilessly. Over two centuries before this remarkable emperor, the gifted Roman poet Lucretius, the self-professed apostle of Epicureanism, preached that man, being entirely made of atoms, would entirely die and therefore had nothing to fear from the gods after his dispersal. But Stoic and Epicurean mortalism was not the highest or the noblest legacy of the ancient world. In their several ways, Plato, Aristotle and Plotinus taught Christianity an impressive

---

[1] For an earlier discussion see A. C. Pegis, "Between Immortality and Death: Some Further Reflections on the *Summa Contra Gentiles*," *The Monist*, 58 (1974), 1-15.

lesson, namely, the lesson that intelligence in man was something immortal
and divine. The center of man's life was not the world of nature around
him, the world of perishable bodies with only a symbolic reality, but a
transcendent world of pure being, divine and matchless in its permanence,
its truth and its beauty. The divine centering of human intelligence is so
true for both Plato and Plotinus that the goal of life, and particularly the
philosophic life, was for them a meditation on death preparing for the long
journey that the soul of man, like another Ulysses, would take to its
heavenly fatherland.

But, precisely, Platonism was to prove both a great teacher and a great
temptation for its Christian followers. The remarkable lesson that Christian
thinkers learned from Plato was the vision of the universe as a hierarchy of
intelligible truth and goodness, and of man as somehow a voyager in such a
world, open to the pull of its supreme term, the transcendent and ineffable
Good. As everyone knows, this Platonic teaching is the backbone of
Augustinian illumination and, to use a Bonaventurean expression, of the
world itself seen as an illuminative highway. On the other hand, the great
temptation of Platonic intellectualism, not to say spiritualism, has always
been to think of man as a soul residing in and governing a body. But, from
Saint Augustine to the mystics of the twelfth century, no Christian thinker
ever believed that man was a soul in the sense that the soul alone was the
human person. For early medieval thinkers, the unity of man and his nature
meant the moral or spiritual order of his life; and when one twelfth-century
thinker said that the whole man was almost entirely the soul, he simply
meant to say that, in the spiritual economy of human life, the human soul
was incomparably the nobler and more important reality. The psychology of
early medieval thinkers was really a religious spirituality, it was not a metaphysics.

It was Aristotle who, beginning with the thirteenth century, taught Latin
theologians how to think about the unity of man and his nature. It was
Aristotle who likewise presented them with another sort of temptation, the
temptation to relate the soul to the body so intimately that, being thus im-
mersed in matter, the soul was mortal except for the intellect which was
alone immortal and for this reason not part of the individual human soul.
Even under these restrictions, man in the Aristotelian tradition strove to
immortalize himself as much as possible in intellectual contemplation,
believing that such a contemplation divinized his life in a life of friendship
with the gods. In the history of Aristotelianism before Saint Thomas, the
individual man was mortal, but not entirely: while men were born and
perished as individuals embodying an eternal species, the intellect endured
eternally.

If Saint Thomas chose to follow Aristotle rather than the Christian Platonic tradition on the notion of man, it was because he saw a clear-cut Aristotelian doctrine that he could use to explain the unity of man, including especially the unity of his nature. Admit the fact to be explained. Admit that there is a composite being in nature which, like other bodily composites, is one being in its very compositeness. This composite being is man. Seen in the world of nature, he is a living body, expressing and carrying out through his body the life that he has. His soul realizes itself as a soul through the body that it informs. In this sense, soul and body in man function by dependence on one another: they are coparts of their composite, man. This is indeed why man is one being: soul and body constitute one living nature, of which the soul and the body are parts related to one another as mutually necessary coparts.

Saint Thomas' problem emerges at this point. Following Aristotle, he did explain the unity of man's nature as a specific kind of living bodily nature. But, precisely, how can man be so explained without living and dying within the world of nature, as other composites do? As long as man lives, the unity of his nature seems to function to his advantage. At the moment of death, part of his nature survives and part dies. Did Saint Thomas, then, follow Aristotle up to this culminating moment in order to admit finally that death defeated his metaphysics? To die wholly, as other living bodies in nature do, is an understandable phenomenon. But what is it to die *in part*? And what is a *nature'* that, at death, in part dies but in part lives? And if you say that, after all, death is natural, does this mean that it is in keeping with the nature of man that he should die in part and in part survive? Truly, what is man, as Saint Thomas sees him, that he should present us with such a puzzle? Were his nature such that he died wholly or, alternatively, that he was wholly immortal, we would have no such puzzle. But there he is, a union of immortality and mortality in his very nature. There he is, as Saint Thomas understands him, a being that by nature is both immortal and mortal, both somehow immortal in his mortality and somehow mortal within his immortality. We seem to need to relate immortality and mortality to one another in man in order to understand him. Exactly what sort of being, even when we call him by the name *man*, is Saint Thomas talking about?

III

Part of the seeming Thomistic dilemma about man can be answered in a straightforward way. From Saint Thomas' point of view, it is not true that man lives and dies in the world of nature, and there is a radical sense in

which human death — the death of a person as distinguished from the
death of an animal — is not natural but rather against the unity of man's
nature. So much in Saint Thomas' doctrine seems to me clear enough (as I
shall try to explain), if only because it follows directly from his metaphysics. But the consequences of the doctrine are philosophically not so
clear. I realize, certainly, that, since Saint Thomas was a theologian even in
philosophy, he could and did lead philosophy toward horizons which philosophy itself could not know or reach. The student who has spent some years
in reading Saint Thomas' lucid prose learns not to be surprised to find
Aristotle, who knew nothing about the beatific vision, somehow agreeing
with Saint Matthew and Saint John when they spoke of eternal life as being
the vision of God.[2] After all, what better company could Aristotle, as the
spokesman for philosophy, have? Only it was a theologian who managed
this remarkable meeting, and while a theologian is always free to follow his
own vision in philosophy, and even to raise philosophy to goals beyond its
capacity to see, and still less to reach, even so, since we are trying to make
our way in the philosophy of Saint Thomas, we must also try to follow the
lead of the metaphysical principles that unite us to his theology. These principles are the ground on which the modern student who wishes to be a
philosopher can be joined to a teacher who was, by his own vocation and
commitment, a theologian.

What I am saying, then, is this. Saint Thomas is speaking to us today as
a theologian, and his interest in man follows what revelation has to say
about man the wayfarer on the earth, including what revelation says about
his death.[3] Christ has saved man from death and therefore man can look
forward to the resurrection of his body when, as Job said, he will see his
redeemer in the flesh (Job 19:25-26). But in the midst of this discussion
Saint Thomas the theologian did not forget his metaphysics—I mean, his
own metaphysics. If, earlier in the *Summa contra gentiles*, he was right in
proving that soul and body constituted one being, a genuine composite substance as defined by Aristotle, then what could the metaphysician say about
the unity of this composite at the moment of death? For if the soul is by
nature the substantial form of the body, completing it and in turn being
completed by it, then what is death? The answer is as disconcerting as it is
to the point. It is against the nature of the soul, says Saint Thomas, that it
be without the body: *est igitur contra naturam animae absque corpore esse.*[4]

---

[2] scg 3.25.14-16.
[3] For what follows see scg 4.79, referring back to the discussion in scg 2.68.
[4] scg 4.79.10.

It was necessary for Saint Thomas to say this on straight metaphysical grounds—I mean, again, his own metaphysical grounds. It was necessary because it followed from his defense of the unity of human nature. Yet, even so, even if we are here trying to follow Saint Thomas, it is easier for us— or, at least, for me—to say what he has said than to see it steadily. In the name of the unity of man, so Saint Thomas thinks, it is against the nature of the soul to be without the body. How natural, then, is death? If with Saint Thomas we say that the reason for the human composite lies in the soul, how natural is it for man to die, even when we recognize that it is natural for the body to die? For we seem to be saying, at one and the same time, that death is and is not natural to man. We can only ask at this point: what is man for Saint Thomas that this paradox should confront him?

The answer to the paradox begins to be tangible when we recognize that, in his very existence, man for Saint Thomas is not a part of the world of nature. He is not a part because he exists as a spiritual being even in his compositeness, living as a composite with a spiritual economy within a spiritual existence. At first glance, it might seem to be otherwise. Saint Thomas is so concerned to make the soul the unique existential principle for the whole man that he seems to locate it in the human body as intimately as possible, believing that the soul gives existence to the body in its very materiality and does so out of its own need of the world of matter as the object of its intellectual activity. No thinker, it seems to me, has ever made the human soul more a part of the world of nature than Saint Thomas—and let us remind ourselves that Saint Thomas was a Christian theologian. But, precisely, it is at its own existential level that the soul enters the body and the world of bodies. This entry means, not that the soul comes to be in the body or in the world of nature, but rather that the body exists with the spiritual existence of the soul. Obviously, this is the fact to consider. The human body, for Saint Thomas, has a spiritual existence, it is a body by a spiritual existence and in a spiritual world. On the very earth on which man stands and moves and acts with his body, he is there as a spiritual being, giving to the world around him a meaning that it does not have except in his sight. Man does not make the world to be intelligible—God, as Saint Thomas might have said, did that; but man's presence in the world gives to its order an intelligible visibility that it would not otherwise have. No, the soul is not in the body, rather the body is in the soul, and through his body man is present in nature, not as being part of it, but as making it part of himself by raising it to the level of his humanity.

The possibility of such a doctrine rests on two considerations. One is Saint Thomas' views that the human soul needs the body for its own intellectual activity and thus for its own spiritual completion. Without the complement of the body and its sense organs, the soul would be incomplete in its own intellectual nature; with the body, it is complete, combining sense perception and intellectual understanding to build its own world of knowledge and love. Man is this completed intellectual soul, exercising through the body a spiritual presence on the earth, and needing to walk on that same earth in order to awaken, however slowly, to his own nature and its transcendent thrust. To say, then, that the soul needs the body, indeed needs to live in and with the body, is to say (for Saint Thomas) that the human composite has an entirely spiritual economy and meaning, and thus a spiritual unity of nature. Man is one and whole as a spirit in his very compositeness: so, unless I am mistaken, Saint Thomas believed.

What is more, Saint Thomas had the metaphysics to realize this extraordinary notion of man. The spiritual whole that man is in his very nature exists wholly in and through the soul. *To exist* or *to be* is for Saint Thomas an act and for man to exist is for him to *enact* what he is. It is to exercise (through his very compositeness) an intellectual presence in the world. Man *is*, and he knows it, because to be is not simply to be there, as though located in existence, it is to be *doing* the existence by which man is himself and is likewise present to himself and to the world. A few paragraphs ago I said that man is one being in the spiritual wholeness of his nature; I am now saying that he *is* one being, he is enacting and unfolding his nature in the spiritual existence that he has through his soul. For Saint Thomas, at least, to be is an act, and for man to be in the world is to be exercising an existential presence in the world which is the beginning of his own human openness and response to that world. We are here face to face with what Saint Thomas means by human existence.

As Saint Thomas understands it, for man to be in the world is to be present *in* and *to* the world. This is a difficult notion to grasp for at least two reasons.

In the first place, the abstract character of human knowledge has often been taken to mean that it is a sort of abstract transcript of what we experience in the world. So understood, intellectual knowledge is a second-level translation of experience. But this is not the position of Saint Thomas Aquinas. To know is certainly not to know abstractions, though it is true that human knowing is abstractive in origin. To abstract is the condition of human knowing, but it is neither the reality itself of knowing nor its object. To know is to be present in the world, indeed, to be and to express the world. In the second place, I have never been able to understand the view that with the *cogito* Descartes made what has been called the great shift to subjectivity. Certainly, the "I think, therefore I am" was some sort of turn to subjectivity as the apodictic starting point for a universal science. But what kind of turn was it and what was new in it? What was new, I believe, was the devaluation of existence and of the world in the presence of thought. The *I* is thought and what the *I* knows is ideas. Other than as originating thought, existence plays no role in such a doctrine: the "I am" is no more than a backdrop for "I think," so that the world of thinking has no roots in existence. But why is a subjectivity that methodically knows itself as thought and its world as ideas anything more than an isolation from existence and from the world?

But, in spite of Descartes and Kant, the world is not beyond thought or knowledge, and, in spite of Husserl, the world is not constituted by the knowledge in which it is present. An old Aristotelian principle has it that, in knowing, the soul is other beings than itself, that is, to know is to become and to be what is known. From this point of view, my knowing presence in the world is a self-transcendence, a being-the-world by means of the activity of knowing. Abstraction is not knowledge, it is the specifying means of the activity of knowing and it is related to knowing as human compositeness is related to man's spiritual nature. Abstraction precedes knowledge, it enables man to know, that is, it enables him to express the world by acts that proceed from him—acts in which he is present and in which he transcends himself within himself. Moreover, the immanence of knowledge does not mean for Saint Thomas, as it does for Husserl, that the knowing consciousness constitutes the world as part of its life. The mystery of knowledge is self-transcendence, and the result is, not that the world is in me, and still less that the world is part of me, but rather that by my knowledge I am the world, I make myself into its image and I discover myself in this intentional identity that I have with the world.

I shall not say that Saint Thomas' view of knowledge is an easy doctrine to explain or to defend in today's climate. It is much easier to say, with some philosophers, that the world is beyond knowledge, or, if you insist with Husserl that such a view is philosophical nonsense, to say that the world is constituted by the knowledge that includes it. What is the world in such doctrines except that which I do not know or, alternatively, that which I make by my knowledge? And yet, the wonder of knowledge is not so easily explained—or explained away. To know is, certainly, to be the known things, but to be the known thing by an immanent act of knowing is also to be aware, through that act of knowing, that I who know know both my knowing and that I am not what I know. I am not what I know in the order of the act of knowing: in this order I am myself, including myself as present in and to what I know. But in the order of the specification of my act of knowing, I am truly what I know—I am the world that I know. May I add that this is what I understand by philosophical realism, namely, the polar otherness between the knower and the known in the act of knowing? I say this because I must admit that I do not understand any theory of knowledge in which the world is beyond my knowing or is constituted by my knowing. The world does not transcend my knowledge, but yet, within my knowledge, it is present to me as a transcendent other in relation to a transcendent other.

IV

There are many things to be said about human knowing understood as man's self-transcending presence in the world, but perhaps the most immediately pertinent aspect to consider is that human knowing, being an intellectual presence, experiences in the world that which corresponds to its intellectuality. To an intelligence (I mean an intelligence as understood by Saint Thomas) the world is a world of being, a world of causal relations and purposes, a world which, in existing, raises for man's mind the deepest of questions: what is being? and what am I that I can ask this question? The world raises for me the question of being, and I find myself involved in the question. *I* exist, I say, *I* am a being, indeed I am a being who recognizes being, and whose existence and destiny are therefore involved in the question that I am able to ask.

Since the days of Aristotle metaphysics has had the honor of being the highest human science. Who has not heard that it is the science of being as being or that at its highest moment it reaches to God as the cause of being? But let us remember that we are not simply dealing with a science, even the noblest of the human sciences; we are also—and even more—dealing with man himself and his intellectual life. For metaphysics is a human work, and it expresses what is most personal in man, namely, his search for the meaning of existence, including especially his own. Being is a thread that man can follow, leading him both to its own highest answer and to his own highest understanding of himself. Not every man is a metaphysician, for which we can be thankful, but every man is interested in being, including especially his own. To be a man is to wonder, however uncertainly, what it means to be. Man could not so wonder if his spiritual presence in the world was not intellectually driven by what he experiences in the being of the world. No, metaphysics is not simply the highest of the human sciences, as though man is to be conceived as a mere spectator and living as a sort of spectator sport. Metaphysics touches the deepest and most personal awakening of man, an awakening in which he realizes that for him to exist as an intellectual being—to be involved in the world in his intellectuality— is to be involved within himself in the mystery of being. That involvement is the driving force behind the human search for transcendence. I do not now mean that initial transcendence by which man is present in the world as a knower; I mean that much greater transcendence to which his involvement in the world impels him.

Aristotle and Saint Thomas did not have the same view of man at this highest moment of his involvement in the world, and the difference is not only that Aristotle did not know what the Chrstian revelation was to teach Saint Thomas. Believing in a self-enclosed and eternally completed world, a world that had no other character or destiny than to perpetuate itself within itself, Aristotle had a mortalist view of man and what I can only call a mortalist metaphysics. By this I mean that he was as content to bury metaphysics within itself as he was content to bury man in the world. In that famous discussion in the tenth book of the *Ethics* in which he explains that the speculative life (the life of the wisdom that is metaphysics) is the highest and most divine life, and also the happiest life for man, Aristotle goes on to say that such a life unites man to the gods, being an imitation of their blessedness.[5] It is not easy to say at this point that the Aristotelian metaphysics, which began as a search for the highest causes explaining being, was able to lead man to a mortal imitation of the gods and no higher. That Aristotle did not know that man would receive beatitude from a God whom he likewise did not know is not the question; that Aristotle's metaphysics had no transcendent direction beyond itself is the question. But even for a philosopher metaphysics does not contain the destiny of man: to know being as being is not only to know it from the world, it is also to know it within the perspective of the world. The Aristotelian gods—those exemplary prime movers that have baffled Aristotle's historians—are beyond the world, and neither nature nor the heavens can reach them, except to imitate them, that is, to achieve what they are but to do so in a lesser and self-enclosed way. Only, can man really accept a human imitation of divinity as his destiny?

If I have understood the third book of the *Summa contra gentiles* correctly, Saint Thomas did not leave man resting in that imitation. True, in the present life metaphysics is the highest wisdom that man can reach, but of its own nature this wisdom is an endless pursuit, giving to man an unfinished and time-ridden happiness. The Arabs, and most notably Averroës, tried to remedy this endlessness by adding to it, and to Aristotle's teaching, a union with the world of spiritual substances and thus a beatitude that was final beyond the endlessness of metaphysics. But Saint Thomas was not impressed. In this life man had no knowledge that was not the product of his

[5] Aristotle, *Nicomachean Ethics* 10; 1177a13ff.

composite nature. His knowledge was therefore as rooted in the world as he himself was, which means that it was as unfinished as, here and now, he was himself. Aristotle was quite right to say that the forever incomplete knowledge of metaphysics was the highest wisdom that, here and now, man could reach. What, then? Did man, of his very nature, dream of going farther? Or, supposing that God had not rescued him, would man simply have remained a wandering metaphysician, and after death nothing more than a disembodied and hence a limping one?

There was no wandering metaphysician in the world of Aristotle, if only because man did not have—and did not dream of having—a personal destiny beyond the world. But the metaphysics of Saint Thomas did not close man in the world. On the contrary, by reaching a God who did not simply exist but was existence itself, Saint Thomas made man a witness to the origin of being and hence located him at that point in the universe at which he could see that he existed because God made him to be, that his presence in the world was made possible and reflected the divine presence to him, and that without that creative presence he would be nothing. Here, at this ultimate moment, is man's true location in the world. He is in the world, but in the sense of witnessing it in its origin. He is present to the world, but in the sense of seeing that of itself it is nothing: it exists because it is being given existence. Man, as Saint Thomas understands him, is a witness to the creative presence of God in the world, a witness who lives in the mystery of what he is beholding, and who is tied in his very existence to that mystery. Man keeps asking himself: why should God have created witnesses to his own creative act? Man is such a witness and the meaning of his existence is that his presence in the world is the mirror of its—and his—beginning.

The creationist metaphysics of Saint Thomas has done more than simply transcend the closed world of Aristotle. It has even done more than repeat the traditional Christian teaching that in the beginning God created heaven and earth. In the metaphysics of Saint Thomas, the beginning of creation is *now*, the now in which God is making the world to be. The world is *now* because it has the gift of existence *now*. Of itself nothing, the world *is* because God is giving it existence. But in addition to establishing a new sense of the world, the creationist metaphysics of Saint Thomas has also established a new sense of man. What is man? Let me risk some answers that I think Saint Thomas has taught me. Man is a presence and a witness, a presence to the world in its very being and a witness to the origin of that being. What is man? He is a spirit in whose intelligence being speaks of its origin. What is man? He is an intelligence who knows that at the originating point of being he is present to a creating God. Again, what is

man? He is an intellectual being who, across the world, has awakened to
his final and permanent location in existence, the divine providence. And,
finally, what is man? He is a spirit who, beyond the world, stands in the
presence of God, aware that he cannot know his destiny unless he looks for
it in its beginning, aware, too, that his very existence in the world is,
beyond the world, a presence to a God who is present to him. This is surely
a religious view of man and his existence. But what I wish to emphasize is
that it is a view created by the Thomistic metaphysics at the moment of
assimilating and using Aristotle's teaching.

With the help of Aristotle, Saint Thomas turned the Christian man
toward the world, toward nature, as his proper home. That turning is the
signature of man's composite intellectuality. But the Thomistic man, who is
turned toward the world and is incomplete without it, is turned with the
world both beyond the world and, by means of it, beyond himself. In his
very existence, indeed in his very spiritual openness to the world itself, man
unites the world to himself only to follow the transcendent direction that his
intellectuality contains for him and for the world. If, by means of Aristotle,
Saint Thomas united man to the world in a way that no preceding theologian had done, let us add that the purpose of this union was to make the
world part of man's own spiritual pilgrimage.

v

Of the many questions that this conclusion on the nature of man raises,
perhaps the most important and certainly the most difficult has to do with
the unity of his nature. There is no doubt that in Saint Thomas' theological
teaching man is a spiritual creature destined by God for the beatific vision;
nor is there any doubt that this vision is a gift that God has freely and
gratuitously chosen to give to man. But since such a view of man and his
destiny is part of Saint Thomas' teaching as a Christian theologian, it
would be easy to think that he has bent man himself, and even man's
nature, to the spiritual purpose for which, in Christian teaching at least,
man was created. And yet, this cannot be true, if only because there are
many things that Saint Thomas has said that do not fit the premise. Certainly, as Christian teaching sees it, man is destined for a final beatitude
that includes the resurrection of the body and the completion of man in the
presence of God. Had Saint Thomas, therefore, shaped his conception of
man to suit his Christian and supernatural view of man's destiny, it could
have been argued that, as a theologian, Saint Thomas was simply tailoring
man to suit the purposes of this theology. This view may sound plausible,

since Saint Thomas was indeed a theologian. But this is certainly not what happened in his teaching. If I feel that I am confronted by a problem at this precise moment, the reason is that Saint Thomas offers impressive philosophical evidence for the unity of man's nature. Hence, the present issue is not that Saint Paul taught Saint Thomas that the resurrection of the body would defeat death and that, in a way, grace would defeat the ills of human nature. A divine gift defeating the evils of a fallen nature is an inestimable religious teaching for those who believe it. But my present point is that, after saying that I believe it, I still have a problem with Saint Thomas Aquinas.

There is no doubt that, at the religious level of Christian teaching, Saint Thomas was the disciple of Saint Paul, but it is also true that, at the philosophical level, he was a disciple of Aristotle. From Aristotle he learned a doctrine that he transformed without, however, denying its basic teaching. Man was one being both in his existence and in his nature, and it was impossible to think of the unity of human nature without thinking of soul and body as coparts of that unity. What could Saint Thomas, the philosophical student who accepted such a notion from Aristotle, then say at the moment of death? The body, being material, was corruptible and therefore that the body should die was a perfectly natural outcome. And yet, this was not an answer to the meaning of death, if only because (as Saint Thomas thought) death was against the unity of human nature. And this is my present problem. Believe with Saint Thomas that the intellectual incompleteness of the human soul needs the body in order to become an intellectual whole, and you are forced to believe both that the unity of human nature is intellectual and that death is—may I say it?—an offense against that unity. Once more, this is not Saint Thomas speaking to us as one reaffirming the teaching of Saint Paul; this is Saint Thomas speaking to us as one who is following, in his own chosen way, the philosophical teaching of Aristotle.

Why should Saint Thomas have said that for the soul of man to be separated from the body is against its nature, unless the human essence requires both soul and body for the constitution of that essence? What is death, then? Is it simply a separation of the soul from the body, or is it the breakup of the human essence? On purely philosophical grounds, Saint Thomas stands in the way of conceding the second alternative, and the question is to know how to understand this formidable philosophical fact. Indeed, we seem to be in a dilemma. We cannot deny death as a fact of nature, but neither can we deny that, in constituting the human essence, soul and body belong together. They belong so much together that the Saint Thomas who said that it was against the nature of the soul to be without the body has also said that the separated soul was, according to its nature, in an unnatural condition.[6]

Thus, the more we see immortality and death in the light of the unity of man's nature, the more we wonder what to say about either one. Can we simply let the parts of human nature go their respective ways? Saint Thomas the metaphysician is saying that we cannot. Immortality, even when it involves the separation of the soul from the body, cannot include that separation as part of its meaning. After all, what is an immortality that includes an unnatural condition? And what can we say about the death of the body, even if it be called a natural event in the world of bodies, if that death is against the nature of the soul and therefore the economy of the human essence? Admit the unity of human nature, therefore, as Saint Thomas conceives it, and you cannot think of either the death of the body or the separation of the soul from the body as natural.

What to think at this point is not so easy to see. But the same Saint Thomas who led us to a seeming impasse has not left us without resources. For it is not only at the moment of death that man is a mystery. Indeed, to think of human death as an event in nature is a mystification rather than a mystery. Human death takes place in the same world in which human life exists and death as a spiritual event is more faithful to man than is death as an event in the world of nature. It is more faithful because it follows and expresses the economy of his nature. Man dies, but not in nature; he dies in the same spiritual world in which he is living, so that his death is truly a spiritual event—an event in his life, indeed in his immortal life as a person. It is at this moment that death, far from being an obvious fact of nature, becomes a mystery which, instead of defeating man, enables him to see himself more steadily and to understand his life more clearly.

For man, as Saint Thomas sees him in his compositeness, is no ordinary being, and what is peculiar to him is that he does not have a ready-made nature; he has a nature that he must complete and whose completion by him is part of its meaning and his meaning. The mystery of man is that he cannot know himself until he discovers that his compositeness is the vehicle of an intellectual nature living within a spiritual existence. Even though man stands on the earth, like any other composite, his intellectual nature stands ultimately and finally before God and nowhere else. Man stands there, he must learn to stand there, and he cannot discover himself or be himself

---

[6] ST 1.89.1. As I have tried to show elsewhere, this text marks a turning point in Saint Thomas' teaching on the natural disabilities of the separated soul. See A. C. Pegis, "The Separated Soul and Its Nature in St. Thomas," in *St. Thomas Aquinas, 1274-1974: Commemorative Studies* (Toronto: Pontifical Institute of Mediaeval Studies, 1974), 1: 131-158.

unless and until this presence that is his spirtual existence recognizes and expresses the presence of God to him. It is not easy to think with Saint Thomas about the nature of man. To be a man, as I think I have learned from him, is to be a witness to the creative presence of God in the universe and in man himself. Man does not have a ready-made nature because, in his spiritual openness, it is his nature to give himself a meaning in the presence of God. As Saint Thomas sees him, man exists in that presence and he cannot know what he is until, in the slow way of his compositeness, he discovers that he is indeed a spiritual being, that he was born in the love of a creating providence, and that his existence is nothing less than a question posed to him by God. What is it that God wants from him? This is his question and this is his nature. At least, this is his nature as Saint Thomas sees him. Temporality and death are part of that nature. Man can learn from his existence that God did not create him in order to frustrate him or to let him dangle endlessly in the world of time. This conclusion is, so to speak, the mark of Saint Thomas the theologian raising both philosophy and man to their highest outcome. But the conclusion requires not only a theological humanism but also a metaphysics that is sensitive to the meaning of existence in the world of being. If I have learned anything from Saint Thomas the theologian, and especially from the metaphysics that was the human vehicle of his theology, it is that a God who is pure existence and whose nature is love creates in order to give himself, and that, even at the level of philosophy, man can learn to think that he is truly himself when he learns to live in the world of the divine invitation.

4

Thomistic Natural Law and Social Theory

Paul Sigmund

Princeton University

In this paper I propose to examine the consequences, both logical and historical, for social theory of the natural law view of society and politics developed by Saint Thomas. In order to do so I will first compare Aquinas' social and political thought with earlier Christian social thought in order to determine what is distinctive about the theory of Saint Thomas, then I will discuss and evaluate different˙views as to the implications of that theory, and finally I will review some contemporary attempts to apply Thomistic natural law to modern politics and society, and speculate about the possible significance of the recent decline of interest in Thomistic natural law. Thus I will be combining a historical and analytic method in order to achieve a fuller understanding of the content and historical impact of Aquinas' thought. To anticipate my conclusion, I will argue that in form and content Saint Thomas' social theory was basically moderate in its view of society and politics, giving rise to social and political doctrines which were moderately conservative in their original formulation, and which became, predominantly but not exclusively, moderately liberal in their twentieth-century neo-Thomistic reformulation. In both cases Thomist social thought avoided the more extreme positions of uncritical acceptance of the political order or of radical world-transformation or world-rejection which can be and have been drawn from the Christian message. The moderation of Aquinas' social thought I attribute (1) to his intellectual method of com-bining and harmonizing earlier religious, philosophical, and legal theories which has corresponding effects on his view of society, and (2) to the par-ticular interpretation—some would say misinterpretation—of Aristotelian teleology which distinguishes his natural law theory from most other such theories.[1]

It is customary for writers on Aquinas' social and political thought to emphasize that it forms only a small part of the overall corpus of his work and is subordinated to a much broader religious interest and purpose. The religious context of his thought does not diminish the intrinsic value of his ideas but adds an additional element of interest as an example of the way religion can act as a source of political thought, either to legitimize the political and social order, or to criticize and transform it. In addition, at least until the last decade, the Roman Catholic Church has used variations on the Thomistic method to formulate its response to modern politics and society in papal encyclicals, in seminaries, in Catholic educational institutions, and in public pronouncements which have great significance in areas of Catholic culture. Thus Thomistic social and political thought is worth studying for its intrinsic content, its religious derivation, and its continuing political and social importance.

Aquinas found it necessary to develop a political and social theory because Christianity in the twelve centuries before he wrote had not produced any overall systematic treatment of politics and society as viewed by the Christian. The New Testament contained statements with political implications, but they were often open to contradictory interpretations. If "the powers that be are ordained of God, and he that resisteth the power, resisteth the ordnance of God" (Romans 13:1-2), it was also asserted that "we must obey God rather than men" (Acts 5:29). "My kingdom is not of this world" (John 18:35) but "There will be a new heaven and a new earth" (Apocalypse 21:1). If Christ commands us to turn the other cheek, He also takes up whips to drive the money changers from the temple. Usury was condemned by the Old Testament but in the parable of the talents the wise servant is one who invests his money profitably. Some things are Caesar's and some are God's but the line of demarcation between the two areas was difficult to draw and the New Testament gave little in the way of guidance to popes, kings, and emperors or to the lawyers, both canon and civil, who had vested interests in expanding their own particular areas of jurisdiction. More fundamentally, certain basic Christian doctrines produced ambivalent, not to say conflicting, attitudes toward the social and political order since the world was both created and maintained by a loving and provident God, and marred by man's fall and the consequences of his sin.

---

[1] For the latter view, see Harry V. Jaffa, *Thomism and Aristotelianism* (Chicago: University of Chicago Press, 1952).

As demonstrated on the one hand by the hermits, pillar saints, and even the monastic movement in its origins, and on the other by the Crusades and theocratic tendencies among papalist theorists, Christians could draw quite opposing conclusions as to their duty to participate in social and political life.

The Christian ambivalence about the world was paralleled by a similar ambivalence about classical culture. "What is Athens to Jerusalem?" says Tertullian, but Saint Paul himself gives evidence of familiarity with Stoic philosophy and a version of Stoic doctrine of natural law is incorporated into his writings when he says that the gentiles "show the work of the Law written in their hearts, their conscience bearing witness thereof" (Romans 2:14-15). The reconciliation of a belief in a natural law with the doctrine of original sin led to such conflicting statements in the writings of the Fathers of the Church that Ernst Troeltsch argued that there are two natural laws in patristic thought—one "absolute" characterized, for example, by the "possession in common of all things and common freedom for all men" mentioned by Isidore of Seville, and another "relative" to fallen man and including institutions such as slavery, property, and coercive government.[2] (The distinction is not present explicitly in patristic writings but it is implicit in the Fathers' ambiguous attitude towards nature.)

The most influential previous Christian work with implications for political thought, Augustine's City of God, was more an expression of an attitude than a systematic attempt to develop an analysis of politics and society. The concept of the two cities implies a relativity of the political order and a pessimism about the possibility of achieving the peace that is the "tranquillity of order" (City of God, 19.13) in this world, yet in the same work the Christian emperor is urged to act as a minister of God in spreading the true religion (5.24). Augustinianism has been viewed as related to an attitude of rejection of politics, to a "realistic" pessimism about the inevitability of power politics, and to attempts to create a papal world-state.[3] These interpretations exaggerate and perhaps distort the political implications of Augustine's writings, but the fact that both the theocrat and the Machiavellian can be related to Augustine's political thought demonstrates how ambiguous is the political application of his writings.

---

[2] Ernst Troeltsch, *The Social Teaching of the Christian Churches* (New York: Macmillan, 1931), vol. 1.

[3] Cf. H. X. Arquillière, *L'augustinisme politique*, 2nd ed. (Paris: J. Vrin, 1955); John Neville Figgis, *The Political Aspects of S. Augustine's "City of God"* (London: Longmans, Green, 1921); Reinhold Niebuhr, *Christian Realism and Political Problems* (New York: Scribner, 1953), ch. 9.

It is only with Saint Thomas that a systematic attempt is made to relate the Christian message to classical social, political, and legal thought in a philosophical way. As is well known, the occasion for that attempt was a second confrontation of Christianity with classical culture—in this case, the sudden reintroduction into Western Europe of the corpus of Aristotle's writings. However, as an examination of Aquinas' natural law theory demonstrates, the Thomistic synthesis involved much more than a combination of Aristotelianism and Christianity. It also drew on Roman legal thought and the Stoic natural law conception embodied therein; it placed law, politics, and society in a Neoplatonic hierarchical framework; and it reflected a knowledge of medieval political institutions and controversies, as well.

The combination of these often conflicting theories into a single system was motivated by a fundamental belief in the ultimate possibility of the resolution of conflicting theories, itself the result of Christian faith in a rational God who has created an ordered and purposive universe the nature of which can be understood, if only in a limited fashion, by man's reason. The Thomistic theory of natural law is a good example of Aquinas' synthetic approach. Thus the hierarchical relationship of eternal, natural, and human law, as well as Aquinas' belief in a natural hierarchy in society, in the church, and among the angels show evidence of Neoplatonic influences as mediated by Dionysius and the *Liber de Causis*.[4] In order to harmonize the conflicting formulations of the theory contained in Title 1 of the *Digest* of Roman law in which Ulpian had asserted that natural law was "that which nature has taught all animals" while Gaius had described it as a law laid down by natural reason for all mankind, Aquinas distinguishes the various levels of natural law corresponding to that which man shares with all substances, other animals, and man alone.[5] The carefully nuanced discussion of whether the king is free from the law (*legibus solutus*) again reflects controversy surrounding a Roman law text.[6] The subtle analysis of the relation of divine and natural law indicates Aquinas' awareness of the confusion in the treatment of that relationship in the *Decretum* of Gratian.[7] The numerous references to the role of the community in the making of law and, possibly, calling the ruler to account reflect a knowledge of contemporary political practice and the common medieval belief in the (ultimate) derivation of law and government from the people as a whole.

[4] ST 1.108.4; SCG 4.76.
[5] ST 1-2.94.
[6] ST 1-2.96.5.
[7] ST 1-2.91.4.

The most interesting part of the Thomistic synthesis, however, is the use which he makes of the Aristotelian belief in immanent purposes in nature as the core of his theory of natural law. Alexander Passerin D'Entrèves is right in relating this belief to Aquinas' explicitly stated assumption of Divine Providence,[8] but it is important to emphasize that Providence is described as "a *rational* governance of created things" and that rational creatures are said to share in the divine reason by purposive action in accordance with natural inclinations to "appropriate" actions and goals.[9] How does man determine what are the natural inclinations to fitting actions and goals? He considers the goals (we might say, needs) he has in common with all substances such as self-preservation; with all animals—sex and child-rearing; and as a rational man—to know God and live in society—and on the assumption of a purposive nature created by a rational God proceeds to derive certain norms or laws.[10] The process of derivation is not a strictly logical or deductive one but involves the use of *synderesis* or direct moral intuition to arrive at basic principles and the exercise of the practical reason to apply those principles to varying and contingent circumstances.[11] In this description of the natural law Aquinas takes a number of Aristotelian concepts and combines them in a way which is different from the way that Aristotle himself used them. Whether or not he was faithful to the spirit of Aristotle may be argued, but a comparison of Aquinas' discussion of natural law with the relevant passages in Aristotle's *Nicomachean Ethics* and *Politics* reveals that Aquinas has combined quite disparate elements in Aristotle—the *phronesis* of the *Ethics*, the description of final causality in the *Physics*, its ethico-political application in the discussions of government, slavery, property, and usury in Book 1 of the *Politics*, the ambiguous treatment of natural justice in Book 5 of the *Ethics*, and the description of law as reason in Book 3 of the *Politics*—into a new synthesis that makes the determination of natural ends a central consideration in the development of Aquinas' theory of natural law.

This has been the traditional understanding of Aquinas' natural law theory and I believe that it is the correct one. Those who see in his theory either an attempt to build a deductive theory on the model of a logical system (Morton White) or who maintain that Thomistic natural law involves intuitive perceptions of what is good which, once they are expressed rationally, become *jus gentium* rather than natural law (Jacques Maritain),

[8] ST 1-2.91.1.
[9] ST 1-2.91.2.
[10] ST 1-2.94.2.
[11] ST 1.79.12; ST 1-2.94.

or that natural law is really "the traditional pragmatism ... not a set of
generalizations but a set of individual intelligent actions" (Michael Novak)
either misunderstand what Aquinas plainly says or simply wish to add the
weight of Saint Thomas' authority to their own ethical theories.[12] Aquinas
states explicitly that adultery, homosexuality, usury, drunkenness, gluttony,
suicide, murder, and the breaking of promises are opposed to nature and
therefore forbidden.[13] His argument is not deductive, intuitive, or pragmatic, but teleological—in terms of the nature and purpose of man in
relation to a given type of action. Those purposes can come in conflict, as
Aquinas recognizes, and this is why he allows for a variety of ways of ap-
plying the precepts of natural law, but he believes that those conflicts are
not irreconcilable, and that apparent contradictions can be resolved by the
use of reason. The effort of the philosopher (or better, the moral theologian
because his reason should be guided by faith) is to order those claims, to see
what is the legitimate basis and the extent of each of them, and to harmonize them—because such a harmony is both possible and necessary.

When one emphasizes, as I have, the syncretism and the central position
of final causality in Aquinas' natural law theory, it is easy to see why I
described him earlier as a moderate in political philosophy. Aquinas' tendency to ascribe a cosmic purposiveness to human conduct combines with
his optimism about the possibility of synthesis of conflicting positions in a
rational system to lead him to take an intermediate or moderate position
wherever he can. To give just a few examples: the state has a natural justification and infidel (but not heretic) rulers have a right to rule but the
church has a higher goal and the pope has a special position which combines both spiritual and temporal powers;[14] the best form of government is a
constitutional monarchy, preferably elective in form with a role for the
populus;[15] unjust laws do not oblige but it is better to tolerate an evil ruler
or have him removed by higher authority than to produce the social ills that
result from revolution;[16] property is an addition to the natural law which is
now "necessary to human life"[17] but the wealthy property holder is obliged

---

[12] Morton White, *Religion, Politics and the Higher Learning* (Cambridge, Mass.: Har-
vard University Press, 1959), pp. 124ff.; Jacques Maritain, *Man and the State* (Chicago:
University of Chicago Press, 1951), ch. 4 ; Michael Novak, A Time to Build (New York:
Macmillan, 1967), p. 342.

[13] ST 1-2.94.3; 2-2.47.2; 2-2.64.5; 2-2.78; 2-2.88.3; 2-2.148.2; 2-2.154.2.

[14] ST 1.96.4; 2-2.10.10; 2-2.12.2; *De regimine principum*, 14; ST 2-2.60.6; *In 2 Sent.* D
44.3.4.

[15] ST 1-2.95.4; 1-2.105.1.

[16] *De regimine principum*, 6.

[17] ST 2-2.66.2.

by natural law to provide for the poor, and the starving man may take what he needs to stay alive;[18] slavery is the result of sin and it is useful for the slave to have the guidance of a wiser master, but "all men are equal by nature" and the slave's rights of self-preservation, marriage and family life are not subject to abridgement;[19] usury and prostitution are wrong but may be tolerated to avoid greater evils.[20] On warfare, Aquinas opposes individual violence or private warfare but espouses the just war theory, provided that it is carried out "from a desire for peace."[21] Society is hierarchically and organically structured and divided into classes[22] and government is based on natural differences of capacity among men[23] but as noted above, "all men are equal by nature" and "all should have some part in government."[24]

More generally the philosophical assumptions of Aquinas and those influenced by him are likely to lead them to take a moderate position in political and social theory, and extreme political positions such as papal theocracy, divine right monarchy, absolute popular sovereignty, or modern totalitarianism are completely opposed to the basic method and content of their theory. Here as elsewhere Aquinas and his followers are faithful to their mentor, Aristotle, in the belief that in ethics and politics virtues lies in the happy medium ("mean").

Yet having said this, have we said very much? For are not most political and social controversies located elsewhere than at the extremes? The conflict between left and right, liberal and conservative, is the basic stuff of modern politics and if we look at the continuing influence of Saint Thomas on social thought, and in particular his influence since the end of the nineteenth century from the point of view of a liberal-conservative dichotomy, I think we may draw some interesting conclusions. For scholasticism in general and Thomistic natural law theory in particular provided the conceptual framework on which were erected the papal critiques of liberalism, industrial capitalism, and socialism, and the ideologies and programs

---

[18] ST 2-2.66.7.
[19] ST 2-2.57.3; 2-2.104.5.
[20] ST 2-2.78.1; 2-2.10.11.
[21] ST 2-2.40.1.
[22] ST 1.108.4.
[23] ST 1.96.3; SCG 3.81.
[24] ST 2-2.105.1. On the pronounced hierarchical cast of Aquinas' social thought, see Katherine Archibald, "The Concept of Social Hierarchy in the Writings of St. Thomas Aquinas," *The Historian,* 12 (1949-1950), 28-54. For a balanced view of the organic aspects of medieval thought, see Ewart Lewis, *Medieval Political Ideas* (New York: Alfred Knopf, 1954), vol. 1, ch. 4.

for both right-wing authoritarians and center-left Christian Democrats in Europe and Latin America. Regimes and parties of the moderate (and sometimes, as in Chile since the coup, not so moderate) right and moderate left have drawn their inspiration from the Thomistic vision of society and politics, as transmitted and reinterpreted by Catholic writers and by the papacy itself.

If we analyze the social thought contained in the two influential papal social encyclicals, *Rerum novarum* of Leo xiii (1891) and *Quadragesimo anno* of Pius xi (1931) we see the papal response to modern industrialism couched in terms of an approach to private property which consciously adopts an intermediate position between what is described as the excessive individualism of liberal capitalism and the statist collectivism of socialism. In terms that recall Saint Thomas' discussion, the social encyclicals defend private property as fulfilling a natural need in man, but limited by its social aspect.[25] The popes endorse the "natural" right of the worker to form associations to protect his right to a living wage for himself and his family; and advocate intermediate structures of decision making based on Pius xi's principle of "subsidiarity" (lower associations should be encouraged and the state should only intervene as a last resort) and the formal recognition of labor-management associations ("orders") in each industry, trade, or profession which will be self-regulating, although "coordinated" by the state.

The nature of that recognition and "coordination" is, of course, crucial to whether a system built on this model results in a quasi-fascist corporatism à la Spain or Portugal or Austria in the early thirties or in an effort to institutionalize the democratic representation of functional groups as in the Economic and Social Council in the Fourth and Fifth Republics in France (and in De Gaulle's unsuccessful effort to restructure the French Senate in 1969). Both corporatism and pluralism can claim to be inspired by a Thomistic natural law theory—although were it not for the statist character which it seems to acquire in modern practice, the corporatist version would seem to be closer to the social thought of Saint Thomas—given his belief in order, hierarchy, and integration in a harmonious and non-conflictual structure. On the other hand, the papal theory has inspired the European and Latin American Christian Democrats to propose the creation of worker-managed and owned factories which in some versions (e.g., some

---

[25] Leo xiii, however, uses a labor theory argument for private property, the best known formulation of which appears in John Locke's *Second Treatise of Civil Government*, ch. 5. Did Leo derive his argument indirectly from Locke, or did Locke borrow it from the scholastics?

of the Chilean Christian Democrats) have a considerable similarity to the Marxist-inspired Workers Councils of Yugoslavia. Similar Catholic theories also influenced the Peruvian military in drawing up the Industrial Community Law in 1970 providing for the gradual transformation of most companies in Peru into worker-management cooperatives, and the Social Property Law of 1974 mandating the establishment of worker self-managed factories. The Peruvian National System of Social Mobilization (*Sinamos*) and the Chilean Christian Democrats' 1964 program of *Promoción Popular* are two contrasting examples of Catholic-influenced efforts to encourage, finance, (and control?) intermediate organizations between the individual and the state.[26]

The political institutions advocated by neo-Thomists since the revival of interest in Aquinas' thought also cover a broad range on the left-right spectrum. A straight reading of Aquinas indicates a clear preference for a limited monarchy, but neo-Thomists such as Mortimer Adler, Jacques Maritain, and Yves Simon have drawn the conclusion that democratic government is the logical conclusion to be drawn from Saint Thomas' natural law theories. The argument is based on a teleological analysis of human freedom which is only implicitly present in Aquinas' thought, but which provided a philosophical basis for the long-overdue accommodation between the Catholic Church and liberal democracy in France, Italy, and Latin America which only was brought to completion in the middle of this century. In the thought of Maritain, Saint Thomas' teleological argument derived from natural inclinations received a thoroughgoing reworking to produce a Thomistic theory of human rights which claimed an ontological foundation more lasting, and in the case of the property right a formulation more applicable to contemporary conditions, than those of the natural rights theorists of the eighteenth century.

The philosophers of Christian Democracy did not go uncriticized by Catholics of a more conservative orientation who also claimed to base their thinking on Saint Thomas. To give one example drawn from Latin America, Christian Democratic theories were attacked in Chile as opposed to Saint Thomas' belief in order and hierarchy, since they were based instead on "the equalitarian liberalism of the French Revolution, poorly disguised by

---

[26] For examples of the divergent interpretations of neo-Thomistic social thought in Latin America, see Paul E. Sigmund, ed., *Models of Political Change in Latin America* (New York: Praeger, 1970), pp. 310-316, and idem, *The Ideologies of the Developing Nations*, 2nd rev. ed. (New York: Praeger, 1972), pp. 407-410, 454-465.

the varnish of Christianity concocted by the philosophical talent of Maritain."[27]

Maritain himself had difficulty with the relation of the liberal democratic state to religion. While he was able to argue for religious pluralism on Thomist grounds he could not accept a state that was neutral between religion and irreligion. The papacy did not endorse religious freedom until Pope John's encyclical, *Pacem in terris*, in 1963 and the Declaration on Religious Freedom of the Second Vatican Council in 1965. The natural law doctrine of Aquinas as reinterpreted by the neo-Thomists provided much of the argument for religious liberty, but it was difficult to reverse the traditional teaching of the papacy (and of Aquinas' own statements) on the duties of the state to the true religion. As in the corporatist-pluralist debate and the controversy over equalitarian democracy, Aquinas' teaching could be cited by both liberals and conservatives.

From the perspective of the mid-seventies, one may now ask whether the Second Vatican Council did not mark the end of the period in which Thomistic natural law theories exercised an important influence on social thought. The negative reaction of Jacques Maritain in *The Peasant of the Garonne* to the new theology of the 1960s indicated that he was aware of what those changes might mean for Thomism, as well as for Catholicism. Already in Pope Paul vi's encyclical, *Populorum progressio*, one is struck by the absence of the natural law vocabulary used in earlier papal documents and by the fact that Pope Paul does not follow Leo xiii and Pius xi in advocating a third position between simplistically portrayed caricatures of individualist capitalism and collectivist socialism. The ecumenism which was encouraged by the council also resulted in an increased attention to the bases of Catholic social thought in scripture and the early Church which echoed Protestant criticisms of the corruption of the Christian message resulting from the introduction of Greco-Roman elements. In philosophy, greater attention is now given by Catholic thinkers to the epistemological criticism of natural law which have been current in modern philosophy since Hume. Probably the most important source of attacks on teleological natural law theories came in the course of the dispute over the papal con-

---

[27] Jorge Iván Hübner Gallo, "Catholic Social Justice, Authoritarianism and Class Stratification," in *The Conflict Between Church and State in Latin America*, ed. Fredrick B. Pike (New York: Knopf, 1964), p. 199. Thomistic theories of democracy appear in Mortimer Adler, *A Dialectic of Morals* (Notre Dame, Ind.: The Review of Politics, University of Notre Dame, 1941), ch. 7; Yves Simon, *Philosophy of Democratic Government* (Chicago: University of Chicago Press, 1951); and Jacques Maritain, *The Rights of Man and Natural Law* (New York: C. Scribner's Sons, 1943), and idem, *Man and the State*, ch. 2-6.

demnation, principally on natural law grounds, of artificial birth control. Scholastic natural law was criticized for its dualism—the artificial division which it implies between the natural and supernatural—its legalism, its excessively abstract analysis of the procreative function apart from the needs of the human person as a whole, and its lack of a scriptural foundation. It was not long until one of the *periti* at the council could write, "While I affirm the reality called 'natural law' it seems to me that it is neither natural nor law."[28]

At the same time the Christian Democratic parties of Europe and Latin America, recognizing that their Catholic associations, while helpful in providing an inspirational base and in attracting the young, were preventing them from broadening their appeal to non-Catholics, became increasingly secular in tone and uninspired in ideology and programs, often losing their more innovative and reform-minded members to movements further to the left, especially those of Marxist inspiration. In Europe, the Christian Democratic parties became identified with the establishment right, losing the reformist impulse which had characterized them following World War II.[29] In Latin America, Christians for Socialism, Third World Priests, and Marxist-Christian dialogues replaced the earlier search for specifically Christian solutions to contemporary problems drawn from Thomistic social and political thought. In areas of Catholic culture, there is now a new openness and willingness to discuss a wider range of alternatives on both left and right outside the (relatively broad) boundaries set by the natural law formulations. Whether this is a positive development depends on one's concept of the relation of religion and politics, but it may mean the end of the last vestige in Europe and North America of the moderating influence of the natural law tradition.

On the other hand, as the recent Peruvian experiments in worker participation and the continuing Chilean debates on the same topic indicate, it may be a little premature to announce the death of social and political

[28] Gregory Baum, "Remarks on Natural Law," in *Natural Law in Political Thought,* ed. Paul E. Sigmund (Cambridge, Mass.: Winthrop Publishers, 1971), p. 203. For criticism of the natural law basis of the papal position on birth control, see Louis K. Dupré, *Contraception and Catholics: A New Appraisal* (Baltimore: Helicon Press, 1964), and G. Egner, *Contraception vs. Tradition: A Catholic Critique* (New York: Herder and Herder, 1967), ch. 3. See also John T. Noonan, *Contraception* (Cambridge, Mass.: Harvard University Press, 1965), ch. 15.

[29] The recent controversies in Germany over the expansion of worker participation in management (*Mitbestimmungsrecht*) from one-third to one-half of company boards of directors indicate that the reformist aspects of Catholic social thought continue to exercise some influence in Europe.

thought inspired by Thomistic natural law concepts. Indeed the renewed interest in corporatism on the part of students of the developing nations may indicate that new versions of Thomist-inspired social thought may have a special applicability in the Third World and may adopt forms which are closer to the conservative than to the liberal interpretations of Thomism, and more authoritarian than libertarian in content.[30]

It would be unfortunate if Thomistic thought no longer gave rise to new social and political formulations, because, along with Marxism and the liberal humanism of the enlightenment, Christianity has been a principal source of symbols and motivation for the transformation of society, especially in times of crisis, and the Thomistic formulation of Christian social and political theory remains one of the more appealing, moderate, and flexible ways to relate the Christian message to contemporary politics and society. More fundamentally, the belief that it exemplifies that human beings can perceive a purposive order and essential regulative principles for their life in community is one that has attracted man throughout the ages— and if that belief disappears one has reason to fear for the future of democracy—or even of our civilized life together.

---

[30] Corporatism derives from many other sources besides Saint Thomas, but it shares Saint Thomas' emphasis on the need for unity and hierarchy as well as his belief in a "natural" order of harmonious cooperating parts in society and politics. For a discussion which emphasizes the importance of Catholic social thought for Latin American corporatism, see Howard Wiarda, "Toward a Framework for the Study of Political Change in the Iberic-Latin Tradition: the Corporative Model," *World Politics*, 25 (1972-1973), 206-250. For an attempt to relate the natural law tradition to contemporary protest movements in the West on the basis of a theory of "human needs and potentialities," see the concluding chapter in my *Natural Law in Political Thought*, ed. Sigmund.

5

The Thomistic Theory of Property, Regime, and the Good Life

Anthony PAREL

University of Calgary

The relationship between property, regime, and the good life has greatly interested all major political theorists. For property relations constitute an integral part of the subject matter of political theory. Property is man's link to nature. Our physical or, as Aquinas would put it, our bodily existence depends upon the continual consumption and conversion of matter into vital energy. Property is a material necessity of human existence. Psychologically, the love of property, as Aquinas observed, has the potential to emerge as even the very rival of the love of God. Property is also a link between man and man and a basis of our social existence. Our social life, at least in much of its external aspects, constitutes a network of productive and exchange relations of property. These very relations become the subject matter of justice and ethics. As Aquinas, commenting on Aristotle, states, "external goods that are used purposively by man have a moral character."[1] Property then, conceived of as *things*, and as implying *relations between things and persons, between persons and persons, between persons and groups*, constitutes the material basis of social and political life. And property contributes towards the shaping of the character of political regimes and to the definition of the good life.

---

[1] *Ethicorum*, 1, lect. 3, no. 34. All quotations are taken from Thomas Aquinas, *Commentary on Nicomachean Ethics*, trans. C. I. Litzinger, 2 vols. (Chicago: Henry Regnery Co., 1964).

There have been, broadly speaking, at least three views expressed on what the relationship between property and the good life ought to be: the liberal, the socialist, and the Aristotelian-Thomistic, with Plato forming a category all by himself.

Liberalism looks upon the individualistic pursuit of property as the moral basis of the good life. The "great and chief end," Locke's famous line runs, "of men uniting into commonwealths and putting themselves under government is the preservation of their property...."[2] Socialism holds the radically opposite view: private property is the *fons et origo* of all social conflicts and of the dehumanization of man; and its abolition is a necessary condition for the attainment of the good life. To take but one sample from Marx:

> There is communism as the positive abolition of property and thus of human self-alienation and therefore of the real reappropriation of the human essence by and for men.... Communism as completed naturalism is humanism and as completed humanism is naturalism. It is the genuine solution of the antagonism between man and nature, man and man. It is the true solution of the struggle between existence and essence, between objectification and self-affirmation, between freedom and necessity, and between individual and species. It is the solution of the riddle of history....[3]

Aquinas, and before him Aristotle, holds the view that the *use* of property is a necessary means, and private property within the bounds of virtue a *relatively* better means than common property, of attaining the end of human existence, which is the full development of specifically human powers of love and knowledge. The use and possession of property must be subject to one proviso, however, namely that the good contained in it must not be viewed as an end in itself (neither as *bonum honestum* nor *bonum delectabile*) but merely as a means (*bonum utile*) to its proper end, namely the attainment of full human development.

The modern liberal democratic view of property, regime, and the good life, as distinct from classical liberalism, tries to combine some of the elements of the first and the third views. As C. B. Macpherson has argued, it conceives of the good life as Possessive Individualism, as both maximization of individual utilities and maximization of individual powers.[4] The contradiction inherent in this formula is revealed by the fact that in the actual realization of Possessive Individualism it is the maximization of utilities that has triumphed over the maximization of human powers. For

---

[2] John Locke, *Second Treatise of Civil Government*, no. 124.

[3] Karl Marx, *Early Texts*, ed. David McLellan (Oxford: Blackwell, 1971), p. 148.

[4] C. B. Macpherson, *The Political Theory of Possessive Individualism: Hobbes to Locke* (Oxford: Clarendon Press, 1962).

"the false image of man as an infinite consumer and infinite appropriator"[5] has in no way been shaken by the liberal claim that the full development of man is also the aim of the good life. On the contrary, Possessive Individualism has merely led to a situation in which some can maximize their utilities only at the expense of the utilities of others. There is a net transfer of utilities because of which some men's human powers are impeded from their full development. In Aquinas' view, as we shall see later, such a state of affairs is inevitable, since one can accumulate superfluities only by depriving others of necessities—the accumulation of superfluous property being, to use a current phrase, a zero-sum game.

What I am arguing here is that Aquinas' theory of property, regime, and the good life challenges the Possessive Individualist position, as indeed it also challenges the second, the socialist, position. Specifically, I shall argue that liberalism has perverted and inverted the Thomistic order of things, which is that maximization of utilities or consumption of property should be subservient to the requirements of maximization of human powers or the development of man's properly human potentials. Aquinas views man as an active, developmental being, and property as only an extrinsic means in the process of human development. But he also recognizes that if property poses as an end in itself, it can and it would impede human development. He therefore rejects any social order which conceives of consumption of property as the chief end of existence as inhuman and unethical and as one that would stunt and diminish man. There is, therefore, a theoretical justification for examining the Thomistic position for those of us who live in a liberal democratic society.

There is also another reason which I would like to call, perhaps temerariously, our cultural link with Aquinas' society. I recognize that I am here on arguable ground. However, despite the vast difference between the Middle Ages and our own age, there is a historical link between Aquinas and ourselves as far as the subject matter at hand is concerned. It must be recalled that his observations on property, regime and the good life were made during a period in history which saw the slow beginning of the burgher culture. Economic historians tell us that there is an organic relationship between that culture and our own liberal culture. Carlo Cippola, for instance, states that the "roots of all subsequent developments, including the Industrial Revolution and its products, can be traced to the urban developments of the Middle Ages."[6] He goes on to add that "our

[5] C. B. Macpherson, *Democratic Theory* (Oxford: Clarendon Press, 1973), p. 38.

[6] Carlo Cipolla, ed., *The Fontana Economic History of Europe*, 1: *The Middle Ages* (London and Glasgow: Collins, 1972), p. 16.

culture is the direct descendent of theirs."[7] Add to this the truth in the observation that Aquinas "virtually ignores the existence of the feudal system" and that "his field of vision is exclusively the medieval town."[8] Of course, he did not approve of all that he observed there, especially the merchants. In fact, he strongly disapproved of the key assumption of the burgher culture, an assumption, it must be added, which is common to it and to our own culture, namely, the validity of the desire for and the justification of unlimited acquisition of property. If the assertion of the organic link is valid, then we can be better assured that Aquinas' social and political theory was based on knowledge of facts, which is comforting to know, especially with regard to a theologian and a metaphysician of his stature.

In developing my argument, I shall begin with Aquinas' notion of the good life, followed by an examination of how, in his view, property can be both a means and an obstacle to the good life. I shall conclude with a brief discussion of the role that the regime plays in bringing about the right relationship between property and the good life.

I. THE GOOD LIFE

The terminology of Aquinas on this point is Aristotelian, but his conception of good life involves a good deal more than what Aristotle had meant by the term. For Aquinas seems to move on three different planes when he speaks of human nature: human nature as it existed *in statu innocentiae*, human nature after the fall, and human nature as graced. The norm of his political theory is human nature before the fall, i.e., human nature as it ought to be. However, it is the actual historical man, infected by sin, who has to realize the full potential of human nature. Aquinas' conception of the good life therefore combines both these views simultaneously. The good life pertains only to this life, and to man's natural life. Aquinas accepts as a fact, though not as derived from reason, that man has a supernatural end. Hence the question of the relation between the good life and the supernatural life, between *felicitas* and *beatitudo*, also arises: "... through virtuous living man is further ordained to a higher end, which consists in the enjoyment of God."[9] Here we feel the full force of Aquinas' doctrine that grace does not destroy nature. If nature and grace are both

---

    [7] Ibid., p. 23.

    [8] Werner Stark, *The Contained Economy; An Interpretation of Medieval Economic Thought*, Aquinas Society of London, papers no. 26 (London: Blackfriars, 1956), p. 11.

    [9] *De regno*, 1.14 (see Thomas Aquinas, *On Kingship, To the King of Cyprus*, trans. G. B. Phelan [Toronto: Pontifical Institute of Mediaeval Studies, 1949], p. 60).

valid orders of human existence, does one and the same act have both natural and supernatural effects? He says, "vivendo secundum virtutem," i.e., leading the good life, man is supposed to arrive at the ultimate end, beatitude. In brief, the discussion of Aquinas' conception of good life must be undertaken with an eye always on man's supernatural destiny as well.

The good life for Aquinas is that life which develops man's natural powers to the full, especially the powers of love and knowledge, and leads man to the end of natural existence, which is happiness or *felicitas*. The development of human powers he calls "virtue." The good life, therefore, is a life of virtue resulting in happiness—"a virtue-oriented activity proper to man in a complete life."[10] Virtue as development of human powers is also termed "operative" or "dynamic" habits or "perfection of powers": "Virtue denotes a determinate perfection of a power."[11] The good life, therefore, is nothing other than the process of human development. It is necessary here to dissociate from the Thomistic notion of virtue any ascetical notion of virtue which seems to inhibit the development of man's natural powers.

Aquinas divides man's powers into bodily or physiological on the one hand and spiritual or psychological on the other. The former is common to man and animals, whereas the latter is proper to man alone, and only the development of the latter is virtue: "Human virtue ... cannot belong to what is bodily, but only to what is proper to soul."[12] This is an important distinction, especially with regard to the question of property. The proper end of property is the sustenance of man's bodily existence. Property does not *directly* contribute to man's genuinely human development. The consumption of property is only a means and a condition for the full development of natural human powers. Hence any materialistic conception of human development, understood to consist in maximizing utilities, is totally alien to Aquinas.

The good life or development is an "ordered" process. That is, each power (*potentia*) of man is said to be in the process of development only insofar as it is directed to the purpose proper to itself: "The perfection of anything ... is considered especially in its relation to its end. Yet the end of a power is its act. A power is said to be perfect, therefore, insofar as it is determined to its act."[13] To direct human powers to "develop" in directions

[10] *Ethicorum*, 1, lect. 10, no. 130.

[11] sт 1-2.55.1 resp. See Anthony Kenny's commentary on Aquinas' idea of perfection as developed in the *Summa theologiae*, Blackfriars ed., vol. 22 (New York: McGraw-Hill, London: Eyre and Spottiswoode, 1964), appendix 9, p. 126.

[12] sт 1-2.55.2 resp.

[13] Uniuscujusque autem perfectio precipue consideratur in ordine ad suum finem. Finis

improper to them is unethical and antihuman. Thus the view that consumption of property is the end of human existence would lead to a disordered and antihuman process of development.

Now the development of human powers is possible only in and through the political community, for without "mutual assistance" and a "common directive principle," a community of free beings cannot fully develop. Thus full human development is not only moral and intellectual but also social and political: "man is helped by the civic group ... not only in regard to bodily needs .. but also in regard to right conduct, inasmuch as public authority restrains with fear of punishment delinquent young men whom paternal admonition is not able to correct."[14] To live well is, above all, the end of the city or of the regime, both collectively with reference to all and severally with reference to each individual.

One important aspect of the good life is what Aquinas, following Aristotle, calls "self-sufficiency," autarky, "vita per se sufficiens." The question of property naturally arises. Granted that property has only an instrumental role to play in human development, the question of the amount necessary for human development has still to be determined. Aquinas gives a negative criterion of determining this issue. In the first place, self-sufficiency means "that which ... makes life desirable and free from wants,"[15] something which "taken apart from other things" is sufficient. This means, once again, that property is justified only to the extent it contributes to human development. Self-sufficiency does not mean the enjoyment of "everything that can come to man." Man's development does not consist in the limitless addition of material things:

> Man can be made better by an additional good. But a man's desire for this does not remain unsatisfied because a desire controlled by reason, such as a truly happy man should have, is undisturbed by the things that are unnecessary even though attainable. Happiness, therefore, has this quality above everything else; it is desirable even when not augmented by other goods.[16]

Secondly, self-sufficiency is inconsistent not only with a limitless desire for material things but also with superabundance:

> Superabundance makes people less self-sufficient, since a man must have the help or service of many servants to guard and manage excessive possessions.

---

autem potentiae actus est. Unde potentia dicitur esse perfecta secundum quod determinatur ad suum actum (sт 1-2.55.1 resp.).

[14] *Ethicorum*, 1, lect. 1, no. 14.
[15] Ibid., 1, lect. 9, no. 114.
[16] Ibid., 1, lect. 9, no. 116.

Besides, rectitude of judgment, by both speculative and practical reason, and external virtuous actions are possible without an abundance of riches.[17]

Aquinas distinguishes between the requirements of the good life considered with reference to the individual and with reference to the state as a whole. In each case, property plays only an instrumental role. With regard to the individual, only two things are necessary:

> The first and most important is to act in a virtuous manner (for virtue is that by which one lives well); and second, which is secondary and instrumental, is a sufficiency of those bodily goods whose use is necessary for virtuous life.[18]

Note that Aquinas says that *use*, not ownership, is necessary. The implication seems to be that use has primacy over ownership. Indeed, in the same context, Aquinas states twice that the end of individual appropriation is the good of the community as a whole, and that private production does not necessarily imply exclusive right of private appropriation: "... whatever particular goods are procured by man's agency—whether wealth, profits, health, eloquence, or learning—are ordained to the good life of the multitude."[19] Again: "... the acquisition of temporal goods ..." is "all ordained to the common good of the multitude."[20]

The instrumental character of property remains unchanged with regard to the "good life of the multitude." To establish virtuous living in a multitude, states Aquinas, three things are necessary:

> First of all, that the multitude be established in the unity of peace. Secondly, that the multitude thus united in the bond of peace, be directed to acting well. ... In the third place, it is necessary that there be at hand a sufficient supply of the things required for proper living, procured by the ruler's efforts.[21]

Aquinas fully endorses the famous Ciceronian conception of community, which came to him through Augustine: "Populus coactus multitudinis juris consensu et utilitatis communione sociatus."[22] The idea here is that a political community is at once a legal bond based on *consensus juris*, and a property bond based on a sharing (*communione utilitatis*). The sharing takes place both through the agency of the ruler *and* through the exercise of the individual freedom.[23] The acquisitive propensity needs the state, i.e., the law

[17] Ibid., 10, lect. 13, no. 2128.
[18] *De regno*, 1.15 (Phelan trans., p. 65).
[19] Ibid. (Phelan trans., pp. 63-64).
[20] Ibid., 1.14 (Phelan trans., p. 62).
[21] Ibid., 1.15 (Phelan trans., p. 65).
[22] Augustine, *De civitate Dei*, 19.21; Cicero, *De republica*, 1.25.
[23] ST 1-2.105.2.

of the regime, not as a corrective as Adam Smith would suggest, but as a directive principle, if it is to serve the just needs of the community. And here we come to Aquinas' conception of the role that law plays in the good life.

The notion of the good life as development and as virtuous life may give the impression that good life is a matter of reason and volition only. The fact is that, for Aquinas, it involves the coercion of law. Here he follows Aristotle faithfully, and brings out the specifically *political* aspect of the good life. He comments:

> ... the best human good, happiness, is the end of political science, whose goal manifestly is activity in accord with virtue. Political science is especially concerned with framing laws and apportioning rewards and punishments in order to develop good citizens and doers of good work. This is to operate in accord with virtue.[24]

In a chapter that would have pleased Machiavelli immensely had he seen it, Aquinas comments, "Passion that—when firmly rooted by habituation—masters man does not yield to argument but must be attacked by violence to compel men to good";[25] "... all men become virtuous by means of law."[26] Law is "necessary" to make men good—the virtuous need it as an incentive, and the insubordinate need it as a deterrent:

> The Law includes coercive power inasmuch as it is promulgated by the ruler or the prince; likewise it is an instruction issuing from prudence and reason which gives guidance towards the good. Therefore, law is obviously necessary to make men virtuous.[27]

There is a further aspect of the good life which reveals the instrumental character of the acquisitive activity. The good pursued in the good life, says Aquinas, is not something found in man himself (*in ipso existens*); it is "extrinsic" to him or lies "outside" him; it is a *finis extra se*, a *bonum exterius*.[28] It is not like health, or truth, or wealth, all of which, Aquinas implies, though found in man only preserve life in its *being* but do not bring it to its *perfection*. Thus a carpenter merely keeps the ship in being by repairing the boards, whereas the captain brings the ship to its perfection, which is its suitability for being taken to the harbour by the captain:

[24] *Ethicorum*, 1, lect. 14, no. 174.
[25] Ibid., 10, lect. 14, no. 2147.
[26] Ibid., 10, lect. 14, no. 2148.
[27] Ibid., 10, lect. 14, no. 2153.
[28] *De regno*, 1.14 (Phelan trans., pp. 58-60).

It is the same with man. The doctor sees to it that a man's life is preserved; the tradesman supplies the necessities of life; the teacher takes care that man may learn the truth; and the tutor sees that he lives according to reason. Now if man were not ordained to another end outside himself, the above-mentioned cares would be sufficient for him.[29]

Thus if health were the end of good life, to rule would have been the task of doctors; or, if knowledge were the end of the good life, professors would have been kings; or, if affluence (*divitiarum affluentia*) were the end of good life, merchants and economists would have been rulers. "It is ... clear," concludes Aquinas, "that the end of a multitude gathered together is to live virtuously. ... And *good life* is virtuous life." If it were otherwise, Aquinas observes tauntingly, all merchants and businessmen living everywhere would constitute a political community, which obviously is not the case: "... only such are regarded as forming one multitude as are directed by the same laws and the same government to live well."[30] The conclusion is that the acquisitive activity, though necessary for the preservation of life, contributes only instrumentally and indirectly and extrinsically to the proper development of man.

The extrinsic character of the good pursued in the good life gives Aquinas a perfect opening to introduce the idea of *beatitudo*, which is totally extrinsic to human nature. If man has a supernatural end, then felicity or the good life can be seen only as an antecedent end, i.e., the end in the next life. The two, felicity and *beatitudo*, are related like the imperfect to the perfect, but not like the means to the end.

The practical conclusion that Aquinas draws from his vision of two ends of man is that *imperium* must be subordinate to *sacerdotium*. And he means both a theoretical and a historical subordination. Aquinas' recommendation of the subordination of the state to the church is at best valid only for his own times. It has no meaning today, especially since the church itself has arrived at a different understanding of its character as an institution. The church does not seem to be unduly worried that its temporal power does not exceed that of San Marino or Bhutan.

The same irrelevance cannot be said to be true of the other aspects of the political theory of Aquinas. For the validity of the theory does not rest on the particular combination it made with thirteenth-century sociology. The theoretical significance is that, given the fact—or even the assumption— that man is ordained to a supernatural end, what then? This is what makes Thomism attractive and intractable. Thomas really wants to have the best of

[29] Ibid. (Phelan trans., p. 59).
[30] Ibid. (Phelan trans., p. 60).

both worlds. He says on the one hand that through natural virtue man cannot arrive at beatitude ("finem fruitionis divinae non consequitur homo per virtutem humanam, sed virtute divina"), yet, on the other hand, and in the same passage, he writes that it is through virtuous living that man arrives at beatitude ("vivendo secundum virtutem ad ulteriorem finem ordinatur ... per virtuosam vitam pervenire ad fruitionem divinam").[31]

The question of the relation between the good life and beatitude is similar to that of the relation between the natural virtues and theological virtues, between reason and revelation, nature and grace. Simply because man has a supernatural end, it does not follow that man may neglect the development of his natural powers. The point is that on the theoretical plane, Aquinas' conception of human development includes and culminates in man's religious development. And one need not even be a Christian to see this. In other words, there is an eschatological element in Aquinas' political theory and in his vision of man. But such an element is no evidence of its historical or sociological irrelevance. Otherwise what sense could one make of such eschatological theories as Marxism or Islam?

Have the place and role of property in any way changed, now that Aquinas has argued that man's final end is beatitude? The answer is "No." Even if man's final end were felicity, property would still have had only an instrumental role to play.[32] It would still not have contributed intrinsically to human development. In the *Summa* Aquinas further clarifies his notion of the role that property should play in felicity and beatitude.[33] In the case of the first (which he calls *beatitudo imperfecta*) such as we can have in this life, property is required, not as constituting the essence of felicity but as a means (*quasi instrumentaliter deservientia beatitudini*). Property is necessary for the sustenance of bodily life, for the performance of intellectual and moral virtues, and for contemplation. But in the case of *beatitudo*, which he calls perfect beatitude, property is required in no way (*nullo modo*). The reason is that the beatific vision does not require a material body, but only either soul, or a spiritual body. In the *Summa*, 2-2.83.6, Aquinas somewhat tones down the sharpness of *nullo modo* and says that, even for the attainment of beatitude, property is required as a means: "Temporal things are lawfully desired, not as our main and final goal, but as helps (*instrumentaliter*) towards eternal happiness, since they may be used to support life of the body and to serve as instruments in performing virtuous acts, as Aristotle says."

---

[31] *De regno*, 1.14.
[32] *Sententia libri Politicorum*, 2.5.
[33] ST 1-2.4.7.

The general conclusion is that Aquinas is consistent in his position that the use and acquisition of property contribute only instrumentally to man's development, and his theological doctrine on man's ultimate end does not contradict but only *reinforces* his philosophical argument about the instrumental character of property.

II. PROPERTY AS MEANS TO THE GOOD LIFE

There are several conditions to be met if property is to be a means to human development. It must be accessible to all, which raises the question of the basis of the right to things. Further, there must be equality in property relations and moderation in use. And, above all, human development must be the justification, and the sole justification, for acquisition and appropriation. This means that the science of acquisition, economics, cannot be autonomous but subject to politics, the architectonic science of human development: "It pertains to *pecuniativa* to acquire money, but to *yconomica* to use it."[34] Again, the distinction between production and right use is most important for Aquinas. It is on the basis of this distinction that he separates natural wealth from unnatural wealth. The first is wealth which has a human, and only a human, end; the second is wealth which is its own end, and therefore becomes antidevelopmental and antihuman.

A. *The Question of Right and Related Issues*

As to the question of right to property, Aquinas gives two specific reasons. The first is the argument from *imago Dei*. Man is the image of God, and therefore analogously shares God's dominion over things. The second is the argument from rationality. Man is a self-developing rational creature and, consequently, he is able to make and use things for his own development, as if things were made for his sake. But these two reasons, *imago Dei* and rationality, give the basis only of use: "... as regards their use, and in this way, man has a natural dominion over external things, because by his reason and will, he is able to use them for his own profit, as they were made on his account...."[35]

The narrower question of proprietary *possession* is not covered by this universal right to *use* things. The right to ownership is confined to questions of production and exchange, *procurandi et dispensandi*. Here Aquinas' language is especially rigorous: "... while use *must* be common,

---

[34] *Politicorum.* 2.6.
[35] ST 2-2.66.1 resp.

ownership *may* be private (*licitum est quod homo propria possideat*)." However, as far as the use of things goes, "... man ought to possess external things, not as his own, but as common...."[36]

The right to private possession, according to Aquinas, is a permissive, relative right, relative to man's historical condition. Its basis is found in human convention, *jus gentium*, and in positive law, and it is in accordance with natural law only in the sense that natural law does not oppose it. The right to private property is like the right to wear clothes. By nature man is naked, and he wears clothes because of habit and convention:

> You speak of something being according to natural right in two ways. The first is because nature is set that way.... The second is because nature does not bid the contrary; thus we might say that it is of natural law for man to be naked, for nature does not give him clothes; these he has to make by art. In this way common ownership and universal liberty are said to be of natural law, because property and slavery exist by human contrivance for the convenience (*ad utilitatem*) of social life (*humanae vitae*), and not by natural law. This does not change the law of nature except by addition.[37]

> Community of goods is ascribed to the natural law, not that the natural law dictates that all things should be possessed in common and that nothing should be possessed as one's own, but because the division of possessions is not according to the natural law, but rather arose from human agreement which belongs to positive law.... Hence the ownership of possessions is not contrary to the natural law, but an addition thereto devised by human reason.[38]

The basis for the relative advantage of private ownership must be carefully noted: private ownership is necessary because it serves the end of human development better than common ownership. Whether it is the question of the universal right to use or the restricted right to proprietary possession, what is uppermost in Aquinas' thought is the human end of property. The central issue in Aquinas is not dominion over things, or the right to ownership, but the proper use of things, namely virtue, i.e., human development. Neither dominion nor ownership per se produces virtue or human development; they are merely rational conditions for human development. In the liberal theory of property, however, dominion and ownership are taken to be the ends of political life. The natural right to property becomes the right to infinite, or limitless, appropriation. For Aquinas, acquisition according to

---

[36] ST 2-2.66.2 resp.
[37] ST 1-2.94.5 ad 3.
[38] ST 2-2.66.2 ad 1.

natural right ought to be self-limiting—anything which has human end cannot be limitless.

The three reasons which he gives for the relative merit of private owner-ship over common ownership all refer to nothing more than pragmatic ad-vantages. In the *Summa*, 1.98.2 ad 3, Aquinas implies that in the state of innocence, i.e., human nature considered as it ought to be, common possession is somehow more natural to man than private possession. How-ever, this is not the case in man's actual historical condition; here common possession gives rise to greater social conflicts and injustice than private possession. The latter is more peaceful (*magis pacificus*), more ordered (*ordinatior*), and provides better incentive (*magis sollicitus*) than the for-mer.[39] In the *Commentary on the Politics*, Aquinas expands his reasoning. He says that in actual societies, private possessions have greater potential to render men friendly and tolerant (*liberales et benefici*) towards each other than common possession, which makes men hostile to each other.[40] Com-mon possession would have to reward equally those who work and those who do not work, which is against justice: "... they do not do equal work and do not receive equal reward."[41]

The evils associated with property relations are more numerous in the case of common possession. According to Aquinas, the determination of "mine and thine" is a precondition for social order. Furthermore, the desire to possess is rooted in one's desire for self-preservation, and so long as this desire is not *magis quam oportet*, it is licit: "... for this desire comes from this, that a man loves himself, for on account of this he desires good things for himself."[42]

It is to be noted that the right to possess something as one's own, in Aquinas' thought, is conditional, not absolute. The condition is that the right be limited, that it should not permit possession of things *magis quam oportet*. Only on this condition would private possession with respect to acquisition and exchange be *socially* beneficial. Only this condition would prevent man from invading others, and from desiring what belongs to others:

> ... While each concerns himself with his own property and not with that of another, quarrels do not occur between men, which generally happen when many have to care for one thing, while it seems it must be done thus to one

---

[39] ST 2-2.66.2.
[40] *Politicorum*, 2.5.
[41] Ibid.
[42] Ibid.

and another way to others; another good thing is that each man increases his possessions more, pursuing that the more carefully as they are his own. And in this way riches will be severally owned, but because of the virtue of citizens who will be both generous and kind, they will be common as to use.[43]

Finally, the question of the right to appropriations through labour. Labour and individual appropriation through labour, it is true, introduce a natural commensuration between the thing which one produces and oneself. Thus a piece of land which one cultivates is more properly one's own than another's who does not cultivate it.[44] However, for Aquinas, the end of labour is not and can never be infinite appropriation, but only livelihood:

> So far as manual labour is directed to obtaining food, it falls under the necessity of precept as necessary for that end, because what is directed to an end derives its necessity from that end, and hence is necessary to the extent that the end cannot be attained without it. Therefore, one who has no other means of livelihood is obliged to work with hand, regardless of his condition. ... One is bound to manual labour by the same necessity by which he is bound to eat. Hence if one could live without eating, he would not be bound to do manual labour.[45]

Aquinas goes on to point out that the necessity for labour arises from the necessity to earn one's livelihood lawfully (*licite*), that is, without having to commit theft, without having to covet other people's property, and without having to resort to unethical business practices (*ad evitandum turpia negotia*). And he concludes by stating that what he said of *manual* labour is true of labour as such:

> But it should be noted that by manual labour are understood all the human activities by which men lawfully earn their livelihood, whether by the use of their hands, feet or tongue. For watchmen, couriers, and such like, who live by their labour, are considered to live by manual labour. Since the hand is the tool of tools, the work of one's hands signifies any occupation by which a man can lawfully earn his livelihood.[46]

The formula of common use and private possession gives the correct basis for both necessary incentive for production and just distribution. The right to common use means that no one may be excluded from the use of things necessary for his development. That is why, according to Aquinas, the reason which permits private property also permits forcible taking of

---

[43] Ibid., 2.4.
[44] ST 2-2.57.3.
[45] ST 2-2.187.3.
[46] Ibid.

necessary things from others without committing the sin of theft.[47] Similarly, it should be beyond doubt that, according to Aquinas, the right to produce and exchange (*procurandi et dispensandi*), does not bring with it the right to exclude others from the use of things which are produced and exchanged, if such things are necessary for their developmental process. In the liberal democratic system the right to produce has become the basis of the right to own, which, in turn, has become the basis for the right to exclude others, regardless of their needs. This perversion of property Aquinas would never tolerate.

B. *Justice or "Equality" of Possession*

The analysis of property as a means to the attainment of good life will remain incomplete if we do not relate it to Aquinas' notion of justice. For, according to Aquinas, justice covers the whole range of man's property relations:

> Justice is about certain external operations, namely distribution and commutation. These consist in the use of certain externals, whether things, persons or even works: of things, as when one man takes from or restores to another that which is his; of persons, as when a man does an injury to the very person of another, for instance by striking or insulting him, or even by showing respect for him; and of works, as when a man justly exacts a work of another, or does a work for him.[48]

Now the important, and the difficult, point is that according to Aquinas the essence of justice, apart from obligation (*ratio debiti*) is equality: "... justice by its name implies equality."[49] "The mean of justice consists in a certain proportion of equality between the external thing and the external person."[50] Conversely, the essence of injustice is inequality: "... the object of injustice is something unequal."[51] Again: "... we speak of injustice in reference to an inequality between one person and another, when one man wishes to have more goods, riches for example, or honors, and less evils, such as toils, and losses...."[52]

Aquinas' identification of justice with equality is especially important with regard to property relations, for it makes sure that every man has, or

---

[47] ST 2-2.67.7.
[48] ST 2-2.61.3 resp.
[49] ST 2-2.58.2.
[50] ST 2-2.58.10.
[51] ST 2-2.59.2.
[52] ST 2-2.59.1 resp.

ought to have, an equal theoretical and practical opportunity to obtain sufficient property. Otherwise his development could not occur. Aquinas does
not conceive of property relations as between the advantaged and dis-
advantaged in the first instance and then introduce the notion of justice, as
Professor John Rawls seems to do,[53] as a means of *reducing existing
inequalities*. If we follow Aquinas strictly, it is difficult to understand how
inequalities come to exist in the first place. Yet inequalities *de facto* exist.
And Aquinas condones them, as for instance medieval slavery (*servus est
possessio quaedam*; a slave is his master's chattel).[54] Hence, there is some
difficulty in dealing with the subject of inequality in Aquinas. I do not see
how Thomas Gilby can sustain the claim that Aquinas "thoroughly disapproved of one man owning and treating another as a utility."[55] What
Aquinas says in the *Summa*, 1.96.4 resp., which Gilby uses in Aquinas'
defence, is that human nature *in statu innocentiae*, i.e., taken in its abstract
perfection, says nothing of slavery; that slavery is the result of human convention. There is nothing in human nature which makes one the chattel of
another. According to nature one man is not ordered for the utility of
another. The reason is "... because everyone naturally values his own good,
and consequently finds it grievous to surrender entirely to another the good
that ought to be his own, it follows that lordship (*dominium*) of this kind
cannot but be punitive to those subjected to it. For this reason, man cannot
have lorded over man in the state of innocence in that sort of way."[56] However, Aquinas condones slavery as it affects historical man. Hence the difficulty in grasping his theory of equality and property.

There appears to be some incompatibility between Aquinas' metaphysics
of human nature and his understanding of the historical institution of
slavery. How are we to understand a theory of equality which, on the one
hand, forbids inequality on the basis of nature yet in practice does not at-
tack it, when inequality in the form of slavery is actually found in history?
Is it that Aquinas gave in too much to the claims of *jus gentium* and
positive law? Or is it that he was merely content with analysis and
clarification, and not bothered with justification? The charitable, and
perhaps even the fair, view seems to be that Aquinas' metaphysics offers the
very tool to correct his error in grasping the institution of slavery.

[53] John Rawls, *A Theory of Justice* (Cambridge, Mass.: Harvard University Press, 1971),
esp. ch. 5.
    [54] ST 2-2.61.3.
    [55] See Gilby's commentary on 1-2.94.5 ad 3, in *Summa theologiae*, Blackfriars ed., vol.
28 (New York and London, 1966), p. 95 n *f*.
    [56] ST 1.96.4.

It is within this "difficult" context, then, that we must turn to his notions of commutative and distributive justice.

Commutative justice covers the whole range of personal property relations and Aquinas gives an exhaustive list of such relations: buying, selling, trade, commerce, interest, loans, wages, price, contracts, fraud, theft, rapine, restitution, false testimony, detractions and, last but not least, seduction. It is the basic principle or theory that must be noted: in these property relations, "... the parties have a claim to equal return";[57] things exchanged must be arithmetically equal: *oportet adequare rem rei* ("it is necessary to equalize thing with thing");[58] whatever is for the common good should not be more of a burden to one than to another, and the value of a thing exchanged must, in the final analysis (i.e., making allowances for labour cost, fluctations in supply and demand, even a moderate profit, etc.), be based on its aptness for human consumption (*humanis usibus apta*).[59]

In his *Commentary on the Politics*, Aquinas fully endorsed Aristotle's distinction between intrinsic value (*usus proprius*) and exchange value (*commutatio*, or *communis usus*). Exchange of commodities was licit provided, of course, it involved only the necessaries of life, and not profit for profit's sake. As he writes in the *Commentary on Politics*:

> For there are two uses for each thing and they agree in this, that each is valid in itself and is not accidental; they differ, in this, that one of them is the proper use of the thing and the other is not, but is the alternate use. Thus there are two uses for a shoe, one certainly being the proper one, namely as a foot cover ... the other however, is not the proper, but the alternate use, namely its exchange use. A man is thus able to use a shoe in exchange for either bread or food; and although this use is not the same as the proper use of a shoe, nevertheless, it is a valid not an accidental use, since he who trades the shoe uses it according to its worth. And as it is said concerning a shoe, thus it must be understood about all other things which can be owned by man.[60]

One could not lawfully raise the price of a thing on account of the need of the individual buyer.[61] The market price can be a just price, provided that there is equality of value between things exchanged; that there is no

[57] st 2-2.61.3.
[58] st 2-2.61.2.
[59] st 2-2.71.1.
[60] *Politicorum*, 1.7.
[61] st 2-2.77.1.

question of profit of profit's sake ; and, finally, that the reason for exchange is human development and nothing else.[62]

As for distributive justice, the basis of equality is geometric, determined by the proportion of the individual's contribution to the common good. This proportion can be judged both with reference to the intrinsic quality of each contribution and with reference to the accepted social evaluation of that contribution. Thus holiness, learning, and wealth, according to their intrinsic value, are put in that order. But the accepted social standards of a community may reverse the order. Thus in an oligarchy a football player may be thought to make a better contribution to society than a bishop or even a professor, "propter potentiam vel industriam secularem."[63] This, according to Aquinas, would not violate commutative justice. What would violate commutative justice in such a society would be if some one was put on the football team merely because he was the relative of the captain, or some other such reason. Such rewarding of a social position would be to act *praeter proportionem*.[64] Thus in the best regime (aristocracy), virtue, i.e., human development, would be the criterion of the proportion; in a democracy, liberty; and in an oligarchy, wealth. Beyond this, Aquinas is not very specific with regard to the criteria of determining the basis of distributive justice.

The conclusion that must be stressed is that, in theory, Aquinas does not permit the *origin* of utilitarian inequality in man's property relations.

c. *Moderation*

Moderation in the amount used is another necessary condition for the instrumental use of property.[65] Moderation simultaneously refers to the amount used or appropriated and to the ethical purpose of use or appropriation. Here we must recall the earlier distinction between natural and unnatural wealth. The latter is necessarily immoderate, that is, in the acquisition of unnatural wealth, wealth becomes an end in itself, and the "invasion" of others follows as a necessary consequence, and a necessary means of such acquisition. In actual fact, however, there may be little difference between the amount moderately acquired and the amount immoderately acquired. The real difference lies in motivation, morality, and in the antidevelopmental social consequence. Aquinas makes this point explicit in the *Commentary on the Politics*:

[62] ST 2-2.77.4 ad 2.
[63] ST 2-2.63.2.
[64] ST 2-2.63.3.
[65] *Ethicorum*, 10, lect. 10, no. 2093.

There is material similarity between natural acquisition (*pecuniativa economica*) and unnatural acquisition (*pecuniativa campsoria*), although they differ formally. In the case of the first, the welfare of the household is the formal end, while in the case of the second, money for its own sake is the end.[66]

He goes on to add that it is the material similarity between the two modes of acquisition that misleads many to pervert the true end of economics.

The rule of moderation does not forbid appropriation of profit which has a social purpose. What is forbidden is the appropriation of profit for the sake of profit, or for purely personal ends. Thus profit sought as a reward for one's efforts (*quasi stipendium laboris*) or for the necessities of the fatherland, or for the purpose of helping the indigent, or for the purpose of saving for one's own future is not immoderate.[67]

Furthermore, property acquired by one's own labour cannot be considered immoderate.[68] Similarly, what is required for the maintenance of one's social position is not immoderate.[69] Here Aquinas is astonishingly specific, for such things include food, drink, clothes, houses, transportation (*vehicula*), etc.[70] In brief, whatever is necessary for each individual's total development cannot be immoderate, for there is in everything, animate or inanimate, a natural inclination to undertake actions commensurate with its powers, and property is a necessary means for such developmental actions.[71]

The particular virtue relevant to moderation is liberality. It corrects the possibility of money becoming the end of human existence, and predisposes one to be friendly towards others.[72] Liberality of the Thomistic variety is the antidote to Possessive Individualism; it prevents one from becoming a lover of money (*amativus pecuniae*) and enables one to use money properly—for oneself, for others, and for God's honor.[73] "The subject matter of liberality," says Aquinas, "is money, and whatever else has monetary value." Since every virtue matches its own objective, liberality as a virtue has the kind of act suited to money. Money, in turn, comes under the heading of goods to be used, because all material goods have as end their use by man.[74] In brief, liberality purifies man's inner affections towards property, curbs the desire for limitless property, and in this way complements justice, which is concerned with man's external property relations.

[66] *Politicorum*, 1.8.
[67] ST 2-2.72.4 resp. and ad 2.
[68] ST 2-2.55.6 ad 2.
[69] ST 2-2.32.6; 2-2.141.5.
[70] ST 1-2.2.1.
[71] ST 2-2.131.1.
[72] *Politicorum*, 1.4.
[73] ST 2-2.117.6.
[74] ST 2-2.117.3.

III. Property as an Obstacle to the Good Life

Aquinas' treatment of property as an obstacle to the good life, to human development, forms an integral part of his political theory. Property becomes dehumanizing when it ceases to be a means, a *bonum utile*, and instead becomes a *bonum delectabile*, an end in itself.[75] The reversal of ends and means is not only due to a moral disorder, to unnatural concupiscence,[76] but is also due to a material factor, namely the emergence of a monied economy. Accordingly, men abandon the *rectum studium bonae vitae*, the life of virtue, and prefer to live any way they please (*qualitercumque*).[77] At the basis of the dehumanization of man through property lies a voluntarist social philosophy, a life based on "wants" unregulated by "intellect," one that is based on an incorrect theory.

In this context, it is necessary to pay attention to Aquinas' views on money, which are based on Aristotle. Money, for Aquinas, is a medium of exchange,[78] and of measurement of property. It is not natural in the sense that it is a practical invention of human reason for the purpose of practising equality in the exchange of property. For through money, it is possible to equalize the value of exchanged commodities: "It is found that coins are in a way certain measures through which excesses and deficiencies are brought back to the mean; that coins are made because of the necessity of exchange."[79]

Being a unit of measurement, money can be used to measure everything. And because of this, it is possible for the disordered man to think, or to desire, that through the medium of money he can acquire possessions without limit.[80] Aquinas seems to imply that the idea of limitless possessions could not have been realized without money. The actual amount possessed will, of course, be limited, but, with money, the desire to possess can become limitless.

"When money was first invented," says Aquinas, " it was used only for the exchange and measurement of necessary things." Later it began to be used for the sake of acquiring money, for *maximum lucrum*, whose "beginning and end"[81] is money itself. Money for money's sake has no human reference, and money acquired on this principle is not "true" wealth. It

---

[75] ST 2-2.118.2.
[76] ST 1-2.30.4.
[77] *Politicorum*, 1.9.
[78] *Politicorum*, 1.7.
[79] Thomas Aquinas, *Tabula libri Ethicorum*, sub "Nummisma."
[80] *Politicorum*, 1.7.
[81] Ibid.

contributes nothing to human development; in fact, it contributes to man's dehumanization. Aquinas drives home the point by citing the fable of Midas (taken from Aristotle), who, because of his "insatiable desire for money" wanted everything he touched to be turned into gold, and upon the wish being granted subsequently died of starvation. Aquinas concludes, "coins are not in truth riches."[82]

Aquinas offers several explanation of why the dehumanizing desire for property is a limitless desire. First, he analyzes the nature of an end (*finis*). A *finis* is "desirable for itself";[83] nothing limits it. Consequently, if money becomes an end, it obviously is desired for its own sake. Secondly, he considers the nature of a means. A means qua means has a necessarily limited character, namely, that determined by its end.[84]

Similarly in the *Summa*:

> ... In all things that are for an end, the good consists in a certain measure, since whatever is directed to an end must needs be commensurate with the end, as, for instance, medicine with health.... External goods come under the head of things useful for an end.... Hence it must needs be that man's good in their respect consists in a certain measure, in other words, that man seeks, according to a certain measure, to have external riches, in so far as they are necessary for him to live in keeping with his condition of life. Wherefore it will be a sin for him to exceed this measure, by wishing to acquire or keep them immoderately....[85]

Thirdly, the inifinite desire for property is the consequence of the wrong application of reason and will. For rational will, according to Aquinas, is a faculty that can desire the opposites: *eadem potentia est oppositorum*, but not the same way. Thus for the will to desire something rationally, it is not necessary that the "good" be objectively good; it is sufficient if it is perceived under the guise of good, *sub ratione boni*.[86] In the pursuit of money for money's sake, fraud and deceit are necessarily involved, and these cannot be practised without the rational faculty. This malicious use of reason has a certain similarity (*similitudo*) to prudence, which of course is the right use of reason (*recta ratio agibilium*).[87] It therefore becomes possible to

---

[82] Ibid. "Ergo denarii non sunt verae divitiae."

[83] *Politicorum*, 1.8; st 2-2.118.7.

[84] Nullius actus instrumentum est infinitum neque multitudine neque magnitudine: ars anim fabrilis non habet infinitos martellos, neque etiam unum martellum infinitum; sed predictae divitiae sunt quaedam organa yconomici et politici, quia eis utuntur ad gubernationem domus vel civitatis, ut dictum est: ergo hujusmodi divitiae non sunt infinitae, sed est eis aliquis terminus (*Politicorum*, 1.6).

[85] st 2-2.118.1.

[86] st 1-2.8.1.

[87] st 2-2.55.8.

desire wealth with no rational limit: "... hence he that desires riches, may desire to be rich, not up to a certain limit, but simply to be as rich as he possibly can."[88]

Finally, the pursuit of property as an end in itself is antihuman, because in such a case man turns all his powers to the pursuit of property. When money is desired limitlessly, it is not possible to satisfy the desire by legitimate means only; moneymaking then becomes the object of every profession—the military, the medical, etc.:

> Since men are sometimes not able to acquire through the art of moneymaking enough of those things by which they satisfy an excess of bodily desires, they try to acquire money by other means, and they do not use whatever the ability that is the virtue, whether a skill or a service, according to its nature....[89]

The conclusion that Aquinas draws from all this is somewhat startling and original: because everything can be measured by money, money acquires a certain primacy (*principalitatem*) among all material things;[90] and because money creates the illusion of being able to possess everything, all material things yield to money, *omnia corporalia obediunt pecuniae*;[91] and in a way money contains virtually all material things and emerges as the rival of felicity—"... in so far as it is useful for obtaining all sensible things, it contains, in a way, all things virtually. Hence it has a certain likeness to happiness."[92] That is not all. It can become the object of idolatry and hence the very rival of God himself.[93] Money can pervert the idea of the good life and human development by giving a false sense of self-sufficiency:

> ... Riches give great promise of self sufficiency ... the reason of which according to the Philosopher (*Ethics* V, 5), is that we use money in token of taking possession of something, and again it is written (Eccles. 10:19): "All things obey money."[94]

It should not surprise us, therefore, if Aquinas concludes that the acquisition of money for money's sake, namely avarice, is the root of all social conflicts. His careful definition of avarice mentions both the moral and material factors involved in avarice: "Avarice ... is the immoderate

---

[88] ST 1-2.30.4.
[89] *Politicorum*, 1.6.
[90] ST 2-2.118.7 ad 1.
[91] ST 1-2.2.1 ad 1.
[92] ST 2-2.118.7 ad 2.
[93] ST 2-2.118.5 ad 4.
[94] ST 2-2.118.7.

greed of temporal possessions which serve the use of human life and which can be estimated in value by money."[95]

Avarice is the root of all social evils, not in the sense that every social evil in every instance originates in it, but in the sense that there is no social evil which does not, at some time, originate in it.[96] Like the root of a tree it draws sustenance for all other evil acts: "They say that in this sense covetousness is the root of all sins, comparing it to the root of a tree which draws its sustenance from earth, just as every sin grows out of the love of temporal things."[97]

The acquisition of superfluous wealth necessarily impedes the possibility of the development of others. One cannot acquire more than one rightly needs without depriving others of what they rightly need, the criterion of right being justice and equality. Material things can be rightly possessed only when equally possessed, otherwise someone is certain to be diminished: "... one man cannot overabound in external riches, without another man lacking them, for temporal goods cannot be possessed by many at the same time."[98] Force and fraud become necessary means of super-fluous appropriation.[99] And Aquinas gives an exact and carefully examined catalogue of social evils stemming from avarice which, incidentally, is the same for sins against justice and equality—restlessness, violence, deceit, lies, perjury, fraud, betrayal, rapacity, and inhumanity.[100]

Finally, avarice leads man into a vicious circle: the more spiritually and morally wanting a man is, the more he desires to make up for such wants by the maximization of utilities. It is as if maximization of utilities becomes a substitute for maximization of human powers:

> ... Covetousness is incurable on the part of a human defect, a thing which human nature ever seeks to remedy, since the more deficient one is the more one seeks relief from external things, and consequently the more one gives way to covetousness.[101]

Of course, for Aquinas it is scarcely necessary to point out the difference between avarice and beatitude; though both are infinitely desired, there is an unbridgeable difference between the characteristics of the two. In the case of beatitude, the more one possesses God the more one loves Him. In the case

---

[95] ST 1.63.2 ad 2.
[96] ST 2-2.119.2 ad 1.
[97] ST 1-2.84.1.
[98] ST 2-2.118.1 ad 2.
[99] ST 2-2.118.3.
[100] ST 1-2.61.2; 2-2.55.6 ad 8.
[101] ST 2-2.118.5 ad 3.

of avarice, the more one acquires, the less desirable acquired wealth becomes and the more one desires other things.[102]

Aquinas' conclusions can scarcely be doubted: the human ends of our existence can be achieved only if property is used instrumentally and moderately, which means justly. But, because of the defect of historical man, because of the *status peccati*, it is possible for him to withhold the moral effort to resist the temptation to use property as an end in itself, immoderately and unjustly. Hence, Aquinas' observation that for a wholesome human development it is more important to check greed than the accumulation of private possessions.[103] In other words, without the cultivation of moral and intellectual virtues, affluence and the most stringent external regulations regarding property cannot possibly produce human development.

iv. Regime, Property, and the Good Life

We now come to Aquinas' conception of the role that the regime ought to play in the process of human development (the good life) and the related questions of the forms of acceptable regimes and the regime's responsibility in maintaining the correct property relations.

According to Aquinas, the full, natural development of man can occur only through the medium of the state. The necessity of the state is a necessity inherent in the social character of man. Though man's ultimate destiny lies outside the state yet the state is the most important thing that human reason is capable of fashioning.[104] Apart from this philosophical reason, the necessity of the regime arises also from the second-level need for order: where many are involved there is the practical need for a "directive principle"; *recta ratio* alone would not suffice.[105] Though human development is primarily an activity dependent on will and intellect, yet it requires the steadying support of coercive public power.[106] In Aquinas one does not find the naive optimism of Adam Smith regarding the alleged capacity for social justice inherent in the acquisitive activity—the propensity to truck and barter; nor the pessimism of Karl Marx regarding the nature of the state as an exploitative, alienating, and transitional institution.

---

[102] st 1-2.2.1 ad 3.
[103] *Politicorum*, 2.9.
[104] *Politicorum*, prologue.
[105] *De regno*, 1.1 (Phelan trans., p. 3).
[106] Ibid. (Phelan trans., p. 6).

For Aquinas, the state will last as long as human nature will last. The particular type of state may vary with historical conditions, but the idea of state is as unchanging a constant of human development as human nature presently constituted.

As far as property and the good life are concerned, the state acts as a link between the two. Only through the mediation of the state, of "the good legislator," can the conditional right to private property and the obligation to put privately acquired property for common use be humanely reconciled:

> Evidently it is much better that possessions be private as to ownership, but that they be made common in some way as to their use; however, the way in which this should be brought about pertains to the care of the good legislator.[107]

In other words, it is only on the hypothesis of the legal regulation of private acquisitive activity that Aquinas is prepared to permit moderate private ownership, moderate capital accumulation.

It should be noted that, for Aquinas, the state which alone represents the common good, corrects the antisocial potential of the acquisitive activity. It would follow that without the positive legislative intervention of the state, economic activities cannot attain their political legitimacy. The state is seen to have the discretion of determining what is socially harmful and socially permissible, and of even tolerating actual social practices which, on moral grounds, may be objectionable. The case in point is usury. If the community benefits by it, it is permissible. And it is the responsibility of the state to make that decision:

> Human laws leave certain things unpunished, on account of the condition of those who are imperfect, and who would be deprived of many advantages if all sins were strictly forbidden and punishments appointed for them. Wherefore human law has permitted usury, not that it looks upon usury as harmonizing with justice, but lest the advantages of many should be hindered.[108]

The idea is found also in the *Commentary on the Politics*: "A lawmaker ought to allow certain evil things, lest he prevent many good things."[109]

Aquinas felt that agriculture was more compatible with virtue and human development than commerce. Here, no doubt, he shows the influence of his aristocratic background on his thinking. However, both as a philosopher and as a "realist," he is prepared to accept trade and commerce as

---

[107] *Politicorum*, 2.4.
[108] ST 2-2.78.1 ad 3.
[109] *Politicorum*, 2.4.

legitimate activities so long as they conform to the requirements of the common good as interpreted by the regime; his conclusion, therefore, is that "the perfect city will make a moderate use of merchants."[110]

Aquinas' arguments leading to the above conclusion should be of interest to the modern reader. In the first place, dependence on trade and commerce for the economic sustenance of the community would undermine the freedom and independence of the regime. Secondly, trade and commerce would increase the influence of foreigners in the internal life of the state. Thirdly, and this is true of his own times only, trade and commerce would destroy the nobility, and with it the military virtues of the community. Fourthly, it would increase the tempo of urbanization and thereby upset the balance between town and country, between agriculture and commerce. Finally, and perhaps most importantly, the spirit of trade and commerce, the bourgeois spirit if you like, would destroy civic virtue:

> Since the foremost tendency of tradesmen is to make money, greed is awakened in the hearts of the citizens through the pursuit of trade. The result is that everything in the city will become venal; good faith will be destroyed and the way opened to all kinds of trickery; each one will work only for his own profit, despising the public good; the cultivation of virtue will fail since honour, virtue's reward, will be bestowed upon the rich. Thus in such a city, civic life will necessarily be corrupted.[111]

However, true to his instinct for balance and realism, Aquinas is not entirely hostile to the new emerging bourgeois culture. He sees two positive values in trade and commerce. First, no state can be self-sufficient, and therefore needs trade and commerce. Here he moves away from Aristotle's ideal of autarky. Secondly, if a given state has an overabundance of some commodities, no matter how acquired or produced, they serve no rational purpose "if they could not be carried elsewhere by professional traders."[112] Note, that for Aquinas the rationality of trade and commerce consists in balancing the distribution of commodities according to the laws of overabundance and scarcity, and not according to those of profit making for its own sake.

It is necessary to point out that Aquinas' views on the role of the state in economic activities are confined to legislation, and do not add up to what might be called "state capitalism." State capitalism would be as alien to his thought as laissez-faire. The function of the state is to legislate the rules ac-

---

[110] *De regno*, 2.3 (Phelan trans., p. 78).
[111] Ibid. (Phelan trans., p. 76).
[112] Ibid. (Phelan trans., p. 78).

cording to which economic activity is carried out: "Therefore it is not the proper or immediate duty of government to produce or acquire food, but it is a proper duty to dispense in the household (or the city) those things according to need."[113]

The burden of economic responsibility that Aquinas imposes on the state is very delicate indeed; even more delicate is the burden imposed on the individual, namely the burden of virtue. Presumably, civic virtue ought to produce the necessary economic incentive to produce enough and even an "overabundance"; the same virtue ought to permit the state to regulate authoritatively the distribution of things. As for the state, its greatest responsibility is to stay above class or private interests and not to allow itself to be aligned with any sectional interest. If one may formulate Aquinas' thought on the relationship between property, state, and the good life, it would read: from each according to his civic virtue, and to each according to his developmental need, as regulated by the requirements of the good of the community as a whole.

Of course, Aquinas was no social reformer. His only advocacy, it is safe to assume, was confined to the theological end of man, namely, the salvation of his soul, and not to the political end of man, which is the attainment of the best earthly regime. This is not to say that Aquinas lacked a theory of the best regime. But he seemed to have been content, in modern eyes at any rate, with analysis of things as they were and as they ought to be, given the existing order.

There can be no doubt that, for Aquinas, the best political regime[114] was that which was conducive to human development, that is to say, conducive to the development of virtue which, as we noted earlier, is synonymous with development of man's properly human capacities. But Aquinas was a political realist in that he recognized that actual political regimes are inevitably shaped by the dominant economic motivations and the moral capacities of their people. If the people do not possess civic virtue, then wealth by default becomes the foundation of political life and social organization. Civic life then becomes polarized between the virtue and property. As he states in the *Commentary on the Politics*, because virtue is not often found in people, one cannot always find virtuous people to whom to entrust the government: "Excellence according to virtue is not always found, so that rulers cannot be chosen on the criterion of virtue alone."[115]

---

[113] *Politicorum*, 1.8.
[114] See M. R. McGuigan, "The Best Form of Government in the Philosophy of St. Thomas Aquinas" (Ph.D. dissertation, University of Toronto, 1957).
[115] *Politicorum*, 2.5.

That being the case, other criteria—originating in property consider-ations—naturally emerge in society. Government is taken over by the nobility (*nobiliores origine*) or the bourgeoisie (*excellentiores divites*). In other words, particular political regimes have only a pragmatic and relativistic justification. However, their moral value, their human worth, is proportionate to their capacity for human development. Whatever the relative advantages or disadvantages of monarchy, oligarchy, and democracy, the basic test of a political regime is its capacity to promote human development.

Although Aquinas wrote seven centuries ago, and wrote primarily as a theologian, his ideas on property, regime, and the good life appear to have a modern resonance. This may be partly due to the organic link between his age and our age that economic historians speak of. This may also be due to the identity of human aspirations and motivations, of human nature if you like. The questions of private property and fair distribution are still with us. Aquinas' distinction between ownership and use, production and use, be-tween property as a means of good life and property as an obstacle to good life, good life as the process of development of human capacities, introduces a certain freshness of approach to the understanding of those questions. In Thomistic thought, economic development is only a means to human development, and the two are not identical at all. Modern bourgeois man has for so long worked on the assumptions of the rationality and morality of the right of limitless acquisition of property as the essence of personal and social development. After working on these essentially materialistic, and what Aquinas would term antihuman views of human development, contemporary man is beginning to realize that it is moral development which gives economic development its purpose, its telos, its human face. As long as these issues are debated, Aquinas will also continue to be debated.

6

Saint Thomas Aquinas
and the Idea of the Open Society

Dante GERMINO*
University of Virginia

It may at first seem strange to hear Thomas Aquinas linked with the "open society," for does he not somehow typify the Middle Ages, those "times o'erworn with rust and ignorance," wherein ecclesiastical dogma allegedly ruled to the exclusion of all free and creative inquiry? Indeed, were we to follow only Karl Popper in characterizing the open society, it would be doubtful that we could make a convincing case for Thomas as a champion of openness. Lord Acton may have struck off a felicitous *mot* in calling Saint Thomas the "first Whig," but it would be considerably less accurate to describe him as a secular liberal before his time, which one would virtually have to do to satisfy Popper's criteria for defenders of the open society. In fact, in the only three references to Aquinas listed in the index of *The Open Society and Its Enemies*, Popper seems to regard the good Doctor as anything but Angelic—i.e., as definitely more of an enemy than a friend of the open society.[1]

* The author wishes to thank the Guggenheim Foundation, whose award of a Fellowship made it possible to complete research on this article in Rome.

[1] K. R. Popper, *The Open Society and Its Enemies*, 5th rev. ed. (Princeton: Princeton University Press, 1966), 1: 237, 316; 2: 237. In these passages Popper criticizes the "confusing use" of "natural law" by modern Thomists (and presumably Thomas himself) as well as "the small emphasis they put on equalitarianism." He also objects to Thomas' use of the medical analogy to characterize society as "diseased." Thomas' alleged adoption of "love" and "happiness" as "political ideals" is said by Popper to "lead invariably to the attempt to impose our scale of 'higher' values upon others, in order to make them realize what seems to us of greatest importance for their happiness; in order, as it were, to save their souls."

Fortunately, however, there is another interpretation of the open society (which even antedates that of Popper) put forward by Henri Bergson and continued with modifications by Eric Voegelin. It is primarily this latter idea of the open society (to which I shall return at the end) which serves as the background of the following discussion of Thomas, although I shall also have occasion to remark upon Thomas' openness from the "secular" perspective of one who is lacking in dogmatism and is open to different perspectives on an issue.

As herein employed, the term "the open society" does not refer to an organized political community at all, but rather to the universal community of the spirit which comprises all mankind in its struggle to comprehend the meaning of human existence and to articulate that meaning in language which illumines the multidimensional character of the reality in which the creature called man participates. There is only one "open society," that of mankind, stretching back into its unknown origins and forward into its unknown future. This existence is illumined along the way by symbols which may be perceived by the philosopher to be "equivalent" to one another, in that they represent attempts, at a similar level of reflection, to articulate the character of the human condition in openness toward the world-transcendent ground of being. History is thus perceived as a "trail of symbols," which, although they are of varying degrees of compactness and differentiation, are roughly "equivalent" in their attempts to articulate meaning gained from the encounter with the ground in the depth of the soul.[2]

According to the foregoing understanding of the open society, the experience of openness toward the transcendent ground of being was maximally articulated through Greek philosophy (and, in particular, through Plato and Aristotle, two of Karl Popper's "archenemies") and through the Judeo-Christian revelation of the hidden God to the community of the faithful. Karl Popper's confinement of the term to modern western constitutional democracy overemphasizes procedures to the neglect of substance. While granting the importance of freedom of speech and the rule of law as well as of institutions and programs for the protection of the poor and the weak, it should be recognized that the secular liberal view of the

---

[2] This concept of the open society is greatly indebted to Eric Voegelin, as expounded particularly in his essay "Equivalences of Experience and Symbolization in History," in *Eternità e storia* (Rome: Istituto accademico di Roma, 1969), pp. 349-362 (to be expanded and included in the forthcoming vol. 5 of his *Order and History*), and in his introduction to *The Ecumenic Age*, vol. 4 of *Order and History* (Baton Rouge: Louisiana State University Press, 1975).

open society as adumbrated by Popper and many others erects only a protective shell which then waits to be filled with a specific moral content.[3] The "secular" ideals which Popper expounds, of tolerance, peaceful cooperation, brotherhood, and social justice have their roots in the "religious" past, and specifically in the notion of the human person as possessing innate dignity by virtue of his being a child of God. Those ideals, furthermore, need to be completed through reference to the experience of the contemplation of and striving for attunement with the highest good which animates the man who pursues the life of reason. Like freedom, openness in the procedural sense is not an end in itself, but a means to the attainment of the only good which is itself not instrumental (or a means to yet some higher good), i.e., the attunement or (in this life only partial) coincidence of human reason with the divine ground of being. Openness in the substantive sense is, then, authentic self-actualization, if the self thus actualized be understood to be open both to the universal spiritual community of mankind and to the ground which is its source. It is clear that, here and now, there will be inevitable disagreement on openness as the end to be sought. I agree with Popper that coercion should not be employed to advance the open society; indeed, I would go further and say that the full conformity of any existing society with the implications of human existence as an "open society" is impossible within history and that, therefore, it remains, as a paradigm beyond our grasp, the "true city" of which Dante (in Canto 16 of the "Purgatory" in the *Divine Comedy*) speaks and whose tower we may see dimly in the distance. Inasmuch as the paradigm of the open society is on principle incapable of being imposed on a given recalcitrant social order, we may seek primarily, as suggested by the Platonic Socrates in *Republic*, 591, to "found it in ourselves," and so indirectly to leaven the existing social order through the quality of our lives. In addition, we may seek to promote structural, institutional reforms that increase the opportunities for achieving a life of openness among those segments of society lacking in the material resources to lead a life of dignity. But we must always recognize that openness and coercion go ill together, and the open society idea is not a program for violent revolution.

We are now in a position to turn to examine major aspects of the political teaching of Saint Thomas as they bear on the theme of the open society. Anticipating our conclusion, we shall argue that Thomas was definitely

---

[3] In addition to Popper's *The Open Society*, I am here drawing on his interview published in *Encounter* in May 1972. See Karl Popper, "On Reason and the Open Society: A Conversation," *Encounter*, 38, no. 5 (May 1972), 13-18.

more of a friend than an enemy of the open society. I do not pretend, however, that there were no elements of closure in Thomas' thought. Even the
greatest thinker, who in important respects manages to transcend his time,
is in other respects timebound. Thomas may no more have been expected to
have reached the conclusions of modern liberalism than Plato, Aristotle, or
Augustine. Thomas lived in a "sacral" age, when enforced religious unity
was the norm and the Inquisition an ugly reality. The repressive features of
his environment, however, did not prevent him from articulating a teaching
which points the way to openness in many of the senses in which we have
been discussing the subject. If the premodern understanding of openness
needs to be supplemented by that of modern liberal constitutionalism, the
modern liberal understanding needs enrichment from the premodern conception of openness as *metanoia* of the consciousness and self-actualization
through the soul's openness to the ground of being. Thomas can help us in
that enrichment process.

THE "OPENNESS OF BEING"

The most striking feature of Saint Thomas' teaching is its openness to
God as the transcendent ground of finite being. In the *Summa theologiae*
Aquinas launches almost immediately into a discussion of the famous "Five
Ways," or reasoned arguments which, in Thomas Gilby's words "open out
the prospect of a world caused by God."[4] Eric Mascall, the Anglo-Catholic
theologian, in his Gifford lectures delivered a few years ago, has aptly
characterized the Thomistic view of the world as predicated on the "openness of being."[5] In Mascall's words, Saint Thomas' Five Ways were presented not as ironclad "proofs" (for which they are frequently mistaken) but as
"persuasive discourse intended to help us grasp the fundamental dependence
of finite beings on infinite being as their ground."[6]

Following Thomas, Mascall holds that "by his natural constitution as a
creature, man has an inherent openness to God."[7] The "contingent world
of our experience manifests the presence, at its metaphysical root, of that
absolute being which Christian theology calls God. That the knowledge

---

[4] Thomas Gilby, "The Five Ways," in Thomas Aquinas, *Summa theologiae*, Blackfriars
edition, vol. 2 (New York: McGraw-Hill Book Co., London: Eyre and Spottiswoode, 1964),
appendix 5, p. 188.

[5] E. L. Mascall, *The Openness of Being: Natural Theology Today* (London: Darton,
Longman and Todd, 1971).

[6] Ibid., p. 89.

[7] Ibid., p. 71.

about God which we can thus acquire is minimal ... I shall not only admit but emphasize. This does not matter; once the point can be located in which finite being manifests the presence in it of the infinite, the knife-blade can be inserted and the cavity widened later on."[8] Thus, continues Mascall, reaffirming the Thomistic principle of *gratia non tollit naturam sed perficit*,

> just because of its radically dependent and non-self-sufficient character, finite being is open to fresh influxes of creative power which will elevate and transform it, but not destroy it. This, as I see it, provides the natural basis for both grace ... and the Incarnation. ... Finite being is essentially dependent, and because dependent incomplete, and because incomplete open to indefinite transformation. Of what kind and degree that transformation may be is not for natural theology to say.[9]

Against the theology of Karl Barth and others, who deny that there is any "point of contact" (*Anknüpfungspunkt*) between the human and the divine, Mascall, following Saint Thomas, argues that "such a point of contact is ... to be found in the sheer element of contingency in all the beings which our senses disclose to us." This experience of contingency "locates the finite world and all its constituents on a foundation of self-existent being on which they themselves are totally dependent."[10]

After Thomas has sought to demonstrate the existence of a being which "everyone understands to be God,"[11] he proceeds, we shall recall, in the next nine questions to argue that this self-existent ground of finite being is simple, perfect, good, infinite, immutable, eternal and one. These attributes of God, comments Mascall, do not state "what God is" (for the finite mind of man cannot know God's essence) but only "how he is related to his creatures." What Thomas has done is to "unpack" what is involved "in the affirmation of the existence of a transcendent self-existent ground of contingent being."[12] Thomas shows, contends Mascall, that this ground of being

> must possess the attributes of thought, will and power, and that it must possess these in a supereminent degree. For to maintain contingent being in existence involves a decision that there shall be contingent being and what kind of contingent being there shall be; and this implies what, however analogically, we can validly describe as an activity of thinking and willing. And the bringing of this decision into effect implies the exercise of what, however ana-

---

[8] Ibid., p. 14.
[9] Ibid., p. 16.
[10] Ibid., p. 118.
[11] ST 1.2.3.
[12] Mascall, p. 119.

logically, we can validly describe as an exercise of supreme power. Taken together, these attributes of thought, will and power justify us in describing the transcendent self-existent being as personal.[13]

By their "very dependence upon God," Mascall declares, "finite beings are inherently open to him; an absolutely autonomous and encapsulated finite entity would be a contradiction in terms. A created universe—and there can be no other—is necessarily not only a finite but an open one. Nature has, simply as nature, a *potentia oboedentialis* for the super-natural."[14]

My purpose in citing Eric Mascall at such length is to provide an example of how, across the centuries, Thomas Aquinas today continues to inspire theologians and philosophers to conceive of the world as an open world and of its entities as open entities, open to one another and to higher levels of existence and activity and ultimately to God, the creative and energizing source of all that exists. What a contrast this presents to the all too frequently encountered portrayal in some histories of philosophy of Thomas as the author of a "closed" and static system! Although Mascall nowhere specifically refers to the concepts of the "open society," he nonetheless gives powerful support to that concept, and he does this as a dedicated follower of Saint Thomas.

In his eloquent conclusion to his *Guide to Thomas Aquinas*, Josef Pieper has properly indicated that, although Thomas argued "systematically," he did not construct a closed philosophical "system." Such a system, of the kind later offered by Spinoza or Auguste Comte would claim to be the "total solution" to all the problems perplexing the human person and would pretend to have penetrated to the essence of things, to have *the* key to the essential reality of the universe. Saint Thomas, however, deliberately never finished his *Summa theologiae*, and his refusal to complete the work, in the face of an experience that revealed to him its provisional character, leaves the *Summa* for all its size, as fragmentary in character.

Not only is the *Summa* shown to lack the character of a closed system because of what is missing, however; as Pieper points out, Thomas' rejection of a closed system is indicated as well by what he explicitly says about the inherent limitations of human knowledge. It was, after all, Thomas Aquinas who wrote the sentence which condemns all attempts to grasp all of reality in the conceptual nets of a "philosopher's" system: *Rerum essentiae sunt nobis ignotae* ("The essences of things are unknown

---

[13] Ibid., p. 120.
[14] Ibid., p. 146.

to us"). Pieper rightly agrees with Marie-Dominique Chenu, that, far from being a system-builder, Thomas harbored *une extrême défiance des systèmes*, or "an extreme suspicion of systems."[15]

THEONOMOUS ETHICS IN SAINT THOMAS

Now let us turn to a consideration of some matters specifically related to political theory in order to see the contribution which Aquinas has made to openness in political activity. The foundation of any comprehensive political theory is a theory of man, or more precisely, a theory of the good person. Without a theory of the good person one cannot develop a theory of the good society, for as Plato shows in the *Republic*, the political community is "man writ large." Societies do not act in the abstract; rulers act for them, and within any given society there are multiple centers or hubs of activity wherein, on a smaller scale, decisions are made by countless individual citizens that affect the quality and tenor of society.

What I understand Aquinas to be teaching us about political ethics, the foundation of political theory is as follows: man is not a self-sufficient, encapsulated entity. It is inconceivable (and here Aquinas, as it were, criticizes in advance the development of secular liberalism from Grotius through Locke to the Enlightenment and beyond) that a dependent being, who did not create himself, could in any ultimate sense be the source of the norms or laws which it seeks to follow. Man is not autonomous, but theonomous: God (*theos*) not the self is the source of law. Autonomy, strictly understood as the bootless chase of the finite creature for self-sufficiency, is not freedom but servitude, not openness but closure.

Just as Aquinas has frequently been misunderstood—by both disciples and critics—as having promulgated a dogmatic, closed metaphysical system, so he has frequently been wrongly judged as having set forth a rigid ethical system comprised of numerous and detailed "natural laws" for every conceivable situation. The notion of a "blueprint" of ethical prescriptions and prohibitions laid out in advance is counter to his basic concept of man. Instead of such a bleak picture of man as the uncritical follower of detailed, apodictic rules, we find in Aquinas the view that man as moral and political actor possesses the faculty of reason through which he is able, as it were, to "participate" or share in the eternal reason of God as the ground of finite being. Moral man to Aquinas is, through his reason, open to and "per-

[15] Josef Pieper, *Guide to Thomas Aquinas* (New York: New American Library, 1962), pp. 140-141.

meable"[16] by the divine reason, which as creative and sustaining activity can "flow" into the consciousness of the open-souled individual.

At the heart of Aquinas' conception of natural law, therefore, we find not a catalogue of detailed injunctions and prohibitions, but a concept of theonomous man as ethical and political actor seeking through his reason to "participate" or share in the divine reason. Or as Thomas expressed the matter in his magistral sentence, "Natural law is nothing else than the sharing in the Eternal Law [i.e., the divine reason] by intelligent creatures."[17] Actually the original Latin conveys more powerfully the notion that the *divine* reason (or the eternal law) is participating in *man's* reason rather than emphasizing the role of man; in any event, the important point Thomas clearly wished to convey is that when he acts aright, man is not alone but is sustained by the help of the divine "partner," without whom his own finite existence is inconceivable.

In stressing the absence of a blueprint or catalogue of instructions in Aquinas, I do not mean to imply that his interpretation of natural law is utterly vacuous or lacking in substance. In the conclusion to the *Summa theologiae*, 1-2.94, for example, Thomas discusses the three-fold "natural inclination" of man to self-preservation, procreation and education of offspring, and development of his distinctively human rational capacities, but the principles are stated in a general way so that the creative application of them to a specific context requires the initiative and resourcefulness of the individual involved. As Paul Sigmund has observed, Thomas is well "aware that the complexities of human life make it impossible to set down a hard and fast rule for every situation."[18]

Thomas' principled flexibility, which eschews both Pharisaism and relativism alike, is particularly evident in his teaching on the virtue of prudence.[19] Here Thomas makes extensive use of Aristotle's *Ethics*, and in particular Aristotle's counsel (which should be engraven over the entrance to every political science department) that "we should not look for the same degree of certainty in all matters, but in each to the extent that the subject allows."[20] Without getting into the complicated question of the extent to

[16] I am here using the term "permeability" in Eric Voegelin's sense of *Durchlässigkeit* in his discussion of Aristotle's notion of *phronesis*, or practical reason. See Eric Voegelin, "Das Rechte von Natur" in *Anamnesis: zur Theorie der Geschichte und Politik* (Munich: Piper, 1966, p. 128.

[17] Lex naturalis nihil aliud est quam participatio legis aeternae in rationali creatura (ST 1-2.91.2).

[18] Paul E. Sigmund, *Natural Law in Political Thought* (Cambridge, Mass.: Winthrop Publishers, 1971), p. 41.

[19] ST 2-2.47-56.

[20] ST 2-2.47.9 (Blackfriars ed., 36: 31).

which Aquinas adopted, transformed, and revolutionized Aristotle, it seems quite clear that in much of his political ethics Thomas finds Aristotle's teaching highly congenial philosophically. The Angelic Doctor did a great service, indeed, in transmitting the spirit of Aristotle's ethical insight to his generation and to later ones as well. Today, in our time of great confusion over moral values, we could do worse than to begin our way out of the crisis by "recovering what has been lost" in the ethics of Aristotle and Thomas. That Aquinas was receptive to the rediscovered Aristotle in his own time—despite the most strenuous opposition to this form of "pagan" wisdom in many sectors of the Church—is a further tribute to his openness to different influences and perspectives. Thus, Alois Dempf has referred to Thomas' *spirituellen Öffentlichkeit*,[21] and F. C. Copleston has praised him for "the use of wide-reaching philosophical principles and categories. He was an eclectic in the sense that he was open to stimulus and ideas from a variety of sources; but he was not an eclectic in the sense of one who adopts a number of different ideas from different philosophies and juxtaposes them. He had to rethink his material coherently and systematically; and in this rethinking he shows his power as a thinker."[22] In other words, the openness of Thomas is not to be confused with mushiness or the acceptance of any influence simply because it was novel or unfamiliar. He was open to the influence of Aristotle because he found Aristotle himself to have been open to man's participation in multidimensional reality and to have provided concepts and symbols which, through creative reworking in the light of reason and the leavening of Christian revelation, could be of incalculable benefit in illuminating the character of the human condition.

In commenting on the spirit of Aquinas' treatise on prudence, Thomas Gilby notes that the work "is not burdened by the anxieties of later moralists" and that it is "relatively carefree compared with most works of spiritual training and edification."[23] This "carefree" approach to existence by Thomas is particularly evident toward the end of the treatise where he takes up the problem of whether prudence calls for "solicitude" about temporal matters. Here Thomas leavens the gravity of Aristotle with the openness of the Sermon on the Mount by citing Matthew 6:31 ("Be not solicitous, saying, what shall we eat or what shall we drink, and wherewith

---

[21] Alois Dempf, *Sacrum Imperium: Geschichts- und Staatsphilosophie des Mittelalters*, 2nd ed. (Darmstadt: Wissenschaftliche Buchgemeinschaft, 1954), p. 386.

[22] Frederick C. Copleston, *A History of Medieval Philosophy* (London: Methuen, 1972, p. 181.

[23] Thomas Gilby, introduction to Thomas Aquinas, *Summa theologiae*, Blackfriars ed., vol. 36 (New York and London, 1974), p. xvii.

shall we be clothed?") and Matthew 6:34 ("Take no thought for the morrow").[24] Even though the treatise is about a form of righteousness, Thomas shows himself eager to combat enclosure of the self in excessive temporal concerns and the rigidities of self-righteousness and Pharisaism. "Prudence" today often has a calculating ring about it; the "prudent investor," for example, is someone who does not take risks and is exceedingly cautious, while the "prudent politician" is governed mainly by expediency. Thomas, however, thought it essential to distinguish between prudence (*prudentia*) and shrewdness or cunning (*astutia*). He also denounced what he called, following Saint Paul in Romans 8:7, "false prudence," or "prudence of the flesh" (*prudentia carnis*).[25] Much that is called prudence in contemporary practice would undoubtedly be gently but firmly criticized by Aquinas as different forms of wordly idolatry. True prudence is a virtue of the practical reason in openness toward transcendence which results in a concrete, responsible ethical decision. It is not a cold, disembodied reason that governs, but rather, as Gilby has expressed it, "the whole man, comprising his mind as receptive of the Spirit, his powers of sense, internal and external, and his affective powers of will and emotion."[26] Prudence for Aquinas, then, Gilby also says, is

> a good habit or settled quality, of the practical reason giving an active bent towards right doing as an individual act; it ranges from our pondering over what should be done, through our judgment of what we should choose to do, and is completed in that being made an effective command. Conscience, or rather sincere and informed conscience, is an act within that ensemble ... and its notion is something more intermittent and less trustworthy than prudence.[27]

Reading through the part of the *Summa* on prudence, one is made aware of the feel for concrete, practical experience which this remarkable, "unworldly" monk had managed to obtain through participating in the affairs of church, state, and university. Although the discussion is general and directed to principles, the contemporary reader can easily fill in the examples of acts of prudence, imprudence, or "sham" prudence from his observation of affairs. For example, when Aquinas discussed how "cunning"

---

[24] ST 2-2.55.6 and 7 (Blackfriars ed., 36: 159, 163).

[25] ST 2-2.47.13 ad 3 (Blackfriars ed., 36: 43).

[26] Thomas Gilby in Thomas Aquinas, *Summa theologiae*, Blackfriars ed., vol. 36, appendix 4, p. 183.

[27] Ibid., appendix 3, p. 180. Gilby points out that conscience (*suneidēsis*) is not the same as *synderesis*, a term made up by Scholastic writers to stand for knowing the first principles of moral practice.

(*astutia*) differs from prudence, one is vividly reminded of the whole sordid "Watergate" affair in the United States by the following passage:

> Cunning uses feints and pretences, not true and open means, to achieve any end which may be either right or wrong. In taking this course there is a double aspect to be considered. First, the plotting of it, and this ... is the function of cunning [just] as ... the planning of right means to a due end is that of prudence. Second, the carrying of it out in deed, and this is for guile. And so guile signifies the execution of cunning, and in this way is part of it.[28]

Thus, true prudence is a large-minded virtue of openness and fair-dealing between men; it is sharply to be distinguished from mere shrewdness and expediency to say nothing of deliberate deception and guile. Prudence for Aquinas closely approximates Thomas Reid's version of "common sense." Reid called common sense a type of rationality, and said:

> There is a certain degree of [this kind of rationality] ... which is necessary to our being subjects of law and government, capable of managing our own affairs, and answerable for our conduct towards others. This is called common sense, because it is common to all men with whom we can transact business, or call to account for their conduct.[29]

Thomas' Christian prudence is not legalistic (although observing a law is often a part of what is involved in it). Prudence cannot be reduced to or exhausted by hard and fast rules, for it often involves the exceptional case, and may be concerned more with what is equitable than what is narrowly legal. "The workings of prudence," observes Gilby, once more testifying to the openness of Thomas, "are not confined to an enclosed system of laws. Open and responsive to the Spirit, they tap springs of justice and law high beyond the channels of legalistic justice."[30]

The conclusions of prudence, of course, are not infallible, any more than human reason is infallible. The practical reason in general and prudence in particular deal with contingencies, with things which can be other than they are. Yet, using our God-given reason, Aquinas held that we could arrive at probable conclusions for moral action amidst the uncertainties of this mortal life which were worthy of the good or mature man, the man whom Aristotle called the *spoudaios*.

---

[28] ST 2-2.55.4 resp. (Blackfriars ed., 36: 155).

[29] Cited in Voegelin, *Anamnesis*, p. 352, from Thomas Reid's "Essay on the Intellectual Powers of Man" (1785).

[30] Thomas Gilby in Thomas Aquinas, *Summa theologiae*, Blackfriars ed., vol. 36, appendix 1, p. 177.

POLITICAL JUDGMENTS

Thus far I have principally discussed the qualities of mind and spirit which Thomas regarded as essential preconditions of right judgment in ethical and political matters. Before proceeding to the final section of my paper which will consider the Thomistic teaching in the light of recent theories of the open society however, I should like to cite a few examples of Aquinas' own political judgments in order to show how he sought to follow his own prescriptions with regard to prudence and the practical reason.

One question with which Thomas dealt concerned the best form of government—whether it be monarchy, aristocracy, democracy, or a mixed constitution. In reviewing his comments on the subject in Book 1 of the *De regimine principum* and in the *Summa theologiae* (1-2.105), one receives the distinct impression from his cautious comments that he is more interested in seeing that the power of government be limited and restrained than in the precise form (monarchy, aristocracy, democracy, or the "mixed constitution") to be preferred. Above all, institutions should be ordered to reduce the danger of tyranny. Examining these passages together, it would appear that Thomas regarded a limited monarchy, with opportunities for participation by both the aristocracy and the common people in public affairs, to be the optimal form of government. Otherwise, one would not know what to make of the apparent contradiction within the same section of the *Summa*. There, on one page he declares the best constitution (*optima politia*) to be a mixed regime, or

> one in which one man, as specially qualified, rules over all, and under him are others governing as having special endowments, yet all have a share inasmuch as those are elected from all, and also are elected by all This is the best ... constitution, a mixture of monarchy, in that one man is at the head, of aristocracy, in that many rule as specially qualified, and democracy, in that the rulers can be chosen by the people and from them.[31]

Immediately thereafter (or literally two brief paragraphs later), however, Aquinas declares monarchy to be "the best form of government, provided it has not become corrupted; but with so much power in the hands of a king it easily degenerates into tyranny."[32] This comment is made in the context of a discussion of the patriarchs of the Hebrew Scriptures and in any event is a more qualified praise of monarchy than is generally found in the short treatise (never finished by Aquinas), *De regimine principum*.

---

[31] ST 1-2.105.1 resp. (Blackfriars ed., 29: 269).
[32] ST 1-2.105.1 ad 2 (Blackfriars ed., 29: 271).

The important point to notice is that Aquinas does not play the ideologue and seek to impose a rigid blueprint on historical reality; what is the "best" constitution depends upon a host of factors; what is crucial is that the government have (1) sufficient unity and force of executive direction and (2) sufficient safeguards against its degeneration into tyranny. Although it cannot be said that Aquinas was an early proponent of constitutional democracy, certainly his political thought was open to the possibility of the evolution of such a political form.

Another example of Thomas' political common sense and awareness of the complexity of many political and moral dilemmas is his treatment of the problem of tyrannicide. Although always careful to stress the advantages of obedience and the dangers of sedition, Aquinas refuses to rule out resistance to and even the killing of a tyrant in extreme circumstances. Thus, in his *Commentary on the Sentences of Peter Lombard,* an early work, Thomas affirmed that "where a person had possessed himself of power through violence, either against the will of his subjects or by compelling their consent, and where there was no possibility of appeal to a higher authority ... one who liberates his country by killing a tyrant is to be praised and rewarded."[33] And in the *Summa theologiae* Thomas comments that the overthrowing of a tyrannical government

> is not strictly sedition; except perhaps in the case that it is accompanied by such disorder that the community suffers greater harm from the consequent disturbances than it would from a continuance of the former rule. A tyrant himself is, in fact, far more guilty of sedition when he spreads discord and strife among the people subject to him, so hoping to control them more easily. For it is a characteristic of tyranny to order everything to the personal satisfaction of the ruler at the expense of the community.[34]

A further illustration, among many possible ones, of the moderation and good political common sense of Aquinas, of his openness to the context of affairs in their practical complexity while at the same time being clear and consistent in his basic principles, is his treatment of the problem of the relationship between the temporal and spiritual powers, *regnum* and *sacerdotium*, or what today we anachronistically refer to as the "church-state" question.

As a Dominincan and loyal son of the Church, Thomas might have been expected to champion the claims of the hierocratic party and to have argued

---

[33] *In 2 Sent.* D 44.2.2 ad 5, as in Thomas Aquinas, *Selected Political Writings*, ed. by A. P. D'Entrèves (Oxford: Blackwell, 1948), p. 185.

[34] ST 2-2.42.2 ad 3 (D'Entrèves, p. 161).

for the widest possible latitude for the papacy in its claim to a general superintendence of affairs. Instead Thomas was generous in his recognition of the autonomy of the temporal power *in suo ordine* and did as much as any thinker of the high Middle Ages to vindicate the Gelasian principle of the two swords.

Thus, in the *Commentary on the Sentences*, Thomas observes:

> Both the spiritual and the temporal power derive from the divine power; consequently the temporal power is subject to the spiritual only to the extent that this is so ordered by God; namely in those matters which affect the salvation of the soul. ... In those matters, however, which concern the civil welfare, the temporal power should be obeyed rather than the spiritual, according to ... St. Matthew (XXII, 21), "Render to Caesar the things that are Caesar's." Unless, of course, the spiritual and temporal power are identified in one person as in the Pope, whose power is supreme in matters both temporal and spiritual, through the dispensation of Him Who is both priest and king.[35]

The last sentence of the above quotation has been interpreted in diverse ways, of course, but it seems to me most plausible to refer to the temporal dominion over the papal states; otherwise the first and major portion of the text would make no sense. Indeed, this final sentence reads like a rhetorical flourish designed to forestall possible papal ire over the generous treatment of the temporal power in the first part. Nonetheless, although Aquinas was no advocate of theocracy, he was not about to embrace political absolutism either. And so, in the *Summa theologiae*, he enunciated that glorious principle which has stood forth ever since against all possible claims by the body politic to totalitarian domination: "Man is not ordained to the political community according to all that he is or has.... But all that man is, and can, and has, must be referred to God."[36]

Examples of Thomas' openness in his judgments on specific practical questions of great importance, e.g. property, the "just war," relations with non-Christians, could be multiplied, although I would not in any way wish to imply either that he was or that he thought himself to be infallible in making them. Particularly in some areas, such as the discussion of slavery

---

[35] *In 2 Sent.* ᴅ 44.3.4 ad 4 (D'Entrèves, p. 187). I am aware that some scholars attach extreme importance to whether Thomas has written something in one of his major or minor works; while this distinction is worth noting, it does not appear to be as relevant for his specifically political observations, which were in any event ancillary to his theology and therefore, in a sense, of "minor" status even in his "major" works. The exception to this observation would be the treatise on law in the *Summa*, which is clearly one of Thomas' most important contributions to political theory.

[36] ѕт 1-2.21.4 ad 3 (my translation).

and the suppression of religious heresy, he appears in retrospect to have been very limited in his perspective. It is time, however, to return to the theme raised at the beginning, viz., the possible contribution of Aquinas to contemporary discussions of the idea of the open society.

THE IDEA OF THE OPEN SOCIETY IN BERGSON AND THOMAS

It is generally acknowledged that the French philosopher Henri Bergson was the first writer actually to employ the term "the open society." In a book published in French in 1932 and in English in 1935, Bergson set forth the distinctions between the "open morality" and the "closed morality" as central to his moral philosophy.[37]

Bergson is in agreement with Thomas Aquinas that man is by nature a political and social animal. Beyond his individual self, man possesses a "social self." Man's nature, however, is an open nature and the society which reflects his nature is "of variable form, open to all progress." Unlike the ant, man is possessed of intelligence; the human society is "intellective" rather than "instinctive."

Although potentially open, however, human societies for the greater part of history have remained closed. Closed societies, which are governed by a "morality of pressure," are more instinctive than intellective. They may be very small (as were the ancient *poleis*) or very large (as have been great nations and empires), but "their essential characteristics is ... to include a certain number of individuals and to exclude others."

By the initial promptings of nature, then, man is not led to the open society. Nonetheless, there is at work in reality as process a creative *élan* which eventually breaks the shell of the closed society (whether large or small) and establishes in the consciousness the experience of oneness with all mankind and with the natural environment as well. This *élan vital* creates the conditions for the emergence of a new personality type: the open-souled hero, whether he be the Buddha, Socrates, the Hebrew prophet, or Jesus, and this "new man" appeals to our "fundamental" rather than to our "surface" selves. The drama of the trial and death of Socrates, who challenged the closed morality of the Athenian *polis* with the truth of philosophy as the love of transcendent, divine wisdom, grips us still today because it teaches a universal lesson. Socrates speaks across the centuries to the depth of our moral experience, arousing within us our best selves. As

---

[37] Henri Bergson, *Les deux sources de la morale et de la religion* (Paris: Felix Alcan, 1932), translated as *The Two Sources of Morality and Religion* (New York: Holt, 1935).

the allegory of the cave illustrates, openness is *metanoia*, a conversion of the soul to new priorities and dimensions of reality.

The closure which the morality of openness seeks to transcend is two-fold in character. In the closed society the person is trapped within the confines both of the city and of the self: in the city because he must conform to the dictates of "my country, right or wrong," and in the self because he seeks above all to preserve, defend and advance the self and its projects through every act and calculation. Closure is self-seeking, while openness is self-fulfillment through sacrifice and love. The contrast between the two moralities was never more vividly presented than in the Sermon on the Mount, with its "Ye have heard it said unto you" and Jesus' answering "But I say unto you" repeated many times.

Bergson speaks repeatedly of the open soul as "breaking" with nature, a nature which "enclosed it both within itself and within the city." He later defines nature as "the *ensemble* of compliances and resistances which life encounters in raw matter." As the very title of his masterpiece suggests, "nature" is one of the "two sources" of morality and religion, while "life" is the other and put this way nature requires completion and indeed qualitative transformation.

Saint Thomas, by comparison, appears to have been rather more generous toward nature than Bergson. Nature is not so intractable; it too is open to leavening. Nature, to be sure, requires to be "perfected" by grace, but it could also be said, in a way which is incompatible with Bergson, that nature prepares the ground for its completion by grace. Despite various qualifications, Bergson seems to emerge as more of an "either-or" man (*either* the open *or* the closed morality), while Thomas more nearly approximates a "both-and" orientation (the open morality as fulfilling or rounding out a more affirmatively envisaged "natural" morality—in Bergson's sense, "closed" morality—that of natural law). Thomas, of course, regarded the Sermon on the Mount as the supreme expression of moral teaching, but in characterizing its tenets as "counsels" rather than "commands," he clearly regarded them as directly and fully applicable only to that small minority of Christians who freely assume the life of self-sacrifice which the Sermon implies. In summary, the distinction (in effect) between the closed and the open morality, while real, is less sharp and cutting in Thomas than it is in Henri Bergson. Aquinas is the more serene thinker of the two: all will be well, eventually, he seems to say, but in God's good time. Bergson, by contrast, although not lacking serenity, fills his pages with strenuous and anguished exhortations to mankind to act on the open morality in the near future.

Because of the peculiar vagueness in Bergon's philosophy, one may read the *Two Sources* in different ways, and one of the "faces" of the book seems compatible with the teaching of Thomas. However, sensitive interpreters of the *Two Sources* were quick to notice profound divergencies between Bergsonism and the Catholicism of which Thomas Aquinas remains the greatest theologian. Thus, Joseph de Toquédec, s.j., in a series of masterful articles in *Etudes*, found Bergson's philosophy closed "to the perspectives of a strictly supernatural faith." Fr. de Touquédec finds that Bergson subordinates the contemplative element in mysticism to innerworldly activism, and that he makes morality independent of belief in God. The closed morality is by definition oriented toward the survival needs of the group, while the open morality "inclines always toward our equals, toward a group of [fellow] creatures." There is little awareness of God's radical transcendence, of the utter dependence of man on God, in Bergson's work. The *élan vital* may either be God or from God, and he quotes the philosopher's statement that "from our viewpoint, in which the divinity of all men is proclaimed, it matters little whether Christ is or is not called a man." He judges Bergson's two moralities to be "incapable of furnishing a moral rule for human activity, because the closed morality is not *moral* (lacking the element of rational choice, and being based on instinct), while the open morality is not a rule. He finds Bergson's cosmopolitanism indiscriminate, declaring that in the order of charity "the love of humanity is not qualitatively different from and superior to the love of one's parents or fellow-countrymen." One loves one's mother not as just a woman among women but because she is *our* mother. And finally, Fr. de Touquédec finds Bergson's open morality lacking in "virility and strength": it sees only the joy in heroism, not the suffering. The suffering of Christ on Calvary reveals a "sadness unto death."[38]

Jacques Maritain, perhaps the most noted follower of Thomas among the philosophers of the twentieth century, also had many misgivings about the *Two Sources*. He concluded that despite the subtlety of the argument, that the work reveals "an attempted reduction of the spiritual to the biological." The sharp distinction between the closed and open moralities gives evidence of a kind of "Manichaean dualism." Despite all protestations to the contrary, Bergson remains an "irrationalist" in philosophy. Similarly to Joseph de Touquédec, Maritain deplores Bergson's excessive emphasis on activism

[38] Joseph de Touquédec, "Le contenu des 'Deux Sources'," *Etudes*, 214 (20 March 1933), 661; 215 (5 April 1933) 34, 35, 42, 43, 51.

and detects in the *Two Sources* a drift toward "Pelagian evolutionism" and "pantheism."[39]

The preceding comments on the part of distinguished Catholic scholars sympathetic to and knowledgeable about the moral teaching of Henri Bergson should give anyone pause who was inclined to argue for a fundamental affinity between Bergson and Thomas. When in this paper I argue that Thomas' teaching is compatible with a theory of the open society that is Bergsonian in inspiration, I mean that, despite its flaws, deficiencies, and incoherencies, Bergson's theory is susceptible to correction and revision, that the germ of the idea of mankind as an open society under the world-transcendent God is implanted in the *Deux Sources*, and that this quintessential quality of openness to transcendence permeates the teaching of Saint Thomas forging a unity of spirit between the monk of the thirteenth and the saintly layman of the twentieth century. For the greatness of Bergson's *Two Sources* is to be found in the impression the whole makes on the reader. Certainly the whole in this instance is greater than the sum of its parts. The whole work gives evidence of theophany, of the manifestation of the divine presence in the consciousness of its author.

One can validly accuse Bergson of immanentizing the transcendent, of biologizing morality, of idealizing the French Revolution and Rousseau, of tending to confuse the open society (a *spiritual* reality) with a globally organized world state (a *temporal* project), and of neglecting the mission of the Prophets and/or the Church to serve as a bulwark against claims by even the most beneficent political regimes over the whole man. In doing so, if one were true to the accommodating spirit of Saint Thomas, one would still have to acknowledge Bergson's great service in resisting the drift of philosophy in his time toward positivism and a crippling rationalism. Bergson fought, however imperfectly, to restore the vision of man, so dear to Saint Thomas, as having been made in the image of God. How incomplete, how dogmatic, how sectarian, how unhistorical does much of Karl Popper's account of the open society appear when compared to that of Bergson; how rich, how fluid, how catholic, how responsive to the durational element of reality is Bergson's exposition by contrast. Bergson was no Thomist, but he shares much of the grandeur, the multidimensionality, the freshness, the transparency, the buoyancy, and the affirmative quality that pervades the teaching of Thomas.

---

[39] Jacques Maritain, "La morale de Bergson," in *De Bergson à Thomas d'Aquin* (Paris: Paul Hartmann, 1947), pp. 71, 76-77, 83, 87, 98.

To compare the theories of the open society put forward by Henri Bergson and Karl Popper after reading in the works of Thomas Aquinas and pondering the saint's life is to be struck with the extent to which Popper's teaching represents an impoverishment of the Bergsonian teaching, so much so that we might even call it the "poverty of Popperism." To be sure, Popper's idea of the open society is simpler and more straightforward than that of Bergson. Openness for Popper is a world without transcendence, without mystery, and without an opening onto ontological reality. It is a no-nonsense kind of world in which the individual human being, brittle and hard, is thrown entirely upon his own resources. The "reason" of Popper is a practical problem solving rather than an inquiring faculty. It is not the contemplative, speculative reason of the author of the *Summa theologiae*. After all, an inquiry such as the *Summa* raises far more problems than it solves. If Sir Karl Popper were to enter into the spirit of the *Summa*, he would have to abandon his autonomous decisionist ethics, his Pelagian view of self-sufficient man, his caricature of Judaism and institutional Christianity, and his closure to the achievement of Aristotelian philosophy. He would have to reflect upon the "Five Ways," in a spirit of openness to the possibility that the finite, phenomenal world suggests more than it contains and is not comprehensible as reality in its own terms. Then he would be able to provide sorely needed philosophical substance to the procedural focus of his theory of constitutional democracy as an "open society."[40]

Yes, Thomas Aquinas, if read seriously again, would aid us in "un-bracketing the divine alternative," to use Arnold Brecht's somewhat inelegant phrase. As we became more deeply acquainted with the *Summa* we would see how this incredible masterpiece was anything but a closed deductive system, how its rational structure radiated the theophanic experience of divine Reality which we find reported in Exodus 3 with Moses and the Burning Bush and in Acts 22 with Paul's vision of the Resurrected Christ. As Eric Voegelin (who frequently cites Thomas in his great *Order and History*) has taught us, theophany and "religion" are not coterminous and secularist historians such as Popper may not validly split the symbols of "religion" from the theophanic experience that motivated their articulation and then reject the deformed symbols as a list of moralistic taboos or propositions about the phenomenal world. To read Thomas again is to break the silence about—even the "taboo" against—theophany in contemporary

---

[40] For relevant passages in Popper's *Open Society* (1962 ed.), see inter alia 1: 61, 66, 153-156, 194-200; 2: 22-26, 230-231, 270-271, 302-303, n. 61.

secularist, instrumentalist culture and to enrich that culture by opening it out to a "world caused by God."

According to the acts of canonization, Saint Thomas deliberately laid aside the still unfinished *Summa theologiae* after Mass on the feast of Saint Nicholas in 1273, a few months before his death. He declared that he would write no more. When pressed by his friends to state the reason for his silence, he is supposed to have replied, "All that I have written seems to me nothing but straw ... compared to what I have seen and what has been revealed to me."[41] With such a teacher, we may learn to open our ears to the music of theophany and to open the eyes of our rationalist culture to the vistas of the spirit. Then we should not have to "define" the open society; we would be conscious of living in it.

[41] Josef Pieper. *The Silence of St. Thomas* (New York: Pantheon, 1957; Chicago: Henry Regnery Co., 1965), p. 40.

7

The Spiritual Community of Man: The Church According to Saint Thomas

Avery DULLES, S.J.
The Catholic University of America

As an inevitable effect of the forces of history, the spiritual community of man has become a major concern in our day. World trade, global travel, and instant communications have, on the one hand, established ties and sympathies that transcend all national and continental boundaries and have, on the other hand, aggravated the tensions and antipathies among the various "worlds" into which our one world is divided. In the present generation, the major spiritual and cultural movements have been global in character. Rock music, transcendental meditation, neo-Marxism, and charismatic Christianity—to cite but a few widely disparate examples—all aspire, in one way or another, to a union of minds and will that knows no linguistic or geographical frontiers. International conferences and agencies such as UNESCO strive to institutionalize whatever cooperation or consensus can be achieved in the spheres of education, science, and culture.

Other papers in this symposium have dealt with the ideas of Thomas Aquinas concerning the civic and political community. Civic peace and cooperation, according to Saint Thomas, depend on a kind of natural friendship arising out of a common sharing of the same human nature.[1] But Saint Thomas, as a Christian and a theologian, looks upon this natural or political community as incomplete. The perfect friendship of charity, he contends, derives from the fact that all human persons are gratuitously ordered to the vision of God.[2] If we love God above all else, and love our neighbor in God, we create the possibility of achieving perfect concord and peace among the human family even here on earth.[3] A fuller investigation of that deeper unity among humankind which flows from the gifts of grace will take us into a study of Saint Thomas' doctrine of the Church.

[1] scG 3.125; cf. st 2-2.29.3 resp.
[2] st 2-2.26.2 resp. and 3.
[3] st 2-2.29.1 ad 2 and 2-2.29.3 resp.

In the course of the past century it has often been asked whether Aquinas had an ecclesiology. Joseph Kleutgen, for example, maintained that he failed to develop this treatise and that his *Summa theologiae* stands in need of a fourth part, which would supply what is lacking in Parts One to Three.[4] More recently, Alois Dempf declared that in Thomas' system the Church is forgotten.[5] On the contrary, J. R. Geiselmann held that Thomas was the creator of a new and original ecclesiology.[6] Yves Congar argues that "everything in the thought of St. Thomas has an ecclesiological phase" and that it is probably a deliberate act on Saint Thomas' part that "he refused to write a separate treatise *De Ecclesia*, seeing that the Church pervaded his theology in all its parts."[7] Congar would seem to be substantially correct. It is indeed possible to find in Thomas' writings statements that touch on almost any question about the Church that would have arisen naturally out of the circumstances in which he lived and wrote. On the other hand we cannot help regretting, from our modern point of view, that he did not treat certain ecclesiological questions more thoroughly and connectedly.

As one would expect from an acquaintance with other areas of his thought, Aquinas' ecclesiology is an extraordinary brilliant synthesis or harmonization of elements derived from many diverse sources—the Bible, the Church Fathers (notably Augustine and Pseudo-Dionysius), the medieval canonists, and the early scholastic theologians. To assemble the full thought of Saint Thomas on the Church one would have to peruse almost the entire corpus of his writings. Questions would then arise as to whether he successfully integrated the various authorities he sought to bring together and whether, in his various treatises, he was fully consistent with himself. In the present paper it will not be possible to explore questions such as these in suitable depth. We shall have to be content with a basic overview of our subject matter.

Following some of the main headings that would appear in a modern textbook on ecclesiology, I shall present, in the main body of this paper, a brief survey of Aquinas' views on a number of major topics: the nature of the Church, its relationship to the Holy Spirit, its relationship to Christ; the sacraments; worship and ministries; the papacy; and Church-State relation-

---

[4] J. Kleutgen, *Institutiones theologicae* 1 (Ratisbon, 1881), p. v.

[5] A. Dempf, *Sacrum imperium*, 2nd ed. (Darmstadt: Wissenschaftliche Buchgemein-schaft, 1954), pp. 230-231.

[6] J. R. Geiselmann, "Christus und die Kirche nach Thomas von Aquin," *Theologische Quartalschrift*, 107 (1926), 198-222; 108 (1927), 233-255; see p. 254.

[7] Y. Congar, "The Idea of the Church in St. Thomas Aquinas," chapter 3 of *The Mystery of the Church* (Baltimore: Helicon Press, 1960), p. 117.

ships. Then in a concluding section I shall make some observations on the current value of the ecclesiology of Aquinas.

1. THE CHURCH: ITS NATURE AND STATES

The term "Church" in our time suggests in the first instance an institution. For Saint Thomas the Church was far more than this. It was above all the way by which the rational creature returns to God, the source of its being. One makes one's way back to God, according to Aquinas, by appropriating the divine life—a life of grace offered in Christ, who is preeminently the way to God. The term "ecclesia," as Thomas uses it, has reference directly to the "plane of grace and divine life (*vie théologale*)."[8]

Yet the Church is also a community. Just as in the natural order man is a social and political animal, so too in the supernatural order, he achieves his highest fulfilment in community.[9] The Church, then, may be called the community of those who are brought into union with God by the grace of Christ. In this sense it may be designated by expressions such as *congregatio fidelium* and *societas sanctorum*.[10] Corporately, the Church is a people in much the same way as are the citizens of a sovereign state. Yet the juridical and sociological aspects of the Church pertain only to its present state of pilgrimage and fail to express the inner life of faith, hope, and charity, which is the heart of the Church's existence.

Many theologians today think of the Church as having some goal beyond itself, such as the Kingdom of God or the heavenly city. According to the mind of Saint Thomas it seems fair to say that the Church, inasmuch as it unites with God, is its own justification. Christ, he holds, came into the world in order to found the Church.[11]

For Aquinas it would be no more true to say that the Church exists for the sake of the Kingdom of God than to say that the Kingdom exists for the sake of the Church. In fact, he identifies the Kingdom of God in its inmost reality with the Church itself. The term "Kingdom of God," he explains is used biblically in four senses. First, it signifies Christ Himself dwelling in us by His grace; second, it means the Scripture insofar as its teaching leads

[8] Y. Congar, "'Ecclesia' et 'Populus (Fidelis)' dans l'ecclésiologie de S. Thomas," in *St. Thomas Aquinas, 1274-1974: Commemorative Studies* (Toronto: Pontifical Institute of Mediaeval Studies, 1974), 1: 159-173.

[9] *De regno* 1.1 (Parma ed., 16: 225). For the reader's convenience, references will be given to the Parma edition (25 vols., 1852-1873) of all the works of Saint Thomas cited in the following pages, except in the cases of the *Summa contra gentiles* and the *Summa theologiae*, which are easily accessible in numerous editions.

[10] A. Darquennes, *De Juridische Structuur van de Kerk, volgens Sint Thomas van Aquino* (Louvain: Universiteitsbibliotheek, 1949), pp. 23-38.

[11] *In Matth.* 16.18 (Parma ed., 10: 154).

to the Kingdom; third, it denotes the present militant Church, which is constituted in the likeness of the heavenly Church; and finally, it designates the heavenly court itself, which Saint Thomas identifies with the glorious Church.[12]

The term "Church" in the vocabulary of Aquinas transcends the limits of time and space; it has its fullest and most perfect realization in the glory of heaven. "The true Church," he writes, "is the heavenly Church, which is our mother, and to which we tend; upon it our earthly church is modelled (*exemplata*)."[13] His works abound in comparisons and contrasts between the earthly and the heavenly Church, the Church of grace and the Church of glory, the Church militant and the Church triumphant, the Church in the wayfaring state (*ecclesia viatorum*) and in the homeland (*in patria*). The institutional features of the Church, which for so many of our contemporaries define its very essence, are for Saint Thomas proper to its earthly, and inferior, condition. In heaven "all prelacy will cease" and the sacraments, insofar as they are ordered to the worship of the present Church, will disappear.[14] Referring to the Pauline statement that the Church, as cleansed by Christ, is to be without spot or wrinkle (Ephesians 5:27), Saint Thomas remarks, "This will be true only in our eternal home, not on the way to it, for now we would deceive ourselves if we were to say that we have no sin, as 1 John 1:8 points out."[15]

For Saint Thomas, as for subsequent ecclesiologists, the Church is distinguished by four properties, which he calls *conditiones*: "It is one, it is holy, it is catholic, i.e., universal, and it is strong and firm."[16] The holiness and unity of the Church, as we shall see, are especially attributed to the active presence within it of the Holy Spirit.

The note of firmness, in Thomas' enumeration takes the place of what in the Constantinopolitan Creed is called "apostolicity." By the firmness of the Church Thomas means the indestructibility that pertains to it inasmuch as it is founded upon Christ and the apostles.[17] So solid is the Church, he holds, that it will endure to the end of time. The universal Church, built upon the teaching of the apostles, cannot fall into error. Universal councils and popes, inasmuch as they represent the universal Church, are protected against error. Whether this doctrine of Saint Thomas implies conciliar or papal infallibility is a question we shall later have to consider.

[12] *In Matth.* 3.2 (Parma ed., 10: 30).
[13] *In Eph.* 3.10, lect. 3 (Parma ed., 13: 471).
[14] ST 3.61.4 ad 1; 3.63.5 ad 3.
[15] ST 3.8.3 ad 2.
[16] *Expos. in Symb.*, art. 9 (Parma ed., 16: 147).
[17] Y. Congar, "L'apostolicité de l'Eglise selon S. Thomas d'Aquin," *Revue des sciences philosophiques et théologiques*, 44 (1960), 209-224.

We generally think of the Church as existing in a particular segment of history—from the glorification of Christ to the end of the world. Some authors speak in this connection of the "time of the Church."[18] For Saint Thomas the Church, even in the historical aspect of its existence, is far more comprehensive. "It is universal in time," he says, "enduring from Abel to the end of the world, after which it will continue in heaven."[19]

The wayfaring Church, however, exists in different forms corresponding to the several stages of salvation history. It was "of a child's age in Abel's days, is young with the patriarchs, and has grown up with the apostles; it will attain old age at the end of the world."[20] From another point of view the stages of Church history may be divided into three: before the Law, under the Law, and under grace.[21] The Church exists most perfectly in this last stage, when it has been enriched with the teaching and sacraments of Christ.

For Aquinas the inclusion of the believers of every age in one Church is not a mere matter of teminology. It is of critical importance in his system that the Church should be so defined as to manifest the inclusion of all those who belong to the order of salvation, which embraces in its differentiated unity both angels and men, both time and eternity.[22] Existing in the same order of redemption, the Fathers of the Old Testament lived by the same faith as Christians do, hence they are to be reckoned as belonging to the same Church.[23]

II. THE CHURCH AND THE HOLY SPIRIT

Saint Thomas' teaching concerning the relationship between the Church and the Holy Spirit was formulated, in part, in the context of polemics. The disciples of the Calabrian Abbot, Joachim of Fiore (ca. 1130-1202), were promoting a theology of history very different from that of Saint Thomas.

---

[18] O. Cullmann, *Christ and Time* (Philadelphia: Westminster Press, 1950), pp. 144-147; idem, *Salvation in History* (New York: Harper and Row, 1967), pp. 304-313; H. U. von Balthasar, *A Theology of History* (New York: Sheed and Ward, 1963), pp. 79-107.

[19] *Expos. in Symb.*, art. 9 (Parma ed., 16: 148). See Y. Congar, "Ecclesia ab Abel," in *Abhandlungen über Theologie und Kirche. Festschrift für Karl Adam* (Dusseldorf: Patmos, 1952), pp. 79-108.

[20] *In Ps.* 36.18 (Parma ed., 14: 286).

[21] ST 3.53.2 resp. Elsewhere (ST 1.73.1 ad 1) Thomas speaks of three completions: *consummatio naturae*, *consummatio gratiae* and *consummatio gloriae*. The Church belongs to the second and third of these completions.

[22] M. Seckler, *Das Heil in der Geschichte* (Munich: Kösel-Verlag, 1964), p. 222.

[23] ST 3.8.3. ad 3.

According to Joachim's view there were three stages of world history corresponding to the three divine persons. The first, the age of the laity, lasted from Adam through the Patriarchs. The second, the age of the clergy or the Church, began with Uzziah and flourished since the time of Jesus. The third, the age of the monks or of the "eternal gospel," began with Benedict and was to emerge about 1260 into full clarity. The Church of Christ, therefore, was about to give way to a new community of the Holy Spirit.[24]

For Saint Thomas the Church of the New Law, as established by Jesus Christ, was already the Church of the Holy Spirit.[25] There was no need to expect any fuller outpouring of the Spirit. The Church is already, through and through, a Spirit-filled community. In his exposition of the Creed, Thomas treats the Church under the article, "I believe in the Holy Spirit." To say "I believe in the holy catholic Church" is in his view an elliptical statement meaning, "I believe in the Holy Spirit sanctifying the Church."[26] Properly speaking it is better to say not that we believe *in* the Church but rather that we believe the Church, for only the divine persons are, in Saint Thomas' perspective, of such a nature that we can believe *in* them.

What has been given in Christ is the "New Law." This Law, unlike that of the Old Testament, is not a series of prescriptions but an interior prompting of the Spirit. Thomas refers to it variously as the "law of love," the "law of freedom," the "law of faith," the "law of perfection," and the "law of the gospel."[27] The New Law, therefore, may be designated indifferently as the Law of Christ and that of the Holy Spirit.[28] The working of the Holy Spirit was not entirely absent prior to the time of Christ. Those Old Testament figures who were animated by the Holy Spirit, even without explicitly believing in Christ, belonged already to the Law of the Gospel.[29]

As compared with many of the Franciscan theologians, including even Saint Bonaventure, Saint Thomas was inclined to stress the continuing identity and stability of the Church from the time of Christ to the end of the world. On guard against the unhealthy apocalypticism rife in his time, Saint Thomas insisted that the passage of generations does not by itself

---

[24] On Joachim see Y. Congar, *L'Eglise de Saint Augustin à l'époque moderne* (Paris: Editions du Cerf, 1970), pp. 209-214.

[25] J. Mahoney, "'The Church of the Holy Spirit' in Aquinas," *Heythrop Journal*, 15 (1974), 18-36.

[26] ST 2-2.1.9 ad 5.

[27] See the texts gathered by M. Grabmann, *Die Lehre des heiligen Thomas von Aquin von der Kirche als Gotteswerk* (Regensburg: G. J. Manz, 1903), pp. 97-98.

[28] ST 1-2.106.4 ad 2 and ad 3.

[29] ST 1-2.106.1 ad 3.

bring humanity closer to God. God's proximity depends rather on his own free interventions. The goal of history is transcendent; it lies above and beyond all history, but it has inserted itself in history in the person of Christ.

The time of Christ, for Aquinas, was the time of fullness (cf. Galatians 4:4). Those who were closest to Christ, either before Him, like John the Baptist, or after Him, like the apostles, had the fullest insight into the mysteries of faith. In this respect salvation history parallels the history of individual men who, according to Saint Thomas, attain their greatest perfection in young adulthood.[30] "It is not to be expected that there will be any future state in which the grace of the Holy Spirit will be had more perfectly than it was already had, especially by the apostles, who received the first fruits of the Spirit earlier in time and more abundantly than others, as stated in the Gloss on Roman 8 [:23]."[31]

In Thomistic theology, as in the encyclicals of Leo XIII and Pius XII, the Holy Spirit is viewed as the inner principle or soul of the Church. Building on the prior work of Augustine,[32] Thomas in his commentary on the Creed calls the Holy Spirit the "soul" vivifying the body which is the Church. Elsewhere he says that just as the soul is the chief and ultimate perfection of the natural body, so is the Holy Spirit for the Mystical Body.[33]

In a special way, Aquinas attributes the inner unity of the Church with its head and of the members with one another to the influence of the Holy Spirit.[34] This would be true to some extent if the Spirit were merely the giver of faith, hope and charity, all of which are unitive virtues, and of sanctifying grace, which is specifically the same in all. In an even deeper sense, however, the Spirit unifies the Church by bestowing Himself as uncreated grace. He is numerically one in all the faithful and thus unites them very intimately to one another and to Christ their head.[35] Identically the same person of the Holy Spirit is present and active both in Christ the Head and in all the faithful as members.

The personal indwelling of the Holy Spirit, is so intimate that it makes Christ and the Church, in a certain sense, "one mystical person."[36] This

---

[30] ST 2-2.1.7 ad 4.

[31] ST 1-2.106.4 resp.

[32] Augustine wrote: "Quod autem est anima corpori hominis, hoc est Spiritus Sanctus corpori Christi, quod est Ecclesia" (*Sermo* 267.4; PL 38: 1231).

[33] *In 3 Sent.* D 13.2.2 sol. 2 (Parma ed., 7: 142).

[34] E. Vauthier, "Le Saint-Esprit principe d'unité de l'Eglise d'après saint Thomas d'Aquin," *Mélanges de science religieuse*, 5 (1948), 175-196; 6 (1949), 57-80.

[35] *De ver.* 29.4 resp. (Parma ed., 9: 451); *In 3 Sent.* D 13.2.2 (Parma ed., 7: 142).

[36] *De ver.* 29.7 ad 11 (Parma ed., 9: 456); ST 3.19.4 resp.; *In Col.* 1.24, lect. 6 n. 61

union between the head and the members, effected by the Holy Spirit as immanent unifying principle, enables the merits of Christ to be efficacious on
behalf of the Church and allows the Church, by an interchange of
predicates (*communicatio idiomatum*), to be designated by attributes proper
to Christ. Those who, through charity, are animated by the grace of Christ,
are most closely identified with the divine Head. The Holy Spirit therefore
unifies the Church precisely by sanctifying it.

To illuminate further the role of the Holy Spirit, Saint Thomas sometimes uses the metaphor, "heart" of the Church[37]—an expression that
seems to have been original with Thomas himself.[38] Just as in the human
organism the heart, according to Aristotle, is the interior source of life and
movement, so in the Church, Aquinas maintains, the Holy Spirit is the immanent principle of vital activity.[39] Just as the heart is hidden in the most
intimate depths of the body, so the Holy Spirit is invisible and interior in
the Church.

Following the example of Saint Paul, who had treated the unity and
variety of ecclesiastical ministries under the rubric of the Body of Christ,
Saint Thomas attributes the diversity of tasks, states, and grades to the
prodigality of the Holy Spirit. All the gifts are maintained in peace and
unity by the Holy Spirit, who is in all the members making them mutually
solicitous for one another.[40] The Holy Spirit at Pentecost descended upon
the infant Church in the form of fiery tongues, which visibly symbolized the
empowerment of the apostles to spread the Church by the ministry of word
and sacrament.[41] As the abiding dynamic principle of the Church, the Holy
Spirit continually gives efficacy to all its ministries and sacraments.[42]

The life of the Spirit is the primary goal of all the institutional aspects
of the Church. "The most important element in the Law of the New
Testament, and the one in which its whole virtue consists, is the grace of
the Holy Spirit, which is given by Christian faith. And thus the New Law
consists principally in the grace of the Holy Spirit, given to Christians."[43]
With regard to the institutional elements, Thomas writes: "The New Law

---

(Parma ed., 13: 538-539). Additional texts are mentioned by H. Mühlen, *Una mystica Persona*, 3rd ed. (Paderborn: Schöningh, 1968), pp. 40-43.

[37] E.g. ST 3.8.1 ad 3.
[38] Grabmann, *Die Lehre*, pp. 184-193.
[39] *In 5 Meta.*, lect. 1 (Parma ed., 20: 381).
[40] ST 2-2.183.2 ad 3.
[41] *In 1 Sent.* D 16.1.2 ad 4 (Parma ed., 6: 130); D 16.1.3, sol. (Parma ed., 6: 131).
[42] Cf. Congar, *The Mystery of the Church*, pp. 102-103.
[43] ST 1-2.106.1 resp.

does, however, have elements that are dispositive toward the grace of the Holy Spirit, and that pertain to the use of that grace, and these are, so to speak, secondary elements of the New Law, in which the faithful should be instructed by words and Scriptures."[44] The sacraments are conducive to grace; the commandments enjoin acts that are in conformity with grace.[45]

Some have objected that by thus subordinating the institutional to the invisible, Aquinas inordinately spiritualized Christian grace and the Church.[46] It might equally well be argued, however, that by this expedient Saint Thomas effectively answered the "spiritualizing" Joachimites, who denied that the presently existing Church is that of the Holy Spirit, and wished to see it superseded by a truly spiritual community. Saint Thomas was in effect defending the institutional Church by arguing that the externals are necessary to prepare for grace and to attune to the promptings of the Holy Spirit. At any event, he insists that the visible and institutional elements are unconditionally necessary to the existence of the Church in the present stage of human existence. Only in heaven will the need for laws, ministries, and sacraments cease. What the Joachimites claimed for the third age of temporal history is more than fulfilled in Aquinas' concept of the glorious Church.

Like the Joachimites, Saint Thomas accepts the superiority of the spiritual over the material, the interior over the external. This is perhaps an effect of his Hellenistic philosophical heritage, but it should not be casually dismissed as an error or as contrary to the New Testament. Rightly or wrongly, Aquinas affirms that the Kingdom of God consists, not exclusively but primarily, in interior acts. Although the Kingdom of God is interior justice, peace, and spiritual joy (cf. Romans 14:17), it involves externals insofar as they are conducive to, or expressive of, these interior gifts.[47]

III. THE CHURCH AND CHRIST

Having seen something of the Church's relationship to the Holy Spirit, we may now ask how Saint Thomas views its relationship to Christ. His ecclesiology is strongly Christocentric. Christ, he asserts, "is the whole treasure of the Church (*totum Ecclesiae bonum*)," so that He is worth as much by Himself alone as together with the rest of the Church.[48] Thomas

---

[44] Ibid.
[45] ST 1-2.108.1 resp.
[46] So F. Malmberg, *Ein Leib—Ein Geist* (Freiburg: Herder, 1960), pp. 199-219.
[47] ST 1-2.108.1 ad 1.
[48] *In 4 Sent.* D 49.4.3 ad 4 (Parma ed., 7: 1229).

continually returns to the Pauline images of the Church as Bride and Body of Christ. In accordance with the terminology of his day, he distinguishes between the Eucharist as the "true" body of Christ and the Church as His "mystical" body.[49]

The Church of the New Law, according to Saint Thomas, was born on Calvary from the pierced side of Christ.[50] Christ is the source of our redemption not simply by reason of His inner spiritual acts but by what He did and suffered in the flesh. Christ's humanity has a part in His redemptive work, for it is the conjoint instrument of His divinity. It is instrument not simply insofar as it is soul, but in its fullness as soul-body composite.[51] As a visible and palpable man Christ became the sacramental organ of salvation. The Church depends continually on Christ as its historical source and abiding head. He is the principal minister in every sacramental action of the Church militant. Even in heaven, it is the complete humanity of Christ, body and soul, that will bring blessedness to the elect.[52]

The physical and sacramental mediation of Christ corresponds to man's nature as a spirit-body composite. Man is of such a nature that he rises to spiritual things through the mediation of those that are bodily. Thus it is necessary that grace should be incarnationally structured.[53]

In no context does Aquinas discuss the Church more explicitly than when he treats of the grace of Christ. In the third part of the *Summa* he explains that in three respects Christ's grace was one of headship (*gratia capitalis*).[54] First, He was the primary recipient of grace, for He was closest to God. Second, He had the fullness of grace, as is said in John 1:14. Third, He has active influence on others. All this implies that the body of Christ is constituted of those who receive grace through Christ, have it in lesser degree, and are governed by Him.

In treating of those who actually belong to the body of Christ, Saint Thomas divides them into three classes. First and most perfectly, the body includes those who are united to Christ in eternal glory; second, those who are united by living faith, or charity; third, and least perfectly, it includes those who have faith, but are in a state of sin. These three classes comprise the actual members of Christ's body—whether they be Christians or

---

[49] Cf. H. de Lubac, *Corpus mysticum* (Paris: Aubier, 1944), pp. 127-137.

[50] ST 3.64.2 ad 3; cf. *In Joan.* cap. 19, lect. 5 (Parma ed., 10: 622).

[51] Cf. J. Hamer, *The Church is a Communion* (New York: Sheed and Ward, 1964), pp. 74-75.

[52] Ibid., pp. 78-79, with references to Saint Thomas.

[53] Ibid., p. 77; cf. Seckler, *Das Heil*, p. 244.

[54] ST 3.8.3 resp.

nonevangelized believers. In a wider sense Christ may be called head of all who ever will be united to Him in any of these three ways, and in the widest sense all men belong to the body of Christ, insofar as they are at least in potency to be incorporated into Him, unless they are definitively damned.

It is noteworthy that the term "body," in divisions such as these, signifies a variegated functional whole (*multitudo ordinata in unum*), but is not necessarily material and visible.[55] Thus Saint Thomas would not have said, as Leo XIII and Pius XII were to assert, "By the very fact that it is a body, the Church is visible."[56] The Mystical Body for Aquinas includes the separated souls of the blessed and even, in a certain sense the angels, though with regard to the angels Saint Thomas remarks that they belong to the body of Christ in a different fashion than men, for there is no specific unity of nature between them and the humanity of Christ.[57]

The general treatment of incorporation in the Church under the rubric of Christ's grace of headship is completed and in some respects further nuanced by the theology of the sacraments, to which we may now turn.

IV BAPTISM AND EUCHARIST

The sacrament of initial incorporation into the Church is baptism. Although one may be truly incorporated by faith and charity, even without baptism, such an incorporation would be merely mental, and therefore incomplete. For its full human and social realization, mental incorporation needs to be complemented by sacramental incorporation, which imprints the baptismal character and assimilates the baptized to the priesthood of Christ.[58] While full incorporation includes both the inner virtues of faith and charity and the sacramental expression of these in baptism, these ingredients are to some extent mutually separable. Thus Thomistic theology provides for many different kinds and degrees of incorporation, more or less perfect and complete.[59]

---

[55] Malmberg, *Ein Leib*, p. 207; Seckler, *Das Heil*, p. 241.

[56] Leo XIII, *Satis cognitum* (*ASS* 28 [1895/6], 710); Pius XII, *Mystici corporis* (*AAS* 35 [1943], 199). Saint Thomas is found to be in conflict with Pius XII by A. Mitterer, *Geheimnisvoller Leib Christi nach St. Thomas von Aquin und nach Papst Pius XII.* (Vienna: Herold, 1950).

[57] ST 3.8.4 ad 1; *Comp. theol.* c. 214 (Parma ed., 16: 60).

[58] ST 3.63.1 ad 3.

[59] Cf. C. O'Neill, "St. Thomas on the Membership of the Church," in *Vatican II: The Theological Dimension*, ed. A. D. Lee (Washington, D.C.: Thomist Press, 1963; originally published as *Thomist* 27 [1963]), pp. 88-140.

From what we have said it evidently follows that the baptized believer can become separated from the Church. Since the Church's unity is perfected by charity, all sin to some degree cuts the sinner off from the Church.[60] Loss of charity through mortal sin weakens but does not of itself terminate membership in the Church, for the sinful believer remains bound to Christ and to his fellow believers at least by faith. The sin of schism, for Saint Thomas, is especially injurious to membership, for it consists in a refusal to recognize the other members as members or the legitimate rulers as rulers.[61] Sins of infidelity are even more destructive of membership, for, by rupturing even the bonds of faith, they sever radically from the community of faith which is the Church.[62] Excommunication is an act of Church authority that excludes from certain types of association with the Church. It separates from the Church, according to Thomistic theologians, in varying degrees according to the severity with which it is imposed.[63] Although excommunication does not by itself terminate every kind of membership, it may officially ratify an existing lack of communion brought about by an offense such as schism or infidelity.[64]

Saint Thomas does not speak of subjection to the pope and the bishops, or of acceptance of the dogmas and disciplinary regulations of the Church, as positive constituents of membership. These conditions come into his discussion only negatively or indirectly, when he is treating of heresy, schism, and excommunication. For Saint Thomas a rejection of Church doctrine or law might involve the sin of heresy or schism, and for that reason sever or weaken the bonds of communion.[65] If inculpable, dissidence would not result in loss of membership or communion.[66] Aquinas seems to assume that a Christian in good faith will easily be able to correct a failure to conform to the doctrine or discipline of the Church once such a failure has been brought to his attention. He does not go into the case of a baptized Christian whose doctrinal errors are, as we would put it today, morally

---

[60] *In 1 ad Cor.* cap. 11, lect. 7 (Parma ed., 13: 248). *In 3 Sent.* D 13.2.2 sol 2 (Parma ed., 7: 142) speaks of sinners as "membra aequivoce." ST 3.8.3 ad 2 calls them imperfectly but actually members.

[61] ST 2-2.39.1 resp. It is noteworthy that Saint Thomas here defines schism primarily as a breach of unity with the pope. Cf. Y. Congar, "Schisme," *Dictionnaire de théologie catholique*, vol. 14, coll. 1286-1312.

[62] ST 3.80.5 ad 2.

[63] Cf. C. Journet, *L'Eglise du Verbe Incarné* (Paris: Desclée, De Brouwer, 1951), 2: 97-117.

[64] ST 2-2.10.9 resp.

[65] ST 2-2.11.3.

[66] ST 2-2.1.3 ad 3; 2-2.2.6 ad 3.

invincible. Thus it is not easy to judge what Saint Thomas would say about the membership of the non-Roman Catholic Christian in the Church. It seems certain that he would grant all baptized, believing Christians some kind of membership.[67]

The sacrament that most profoundly constitutes the Church, according to Saint Thomas, is not baptism but the Eucharist. In this sacrament, he says, the entire spiritual patrimony of the Church is present, for it contains Christ who, as we have mentioned, is the true treasure of the Church.[68]

The specific sacramental effect of the Eucharist, Saint Thomas asserts on many occasions, is the unity of the Mystical Body.[69] For this reason, reception of the Eucharist is necessary for salvation in the same way that the Church itself is.[70] But, as one might suspect, Saint Thomas distinguishes various ways of receiving the Eucharist. Some receive it physically, others by intention or desire (*in voto*). The latter kind of reception is sufficient in cases where one is physically or morally impeded from approaching the sacrament.[71]

If the unity of the Mystical Body is the specific effect of the Eucharist, it might seem problematical how baptism can impart membership. To this difficulty Saint Thomas replies by his doctrine of *votum*.[72] Baptism is objectively oriented toward the Eucharist in such a way that to receive baptism with the required dispositions is automatically to receive the Eucharist *in voto*. Thus the *votum*, for Saint Thomas, is not merely a subjective act of intention, but is an objective dynamism built into the very economy of salvation.

The whole purpose of the Church, as Saint Thomas conceives it, is to unite with God. This union takes place primarily through sanctifying grace, which is effectively communicated by the sacraments. Hence all the sacraments—and not simply the Eucharist—have an ecclesial aspect. They assimilate believers to the People of God and give them specific roles and functions within the Body of Christ.

---

[67] Cf. C. O'Neill, "Membership"; also E. Sauras, "The Members of the Church," *Thomist*, 27 (1963), 78-87; A. Dulles, *Church Membership as a Catholic and Ecumenical Problem* (Milwaukee: Marquette University Theology Department, 1974), pp. 7-12.

[68] ST 3.65.3 resp.; 3.79.1 resp. and ad 1.

[69] E.g., ST 3.73.2 sed c.; 3.83.4 ad 3.

[70] ST 3.73.3 resp.

[71] ST 3.80.1 resp. and ad 3.

[72] See G. Vodopivec, "Membri *in re* ed appartenenza *in voto* alla Chiesa di Cristo," *Euntes Docete*, 10 (1957), 65-104, esp. pp. 72-74.

v WORSHIP AND MINISTRIES

The ecclesial nature of the sacrament is evident especially in the Eucharist, which we have discussed, and in the three sacraments that confer a "character"—a sign of being deputed to acts suited to the present state of the Church.[73] Seen under their cultic aspect, these sacraments qualify their recipients to worship God according to the rite of the Christian religion, and thus bestow a certain participation in the priestly office of Christ.[74]

Baptism, the basic sacrament of incorporation, qualifies the Christian to participate in the official worship of the Church and to receive the other sacraments.[75] Confirmation perfects the powers received in baptism[76] and in addition, effectively symbolizes the grace to profess the faith publicly in a quasi-official manner (*quasi ex officio*).[77] The various minor and major orders confer specific powers for administering the sacraments to others. All the ministries of the Church, according to Saint Thomas, are somehow related to the central sacrament, the Eucharist. The power of actually consecrating the eucharistic elements is reserved to the highest grades of order, namely the two degress of priesthood (the presbyterate and the episcopate).

The two grades of priesthood, according to Saint Thomas, were instituted by Jesus himself and are prefigured in the distinction between the Twelve and the Seventy-two as described in the Gospels.[78] Saint Thomas was quite aware that the terms "presbyter" and "episcopus" in the New Testament sometimes designate the same individual, but he contended that the realities themselves were always distinct even though the terminology was initially somewhat confused.

Priestly ordination, in the view of Saint Thomas, empowers one to consecrate the body and blood of Christ and to give this to the faithful.[79] It includes the power to dispose the faithful to receive the sacrament. The power of the keys, as Thomas explains it, is related in the first instance to the sacrament of penance.[80] Essentially, it means the power of the priestly minister to remit sins and thus to dispose for the reception of the Eucharist. This power is conferred with ordination and is only rationally distinct from

---

[73] ST 3.63.3 resp.
[74] Ibid.
[75] ST 3.63.6 resp.
[76] ST 3.65.3 resp., ad 2 and ad 4.
[77] ST 3.72.5 ad 2.
[78] ST 2-2.184.6 ad 1.
[79] Congar, *L'Eglise de Saint Augustin*, pp. 235-236.
[80] U. Horst, "Das Wesen der 'potestas clavium' nach Thomas von Aquin," *Münchener theologische Zeitschrift*, 11 (1960), 191-201, with references to pertinent texts from the *Commentary on the Sentences* and the *Supplementum*.

the power of order itself, but the actual exercise of the ministry of forgiveness requires the designation of subjects over whom the minister has jurisdiction. A secondary function of the power of the keys is to exclude from communion or to admit to it by the imposition and removal of ecclesiastical penalties. This secondary function may be given to those who are not ordained priests.

The bishop, according to Saint Thomas, has the same power over the Eucharist that simple priests do, but he has larger powers with respect to the Mystical Body. He is a successor of the apostles,[81] a prince within the ecclesiastical order,[82] and a head of the particular church to which he has been assigned.[83] The bishop is in a "state of perfection" not in the sense that he is necessarily faultless, but in the sense that he is obliged to a perfect love of the flock of Christ, even to the extent of being ready to lay down his life for it.[84] The task of the bishop, Thomas explains, is to "instruct, defend, and peacefully govern the Church."[85] His principal duty, as a successor of the apostles is to teach[86]—a gift and a task signified by the descent of the Holy Spirit on the apostles at Pentecost in the form of fiery tongues.[87] Although Thomas rarely uses the term "magisterium" in speaking of bishops,[88] he clearly states that the tasks of public preaching and public teaching have been committed to bishops as successors of the apostles.[89] The teaching office, he holds, is the chief function of the bishops, and, unlike baptism, it may not be delegated by them to subordinates.[90]

In their doctrinal and sacramental functions, bishops have a strictly ministerial authority.[91] Their action is a mere prolongation of that of

---

[81] ST 3.67.2 ad 1; 3.72.11 resp.

[82] ST 3.82.1 ad 4.

[83] ST 3.8.6 resp.

[84] ST 2-2.184.5 resp.

[85] ST 2-2.185.3 resp.

[86] ST 3.67.2 ad 1; quoting Acts 6:2.

[87] ST 1.43.7 ad 6.

[88] The term *magisterium* in Aquinas generally signifies either the teaching function in general, or, in particular, the function of a *magister* or *doctor* who has received the *licentia docendi* in the Church. This usage is illustrated in Thomas' *Contra Impugn.*, cap. 2 (Parma ed., 15: 3-8). Only very rarely does Thomas use the term *magisterium* in connection with the episcopate. An example would be *Quodl.* 3.4.1 ad 3 (Parma ed., 9: 490-491), a text in which he contrasts the *magisterium cathedrae pastoralis*, meaning the episcopal teaching office, with the *magisterium cathedrae magistralis*, meaning the license to teach theology.

[89] *Quodl.* 12.18.27 (Parma ed., 9: 628); cf. E. Ménard, *La tradition: révélation, écriture, église selon Saint Thomas d'Aquin* (Bruges, Paris: Desclée, 1964), pp. 204-210.

[90] ST 3.67.2 ad 1.

[91] T. R. Potvin, "Authority in the Church as a Participation in the Authority of Christ According to St. Thomas," *Eglise et Théologie*, 5 (1974), 227-251.

Christ, who, as we have seen, was in his human nature a "conjoined instrument" of God. Bishops have no power to change or innovate but only
to hand on faithfully what has been committed to them. In the words of
Saint Thomas, "The apostles and their successors are vicars of God with
regard to the government of that Church which has been constituted by
faith and by the sacraments of faith. Hence, just as it is not licit for them to
constitute another Church, so it is not licit for them to transmit another
faith or to institute other sacraments; but the Church is said to be constituted by the sacraments that flowed from the side of Christ as he hung on
the Cross."[92]

When the bishop teaches, therefore, we believe him only insofar as he
bears witness to the teaching of Christ and the apostles. In a certain sense,
that testimony is fully given in Scripture. Thus Aquinas can write: "We do
not believe the successors [of the prophets and apostles] except insofar as
they declare to us those things which they [the prophets and apostles] have
left us in written form (in scriptis)."[93] In a certain sense, then, Saint
Thomas can hold that Scripture alone is the rule of faith.[94] But this tenet
does not contradict what has been said above concerning the ministerial
authority of bishops as public teachers in the Church. The doctrine of the
Church, "which proceeds from the First Truth manifested in Scripture," is
for Saint Thomas an infallible and divine rule of faith.[95] There is no
evidence that he would countenance an appeal to Scripture in opposition to
official Church teaching.

The sacramental powers of bishops are to a great extent identical with
those of simple priests. While sharing with the latter the power to consecrate the Eucharist, bishops have in addition certain sacramental powers
that are reserved to them as princes of the Church. It pertains to them, in
this capacity, to administer sacraments that confer a special mission, as do
confirmation and order.[96] The simple priest does not have this power, at

---

[92] ST 3.64.2 ad 3.

[93] De ver. 14.10 ad 11 (Parma ed., 9: 244); cf. P. E. Persson, Sacra Doctrina: Reason
and Revelation in Aquinas (Philadelphia: Fortress Press, 1970), p. 64.

[94] "Sacra enim scriptura est regula fidei, cui nec addere nec subtrahere licet" (ST 2-2.1.9
obj. 1); cf. ST 1.1.8 ad 2; also In Joan. 21.6 (2) (Parma ed., 10: 645): "Sola canonica scrip-
tura est regula fidei." On the basis of texts such as these, Persson feels entitled to maintain:
"In Thomas, tradition is not complementary but interpretative" (Sacra Doctrina, p. 69).
Against Persson, however, it must be noted that there is a second series of texts in which
Thomas argues that it is necessary to accept apostolic traditions not written down in Scrip-
ture, e.g. In 2 Thess. 2.15 (Parma ed., 13: 580); ST 2.25.3 ad 4; 3.64.2 ad 1; 3.83.4 ad 2.
These two series of texts cannot easily be harmonized.

[95] ST 2-2.5.3 resp.

[96] ST 3.65.3 ad 2.

least by reason of his own order. Yet Saint Thomas acknowledges that the pope, thanks to his "fullness of power" (*plenitudo potestatis*), can delegate to presbyters the power to confirm and to administer at least minor orders.[97] When a simple priest confirms or ordains he does so, it would appear, not by reason of his own power of order, but by a jurisdictional empowerment, which is of its nature transitory.[98]

In addition to their powers as teachers and ministers of the sacraments, bishops have jurisdictional powers. As rulers over their dioceses, they have authority to issue binding regulations as regards worship, fasting, and the like and to enforce these regulations by appropriate penalties.[99] For any exercise of the power of the keys, whether in the sacramental or the non-sacramental forum, jurisdiction is necessary.[100] Like the other great scholastic theologians of his day, Saint Thomas held that the jurisdictional powers of bishops are received not directly from Christ but from the pope.[101]

The superiority of bishops over simple priests, for Saint Thomas, is not a mere matter of jurisdiction, but also one of order. By reason of their rank in the Church, they have certain powers, such as their sacramental powers to confirm and to ordain, which, unlike their jurisdictional powers, they cannot delegate.[102] The power of order is permanent and inalienable.

In holding that bishops excel priests in their power of order, and not merely in jurisdiction, Aquinas anticipates the later teaching of the official Church. But it is interesting to note that, influenced by the authority of Peter Lombard, he shies away from calling episcopal ordination a sacrament, nor is he willing to say that it confers a character in the sense that baptism, confirmation, and priestly ordination do.[103]

vi The Papacy

Until the middle of the thirteenth century, dogmatic theology had contributed little or nothing to the growing claims made for the papacy. These

---

[97] ST 3.72.11 ad 1.

[98] ST 2-2.39.3 resp.

[99] ST 1-2.108.2 resp.; 2-2.147.3.

[100] *In 4 Sent.* D 18.1.1 qla. 2 ad 2 (Parma ed., 7: 809).

[101] J. Lécuyer, "Orientations présentes de la théologie de l'épiscopat," in *L'épiscopat et l'église universelle*, edd. Y. Congar and B.-D. Dupuy (Paris: Editions du Cerf, 1962), pp. 804-807.

[102] *De perf. vitae spir.*, cap. 24 (Parma ed., 15: 100); cf. J. Lécuyer, "Les étapes de l'enseignement thomiste sur l'épiscopat," *Revue thomiste*, 57 (1957), 44-45.

[103] *In 4 Sent.* D 24, esp. qq. 1 and 3 (Parma ed., 7: 887-902) and D 25.1 (Parma ed., 7: 906-907).

claims grew out of practical historical exigencies, including especially the struggle with the emperors, and were enshrined in collections of canonical decrees, some of which were falsely ascribed to ancient authorities.

The mendicant orders of the thirteenth century found themselves dependent for their very life on the protection offered by a strong papacy. Perhaps partly for this reason, friars such as Saint Bonaventure and Saint Thomas became the great architects of the new papalist ecclesiology. Early in life Saint Thomas was compelled by circumstances to take up the pen in defence of the mendicant orders and their papal privileges.[104] Later he spent four years (1261-65) at the papal court at Orvieto and there gained the confidence of Pope Urban IV, who was deeply concerned with achieving reunion with the Greek Churches.

About 1262 Pope Urban was asked to examine a work of a certain Nicholas of Durazzo, bishop of Cotrone, *Against the Errors of the Greeks*. The pope passed this on to Saint Thomas, who composed a prologue and made some observations concerning the use of the authorities cited by Nicholas concerning the procession of the Holy Spirit and the primacy of the Roman pontiff. Aquinas regrettably copied from Nicholas a number of unauthentic quotations from Saint Cyril and other Greek Fathers. In opposition to the Greeks of his own time, he greatly exalted the papal prerogatives. In this tract occurs the famous statement, which was to be repeated and somewhat sharpened by Boniface VIII in *Unam Sanctam*, that it is necessary for salvation (*de necessitate salutis*) to be subject to the Roman pontiff.[105]

Saint Thomas' work *Against the Errors of the Greeks*, being a commentary on the *libellus* of Nicholas of Cotrone, is not the most reliable index of his own personal thought. Aquinas' views on the papacy are more characteristically expressed in the *Summa contra gentiles* and the *Summa*

---

[104] See Y. Congar, "Aspects ecclésiastiques de la querelle entre mendiants et séculiers dans la seconde moitié du xiiie siècle et le début du xive," *Archives d'histoire doctrinale et littéraire du Moyen Age*, [28] (année 1961), 35-152. For biographical data see J. A. Weisheipl, *Friar Thomas d'Aquino : His Life, Thought, and Work* (New York: Doubleday, 1974).

[105] *C. err. graec.*, cap. 38 (Parma ed., 15: 257): "Ostenditur enim, quod subesse Romano Pontifici, sit de necessitate salutis." In Boniface VIII's *Unam sanctam* this becomes: "Porro subesse Romano Pontifici omni humanae creaturae declaramus, dicimus, diffinimus omnino esse de necessitate salutis (*DS* 875). That this pronouncement cannot be regarded as an infallible definition, according to the norms set forth by Vatican I, is shown by George Tavard, "The Bull *Unam Sanctam* of Boniface VIII," in *Papal Primacy and the Universal Church*, edd. P. C. Empie and T. A. Murphy, Lutherans and Catholics in Dialogue, 5 (Minneapolis: Augsburg Publishing House, 1974), pp. 105-119.

theologiae—works in which he does not rely on the falsified texts that weaken the value of the *Contra errores graecorum*. In his major works Saint Thomas rests his high doctrine of the papacy less upon Patristic citations than upon the Petrine texts in the Gospels, interpreted with the help of a hierarchical style of thinking derived from Pseudo-Dionysius and a number of axioms taken from canon law. He contends that the pope is the highest of the bishops (*episcoporum summus*),[106] that he has universal episcopal power, and that he is, under Christ, "head of the whole Church." Aquinas adds, however, that the pope's headship is one of merely external government, whereas Christ alone has the headship of vital influence.[107]

In the *Summa contra gentiles*, an apologetical work, the arguments for papal primacy are taken from philosophy, political theory, and biblical authority.[108] Thomas argues first, that just as the unity of the diocese is secured by mono-episcopacy, so the unity of the entire people of God is secured by the existence of a single chief bishop. Second, he contends, there must be a single head in order to settle disagreements about matters of faith. Third, he asserts that since the peace and unity of any society is best promoted by having one supreme ruler, monarchy is the best form of government.[109] Fourth, he argues that just as there is to be one fold and one shepherd in the heavenly Church, so *a pari* the Church militant needs a single visible head. In answer to a possible objection, he asserts, finally, that Christ's appointment of Peter as head (John 21:17, Luke 22:32 and Matthew 16:19) is undoubtedly intended to endure, as the Church will, to the end of time.

In the *Summa theologiae* and other theological works Saint Thomas makes extensive use of canonical principles, such as the pope's power to decide all "major cases" (*causae maiores*), to convoke all ecumenical councils and to approve their decrees.[110] By virtue of his *plenitudo potestatis* over all ecclesiastical affairs, Aquinas argues, the pope can relax and commute vows and oaths.[111] By this power, also, he can commit to a non-bishop

---

[106] *In 4 Sent.* D 7.3.1 ad 3 (Parma ed., 7: 577-578).

[107] ST 3.8.6 resp. Cf. H. Rikhof, "Corpus Christi Mysticum: An Inquiry into Thomas Aquinas' Use of a Term," *Bijdragen*, 37 (1976), p. 167.

[108] SCG 4.76.

[109] In this context Aquinas says nothing to echo his statements in ST 1-2.105.1 regarding the advantages of the "mixed" form of polity, in which elements of aristocracy and democracy are blended with monarchy. Pursuing this line of thought, Thomas' disciple John of Paris was led to a more corporative and conciliarist theory of Church polity; see Congar, *L'Eglise de Saint Augustin*, p. 284.

[110] ST 1;36.2 ad 2.

[111] ST 2-2.88.12 ad 3; 2-2.89.9 ad 3.

whatever belongs to the episcopal state provided this does not have immediate relationship to the Eucharist.[112]

It is not surprising, then, that Saint Thomas accorded the pope the highest doctrinal authority. From the fact that the pope can convoke and confirm general councils to defend the faith against new errors, Saint Thomas draws the conclusion that when it is impossible, for one reason or another, to call a council, the pope may consult with others and issue, on his own authority, a determination of the faith.[113]

It was disputed at Vatican I, and is still disputed, whether Saint Thomas may properly be invoked as a witness to the doctrine of papal infallibility.[114] In the texts just cited and in the course of a quodlibetic disputation on the canonization of saints,[115] he teaches that, since the pope has authority over the universal Church, his determinations concerning the faith are to be firmly accepted by all Christians. According to Congar, if the pope has power, as Thomas puts it, "to decide matters of faith authoritatively so that they may be held by all with unshaken faith," the dogma of Vatican I necessarily follows.[116] But Congar is also correct in remarking that Thomas nowhere asserts that the pope is infallible, or that the pope cannot err, and it is not certain that Thomas would have been willing to say these things.

VII CHURCH AND STATE

At several points in his works Saint Thomas touches on the neuralgic question of the relationship between the spiritual and temporal powers. On this question there were three general positions which came to be more sharply defined toward the beginning of the fourteenth century.[117] The Guelf position, which was to be asserted in Boniface VIII's *Unam sanctam* (1302), held that temporal as well as spiritual authority was derived from

[112] *In 4 Sent.* D 25.1.1 ad 3 (Parma ed., 7: 906).

[113] *De pot.* 10.4 ad 13 (Parma ed., 8: 212); ST 2-2.1.10 resp.

[114] U. Betti holds that Aquinas may safely be listed as a witness in favor of papal infallibility; "L'assenza dell'autorità di S. Tommaso nel Decreto Vaticano sull'infallibilità pontifica," *Divinitas*, 6 (1962), 407-422. Brian Tierney, in his brief discussion of Saint Thomas, finds that he does not teach infallibility; see his *Origins of Papal Infallibility, 1150-1350* (Leiden: E. J. Brill, 1972), p. 95 n. 3, p. 245 n. 4.

[115] *Quodl.* 9.16 (Parma ed., 9: 599). For an extended commentary, holding that this passage holds for papal infallibility in canonization processes, see M. Schenk, *Die Unfehlbarkeit des Papstes in der Heiligsprechung* (Freiburg, Switz.: Paulusverlag, 1965).

[116] Y. Congar, "St. Thomas Aquinas and the Infallibility of the Papal Magisterium (*Summa theol.* II-II, q. 1, a. 10)," *Thomist*, 38 (1974), 81-105.

[117] With regard to these three position see Weisheipl, *Friar Thomas d'Aquino*, 191-92; Congar, *L'Eglise de Saint Augustin*, pp. 269-295.

God through the pope, who could at his discretion depose kings and absolve subjects of their duty of allegiance. The Ghibelline view held, on the contrary, that all temporal power comes from God through the consent of the governed. According to Marsiglio of Padua, an extreme advocate of this position, the pope has no coercive power and consequently no jurisdiction over the temporal city. A mediating position, which was to be defended in the early fourteenth century by John Quidort of Paris, held that there is a kind of mutual subjection between the two powers. In temporal affairs the priestly authority is subject to the secular ruler, while in spiritual matters the civic authority is subject to the priestly rule. Some writers of this school suggest that the pope has an indirect jurisdiction in temporal matters, insofar as may be needed for spiritual ends.

In this triple classification, Saint Thomas seems to fit best into the third category. His basic position is expressed in his commentary on the *Sentences* (1254), which seems to give equal legitimacy to each of the two powers in its own sphere, while allowing for the exceptional case in which both powers may be conjoined in a single ruler:

> Spiritual as well as secular power comes from the divine power. Hence secular power is subjected to spiritual power in those matters concerning which the subjection has been specified and ordained by God, *i.e.* in matters belonging to the salvation of the soul. Hence in these we are to obey spiritual authority more than secular authority. On the other hand, more obedience is due to secular than to spiritual power in the things that pertain to the civic good (*bonum civile*). For it is said *Matth.* 22:21: Render unto Caesar the things that are Caesar's. A special case occurs, however, when spiritual and secular power are so joined in one person as they are in the Pope, who holds the apex of both spiritual and secular powers.[118]

In a later work, *De regno*, only partly from his own hand, Saint Thomas speaks in more theocratic terms, emphasizing the subjection of all secular governments to the pope.

> To him [the Roman pontiff] all kings of the Christian people are to be subject as to our Lord Jesus Christ Himself. For those to whom pertains the care of intermediate ends should be subject to him to whom pertains the care of the ultimate end, and be directed by his rule.
>
> Because the priesthood of the gentiles and the whole worship of their gods existed merely for the acquisition of temporal goods (which were all ordained

---

[118] *In 2 Sent.* D 44, expos. textus (Parma ed., 7: 790-791); Thomas Aquinas, *On Kingship to the King of Cyprus*, trans. G. B. Phelan (Toronto: Pontifical Institute of Mediaeval Studies, 1949), p. 107. As noted by Dante Germino in the present volume (see above p. 118), the last sentence of this quotation admits of more than one interpretation.

to the common good of the multitude, whose care devolved upon the king), the priests of the gentiles were very properly subject to the kings. Similarly, since in the old law earthly goods were promised to the religious people (not indeed by demons, but by the true God), the priests of the old law, we read, were also subject to the kings. But in the new law there is a higher priesthood by which men are guided to heavenly goods. Consequently, in the law of Christ, kings must be subject to priests.[119]

If the text just quoted is, as most scholars seem to believe, authentic, we may synthesize the doctrine of Saint Thomas somewhat as follows. There are two powers, belonging to two distinct orders. The secular ruler reigns by natural right, and the pope by the positive will of God. The State has a certain autonomy with regard to its own goals, but it must conduct itself in such a way that it does not interfere with the higher goals of the spiritual authority. Absolutely speaking, the *sacerdotium* is superior to the *regnum*. These theses, derived from the convergent testimony of the various texts in which Saint Thomas touches on the theme, correspond closely with what was to become the teaching of Leo XIII in the nineteenth century.

VIII SAINT THOMAS' ECCLESIOLOGY AT ITS PRESENT VALUE

Under the pressure of historical conflicts, Catholic ecclesiology, from the fifteenth century, developed along lines rather different from those sketched by Thomas Aquinas. Cardinal Juan de Torquemada (1388-1468), whose *Summa de ecclesia* set the pattern for many centuries, greatly admired Saint Thomas but put the accent far more on the external, visible features. Cardinal Robert Bellarmine (1542-1621), polemicizing against the Protestants, gave still greater emphasis to the juridical. Thus the theocentric, christological, and pneumatic features so central to Thomistic ecclesiology came to be neglected. Leo XIII, in his encyclicals on the Holy Spirit, the unity of the Church, and church-state relations, initiated a healthy return to the authentic Thomist tradition. In the early twentieth century the rediscovery of the theme of the Mystical Body gave further impetus to this trend. Pius XII, in his encyclical on the Mystical Body, struck a kind of balance between Patristic and Thomistic elements, on the one hand, and on the other elements more characteristic of Bellarmine.

Vatican Council II (1962-65) reaffirmed the place of Saint Thomas as the most authoritative of the doctors of the Church and quoted Paul VI to this effect. It praised him especially for showing how faith and reason give

---

[119] *De regno* 1.14, nos. 110-111 (Parma ed., 16: 257; trans. Phelan, pp. 62-63).

harmonious witness to the unity of all truth.[120] But, generally speaking, the council tended to shy away from the categories of scholasticism. Its theology was chiefly inspired by the New Testament and by the Church Fathers. Yet it read these sources with the help of light derived from Thomas and the scholastic tradition.

Lumen gentium, Vatican II's great constitution on the Church, cites in eleven official footnotes seventeen texts from Saint Thomas. Saint Cyprian is cited thirteen times in twelve footnotes. The only theologian cited more often in this document is Saint Augustine, to whom there are twenty-one references in nineteen footnotes. Since Aquinas himself depended heavily on Augustine, and Augustine on Cyprian, the theological authorities used by Vatican II in its ecclesiology may be said to be Saint Thomas and the predecessors who inspired him. The post-Thomistic sources cited by Vatican II, including the official documents of popes and councils, were often dependent on Aquinas.

Quite apart from the question of citations, one could list numerous Thomistic ecclesiological theses that were officially endorsed by Vatican II. The following list is not intended to be exhaustive:

1. The visible structure of the Church is subordinate to the life of grace, which the Church is intended to foster.[121]

2. The Holy Spirit is soul of the Church, the Body of Christ.[122]

3. The Holy Spirit is the principle of the Church's unity.[123]

4. The sacraments really but invisibly unite us to Christ's suffering and glory.[124]

5. Baptism is the basic sacrament of incorporation.[125]

6. Baptism imprints a character; it consecrates its recipients to Christian worship and obliges them to Christian witness.[126]

7. Confirmation establishes a deeper bond with the Church and imposes a stricter obligation to defend and spread the faith.[127]

---

[120] *Declaration on Christian Education* (*Gravissimum educationis*), no. 10; quoted from W. M. Abbott, ed., *The Documents of Vatican II* (New York: Herder and Herder, 1966), p. 648.

[121] *Lumen gentium*, 8, citing Leo XIII, *Satis cognitum* (Abbott, p. 22).

[122] *Lumen gentium*, 7, quoting verbatim, in an official footnote, Saint Thomas, *In Col.* 1.18 lect. 5 (Abbott, p. 22).

[123] *Unitatis redintegratio*, 2 (Abbott, p. 344); compare *Lumen gentium*, 7 and 49.

[124] *Lumen gentium*, 7 (Abbott, p. 20), referring to ST 3.62.5 ad 1.

[125] *Unitatis redintegratio*, 3 (Abbott, p. 345), and 22 (pp. 363-364); *Lumen gentium*, 15 (pp. 33-34).

[126] *Lumen gentium*, 11 (Abbott, p. 28) referring to ST 3.63.2.

[127] *Lumen gentium*, 11 (Abbott, p. 28), with references to ST 3.65.3 and 3.72.1 and 5.

8. The Eucharist is the efficacious sign of "the unity of the Mystical Body without which there can be no salvation."[128]

9. The Eucharist is the center of sacramental life, and contains the whole patrimony of the Church.[129]

10. All the other sacraments and ministries are linked to the Eucharist and directed to it.[130]

11. Bishops are gifted with a grace of state enabling them to exercise a perfect role of pastoral charity.[131]

12. Preaching is preeminent among the duties of bishops.[132]

13. Bishops are by divine institution successors of the apostles.[133]

14. Priests must hand on to the faithful the fruits of contemplation.[134]

15. The priestly character gives a special participation in the priesthood of Christ.[135]

16. It is the prerogative of the Roman pontiff to convoke ecumenical councils, to preside over and to confirm them.[136]

17. In its present earthly condition the Church is not yet spotless but is in need of being purified.[137]

18. All in the Church are called to pursue perfection according to Christ's injunction.[138]

19. Charity gives life to all the virtues; the observance of the evangelical counsels is a singular help to holiness.[139]

20. "By the charity to which they lead, the evangelical counsels join their followers to the Church and her mystery in a special way."[140]

---

[128] *Lumen gentium*, 26 (Abbott, p. 50), with reference to ST 3.73.3.

[129] *Presby. ordinis*, 5 (Abbott, p. 541), with references to ST 3.65.3 ad 1 and 3.79.1 resp. and ad 1.

[130] *Presby. ordinis*, 5 (Abbott, p. 541), with reference to ST 3.65.3.

[131] *Lumen gentium*, 41 (Abbott, p. 68), with references to ST 2-2.184.5 and 6; *De perf. vitae spir.*, cap. 18.

[132] *Lumen gentium*, 25 (Abbott, p. 47).

[133] *Lumen gentium*, 20 (Abbott, p. 40).

[134] *Presby. ordinis*, 13 (Abbott, p. 560), citing ST 2-2.188.7.

[135] *Lumen gentium*, 10 (Abbott, p. 27).

[136] *Lumen gentium*, 22 (Abbott, p. 44).

[137] *Lumen gentium*, 40 (Abbott, p. 66); cf. *Lumen gentium*, 8 and *Unitatis redintegratio*, 6-7.

[138] *Lumen gentium*, 40 (Abbott, p. 66), referring to ST 2-2.184.3.

[139] *Lumen gentium*, 40 (Abbott, p. 71), with references to ST 2-2.184.1, 1-2.100.2 resp. and 2-2.44.4 ad 3.

[140] *Lumen gentium*, 44 (Abbott, pp. 74-75), with references to ST 2-2.184.3 and 2-2.188.2.

21. "Those who have not yet received the gospel are related in various ways to the People of God."[141]

22. Missionary activity has as goals the expansion of the Church and the planting of the Church where it has not yet taken root.[142]

23. The gospel must be preached to all nations before the end of the world.[143]

24. The Church will attain its full perfection at the end of history, when the heavenly city is complete.[144]

These specific affirmations of Vatican II, which so closely correspond to the teaching of the Angelic Doctor, sufficiently demonstrate that Thomas' teaching on the Church remains very much alive in contemporary Catholicism—much more alive, one might add, than many of the systematic ecclesiologists who have written since the time of Torquemada.

On the other hand it must be frankly conceded that the basic inspiration of Vatican II's ecclesiology is not scholastic or Thomistic. While making ample use of the Thomistic images of the Body of Christ and the Bride (which are also, of course, biblical images), the Council preferred to work with the more fluid biblical analogy of the "People of God." In some of its crucial affirmations, moreover, Vatican II departed from the doctrine of Aquinas. Going beyond his teaching, the Council taught that episcopal consecration is a sacrament[145] and that it imposes a sacred character.[146] Unlike Pius XII in *Mystici corporis*, Vatican II refused to endorse the doctrine of Saint Thomas and his contemporaries that episcopal jurisdiction is given to bishops by the pope rather than directly by Christ.[147]

In place of Saint Thomas' pyramidal ecclesiology, with its strong accent on the pope's *plenitudo potestatis*, Vatican II introduced the idea that the pope and his brother bishops constitute a "collegium." As Congar has

---

[141] *Lumen gentium*, 16 (Abbott, p. 34), citing ST 3.8.3 ad 1.

[142] *Ad gentes*, 5 (Abbott, p. 591), with references to *In Matth.* 16.28, *In 1 Sent.* D 16.1.2 ad 2, D 16.1.3 sol., ST 1.43.7 ad 6, 1-2.106.4 ad 4.

[143] *Ad gentes*, 9 (Abbott, p. 596), citing ST 1-2.106.4 ad 4.

[144] *Lumen gentium*, 48 (Abbott, p. 78).

[145] *Lumen gentium*, 21 (Abbott, p. 41).

[146] Ibid., p. 42.

[147] *Lumen gentium*, 21 (Abbott, p. 41) and 24 (Abbott, pp. 46-47). The former text states that the power of teaching and governing is conferred by episcopal consecration, provided that hierarchical communion with the head and members of the episcopal college is maintained; the latter, that bishops receive their teaching and preaching powers fundamentally by reason of being successors of the apostles. *Mystici corporis*, 41 (*AAS* 34 [1943], 211-212) asserted that bishops, although they enjoy ordinary power of jurisdiction, receive this power immediately from the pope.

acknowledged, the Vatican II doctrine of episcopal collegiality finds no basis in Thomistic theology. "On ne peut guère parler pour saint Thomas d'une idée de collégialité épiscopale."[148]

In close connection with the points just made, one may contrast the ecclesiological universalism of Aquinas with the particularism and pluralism of Vatican II.[149] Saint Thomas was concerned with the worldwide Church united under the primacy of the pope. He looked upon dioceses as administrative districts or portions of the people of God rather than as churches in the theological and sacramental sense of that word.[150] Vatican II, on the other hand, revived the ancient idea of the "particular church." Dioceses, from this perspective, are seen as particular realizations of the mystery of the Church which is confessed to be one, holy, catholic and apostolic.[151]

Several of the major ecclesiological themes of Vatican II grew out of concerns that must be recognized as foreign to the thought of Aquinas. The Church in the thirteenth century was clearly dominant, at least in Western Europe, and supremely self-confident. It was more concerned with the pastoral care of the faithful than with mission or dialogue. By the time of Vatican II, the Church, humbled by major losses, had become more conscious of the need of full-scale dialogue on three main fronts: with other Christian bodies, with other religions and ideologies, and with secular civilization.

In his dealings with other Christian groups, Aquinas was scarcely an ecumenist. His tract *Against the Errors of the Greeks*—though the polemical title was not his own—sharply contradicts the views of those who reject the *filioque* and the pope's authority to approve its addition to the creed. As already mentioned, Saint Thomas here insists on subjection to the pope as a prerequisite for salvation. In the *Summa theologiae* he holds that heretics, if pertinacious, are to be excommunicated and turned over to the secular power for capital punishment.[152]

Yet there are some basic principles in Saint Thomas that could serve as a basis for ecumenism. He recognized that all the baptized, unless they have

---

[148] Congar, *L'Eglise de Saint Augustin*, p. 237.

[149] See Congar, "'Ecclesia' et 'Populus (Fidelis)'."

[150] See, for instance, scg 4.76 and *In 4 Sent.* D 24.3.2 sol. 3 (Parma ed., 7: 902).

[151] *Christus Dominus*, 11 (Abbott, p. 403); cf. *Lumen gentium*, 23 (Abbott, p. 44). Y. Congar points out that since Saint Thomas, when he designates particular churches as divisions, is speaking in the framework of his more sociological concept of the Church as "populus Dei," he is not really in conflict with these texts from Vatican II, which are based rather on the sacramental view of the Church. The latter, too, can claim a foundation in Aquinas, who set forth the principle that where the Eucharist is, there is the total spiritual capital of the Church. See Congar, "'Ecclesia' and 'Populus (Fidelis)'."

[152] st 2-2.11.3 resp.

culpably separated themselves, are members of the Mystical Body. He sought to appreciate the riches of the Greek as well as the Latin Fathers. In his *De potentia*, going beyond the positions of the *Contra errores graecorum*, he finds ways of justifying the Greeks' denial that the Son is co-principle of the Holy Spirit, and then concludes, "If one rightly considers the statements of the Greeks, one will find that they differ from us more in words than in meaning."[153] This judgment anticipates the accord reached at the Council of Florence in 1439.

In some ways Aquinas comes close to the insights of the Protestant reformers. His veneration for the Bible as the fundamental rule of faith and the primacy he ascribes to the ministry of the word have found echoes in Protestant theology. Above all, his treatise on the "new law" of the Gospel is, as Congar remarks, "the most extraordinary charter of evangelical theology."[154] Thus it is not surprising that a seventeenth-century author could have written a book entitled, *Thomas Aquinas veritatis evangelicae confessor*,[155] and that a contemporary Protestant, Thomas Bonhoeffer, can affirm, "Thomas Aquinas belongs among the Fathers of Protestant theology."[156]

Can one look upon Aquinas as an apostle of dialogue with the other religions? Some of his statements strike us today as harshly polemical—for instance, his appraisal of Mohammed and of the Koran in the *Summa contra gentiles*.[157] His views on the toleration of non-Christian religions would scarcely satisfy the sensitivities of our time. Yet he did painstakingly study the works of Jewish and Islamic sages; he borrowed extensively from Maimonides and Avicenna. All this he could justify on the profoundly ecumenical principle, "All truth, whoever utters it, is from the Holy Spirit."[158]

Aquinas apparently did not look upon living religions other than Christianity as channels of salvation for their own members, but he did believe that the grace of Christ was at work beyond the limits of the official Church. As we have seen, he maintained that the patriarchs and prophets of

---

[153] *De pot.* 10.5 resp. (Parma ed., 8: 215).

[154] Y. Congar, "Saint Thomas Aquinas and the Spirit of Ecumenism," *New Blackfriars*, 55 (1974), 196-209.

[155] Cf. K. Barth, *Church Dogmatics*, vol. 1, part 2 (Edinburgh: T. and T. Clark, 1956), p. 614.

[156] T. Bonhoeffer, *Die Gotteslehre des Thomas von Aquin als Sprachproblem* (Tubingen: J. C. B. Mohr, 1961), p. 3.

[157] SCG 1.6.

[158] *De ver.* 1.8 in contr. 1 (Parma ed., 9: 17). Saint Thomas attributes this dictum to Ambrose.

old, in their confidence in God's saving love, had been spiritually oriented in an implicit way to Christ as Redeemer and thus belonged in some sense to the Church of Christ. This important principle, more widely applied, could serve as grounds for a somewhat optimistic appraisal of faiths other than that of ancient Israel.

In pondering the relationship between Church and world, the contemporary Christian can find many valuable principles in the Angelic Doctor. Thomas introduced clear distinctions between nature and grace, reason and faith, temporal and spiritual, *imperium* and *sacerdotium*. These distinctions make it possible to vindicate the relative autonomy of scientific investigation, culture, and secular government.

Saint Thomas treated the relationship between the "two powers," but he left it for later authors to explore the relationship between Church and world. Vatican II took up this task somewhat in the spirit of Aquinas. In agreement with the Thomistic tradition the Council taught that the Church "has a saving and eschatological purpose which can be fully attained only in the other world" and that "Christ gave his Church no proper mission in the political, economic, or social order."[159] But Vatican II went considerably beyond Saint Thomas in maintaining that the Church has a mission to direct human society "as it is to be renewed in Christ and transformed into God's family."[160] Since the Council, the 1971 Roman Synod of Bishops went still further in asserting: "Action on behalf of justice and participation in the transformation of the world fully appear to us as a constitutive dimension of the preaching of the gospel, or, in other words, of the Church's mission for the redemption of the human race and its liberation from every oppressive situation."[161] This statement blurs the neat Thomistic distinction between the temporal and the spiritual.

For Saint Thomas there was always room for a ministry of reform, in the sense that pastors and faithful needed to be exhorted to eliminate abuses and to return to authentic evangelical principles. Saint Thomas assumed, however, that the essential articles of faith and the structures of the Church had been fully revealed in apostolic times. Thus he saw very little need to innovate. The only purpose of prophecy since the time of the apostles, he declared, was "the correction of morals."[162] He would not have recognized the importance of the so-called "signs of the times" for an appropriate contemporary understanding of the faith.

[159] *Gaudium et spes*, 40 (Abbott, p. 238).
[160] Ibid., p. 239.
[161] "Justice in the World," *Catholic Mind* (March 1972), p. 53.
[162] *In Matth.* 11.13 (Parma ed., 10: 110); cf. ST 2-2.174.6 ad 3. In the latter text prophecy is said to continue "for the direction of human acts."

The council understood human historicity in a far more radical sense than did Saint Thomas. The Pastoral Constitution recognized that "today the human race is passing through a new stage in its history,"[163] that it has "passed from a rather static concept of reality to a more dynamic, evolutionary one,"[164] and that "historical studies make a signal contribution to bringing men to see things in their changeable and evolutionary aspects."[165] It called upon the Church to move forward "together with humanity"[166] and to keep its understanding of doctrine abreast of the advance of human knowledge.[167]

These new trends in modern thought, which have important implications for ecclesiology, pose serious challenges to the Thomistic theologian. Aquinas, as we have noted, strongly emphasized the element of permanence in the Church—its steadfast adherence to what Christ and the apostles had instituted. He believed that the faith, sacraments, and ministries of the Church had been, in all essentials, established by Christ in the lifetime of the apostles. Modern historical studies have underscored the changeable and evolutionary aspects of ecclesiastical institutions. The contemporary theologian, while admiring the robustly Christocentric character of the Thomistic system, may be permitted to ask whether this Christocentrism could not advantageously be restated so as to harmonize better with the "more dynamic and evolutionary" view of the world acknowledged by Vatican II as a salient feature of our times.

[163] *Gaudium et spes*, 40 (Abbott, p. 238).
[164] Ibid., 5 (Abbott, p. 204).
[165] Ibid., 54 (Abbott, p. 260).
[166] Ibid., 40 (Abbott, p. 239).
[167] Ibid., 62 (Abbott, pp. 269-270).

Bibliography

Only those writings—including those of Saint Thomas—of which specific editions have been cited are listed here.

Abailard, Pierre. *Dialogus inter philosophum, iudaeum et christianum.* Ed. Rudolf Thomas. Stuttgart-Bad Cannstatt: F. Frommann Verlag, 1970.

Abbott, W. M., ed. *The Documents of Vatican II.* New York: Herder and Herder, 1966.

Adler, Mortimer J. *A Dialectic of Morals.* Notre Dame, Ind.: The Review of Politics, University of Notre Dame, 1941.

Alanus de Insulis. *De fide catholica.* PL 210, coll. 305-430.

Alexander de Hales. *Summa theologica seu ... "Summa fratris Alexandri."* Ed. Bernard Klumper, et al. 4 vols. in 5 parts. Quaracchi: Collegium S. Bonaventurae, 1924-1948.

Archibald, Katherine, "The Concept of Social Hierarchy in the Writings of St. Thomas Aquinas." *The Historian*, 12 (1949-1950), 28-54.

Arquillière, Henri X. *L'augustinisme politique.* 2nd ed. Paris: J. Vrin, 1955.

Bacon, Roger. *Opera quaedam hactenus inedita*, 1: *Opus tertium.* Ed. J. S. Brewer. London: Longman, Green, Longman, and Roberts, 1859.

Balthasar, Hans U. von. *A Theology of History.* New York: Sheed and Ward, 1963.

Baronio, Cesare; Odorigo Rinaldi, and Giacomo Laderchi. *Annales ecclesiastici.* 37 vols. Bar-le-Duc, Paris, Freiburg, 1864-1883.

Barth, Karl. *Church Dogmatics.* Vols. 1——. Edinburgh: T. and T. Clark, 1936——.

Bergson, Henri L. *Les deux sources de la morale et de la religion.* 11th ed. Paris: Felix Alcan, 1932.

——. *The Two Sources of Morality and Religion.* New York: H. Holt, 1935.

Betti, Umberto. "L'assenza dell'autorità di S. Tommaso nel Decreto Vaticano sull'infallibilità pontificia." *Divinitas*, 6 (1962), 407-422.

Blaise, Albert; and Henri Chirat. *Dictionnaire latin-français des auteurs chrétiens.* Strasbourg: Le Latin Chrétien, 1954.

Bocheński, Innocentius M. *A History of Formal Logic.* Trans. and rev. by I. Thomas. Notre Dame, Ind.: University of Notre Dame Press, 1961.

Bonhoeffer, Thomas. *Die Gotteslehre des Thomas von Aquin als Sprachproblem.* Tübingen: J. C. B. Mohr, 1961.

Brundage, James A. *The Crusades. A Documentary Survey.* Milwaukee: Marquette University Press, 1962.

Bruno, Giordano. *Cause, Principle and Unity: Five Dialogues.* Trans. by J. Lindsay. Castle Hedingham: Daimon Press, 1962.

Calo, Peter. See Prümmer, Dominicus, et al.

Chenu, Marie Dominique. "'Authentica' et 'magistralia.' Deux lieux théologiques aux XII-XIII siècles." *Divus Thomas* (Piacenza), 28 (1925), 257-285.

———. "Création et histoire." In *St. Thomas Aquinas, 1274-1974: Commemorative Studies*, 2: 391-399. Toronto: Pontifical Institute of Mediaeval Studies, 1974.

———. *Introduction à l'étude de saint Thomas d'Aquin.* Publications de l'Institut d'Etudes Médiévales, 9. Montréal, Paris: Université de Montréal, 1950.

———. *Saint Thomas d'Aquin et la théologie.* Maîtres spirituels. Paris: Editions du Seuil, 1959.

———. *Toward Understanding Saint Thomas.* Trans. and rev. by A.-M. Landry and D. Hughes. Chicago: Henry Regnery Co., 1964.

Chesterton, Gilbert K. *St. Thomas Aquinas.* New York: Sheed and Ward, 1933.

Cipolla, Carlo, ed. *The Fontana Economic History of Europe*, 1: *The Middle Ages.* London and Glasgow: Collins, 1972.

Congar, Yves Marie Joseph. "L'apostolicité de l'Eglise selon S. Thomas d'Aquin." *Revue des sciences philosophiques et théologiques*, 44 (1960), 209-224.

———. "Aspects ecclésiologiques de la querelle entre mendiants et séculiers dans la seconde moitié du XIIIe siècle et le début du XIVe." *Archives d'histoire doctrinale et littéraire du moyen âge*, [28] (année 1961), 35-152.

———. "Ecclesia ab Abel." In *Abhandlungen über Theologie und Kirche. Festschrift für Karl Adam*, pp. 79-108. Düsseldorf: Patmos, 1952.

———. "'Ecclesia' et 'Populus (Fidelis)' dans l'ecclésiologie de S. Thomas." In *St. Thomas Aquinas, 1274-1974: Commemorative Studies*, 1: 159-173. Toronto: Pontifical Institute of Mediaeval Studies, 1974.

———. *L'Eglise de Saint Augustin à l'époque moderne.* Paris: Editions du Cerf, 1970.

———. *The Mystery of the Church.* Baltimore: Helicon Press, 1960.

———. "St. Thomas Aquinas and the Infallibility of the Papal Magisterium (*Summa theol.* II-II, q. 1, a. 10)." *Thomist*, 38 (1974), 81-105.

———. "Saint Thomas Aquinas and the Spirit of Ecumenism." *New Blackfriars*, 55 (1974), 196-209.

———. "Schisme." *Dictionnaire de théologie catholique*, vol. 14 (Paris, 1939), coll. 1286-1312.

Copleston, Frederick C. *A History of Medieval Philosophy.* London: Methuen, 1972.

Cullmann, Oscar. *Christ and Time.* Philadelphia: Westminster Press, 1950.

———. *Salvation in History.* New York: Harper and Row, 1967.

Darquennes, Achilles. *De Juridische Structuur van de Kerk, volgens Sint Thomas van Aquino.* Louvain: Universiteitsbibliotheek, 1949.

Dempf, Alois. *Sacrum Imperium: Geschichts- und Staatsphilosophie des Mittelalters.* 2nd ed. Darmstadt: Wissenschaftliche Buchgemeinschaft, 1954.

Denifle, Heinrich; and E. Chatelain. *Chartularium universitatis Parisiensis.* 2 vols. Paris, 1889-1891.

Dondaine, Antoine. "La lettre de saint Thomas à l'abbé du Mont-Cassin." In *St. Thomas Aquinas, 1274-1974: Commemorative Studies*, 1: 87-108. Toronto: Pontifical Institute of Mediaeval Studies, 1974.

——. *Les secrétaires de saint Thomas.* Rome: Commissio Leonina, 1956.

Dulles, Avery R. *Church Membership as a Catholic and Ecumenical Problem.* Milwaukee: Marquette University Theology Department, 1974.

Dupré, Louis K. *Contraception and Catholics: A New Appraisal.* Baltimore: Helicon Press, 1964.

Egner, G. *Contraception vs. Tradition: A Catholic Critique.* New York: Herder and Herder, 1967.

Eschmann, Ignatius T. "A Catalogue of St. Thomas's Works." In Etienne Gilson, *The Christian Philosophy of St. Thomas Aquinas*, trans. by L. K. Shook, pp. 381-439. New York: Random House, 1956.

Figgis, John Neville. *The Political Aspects of S. Augustine's "City of God."* London: Longmans, Green, 1921.

Foster, Kenelm, trans., ed. *The Life of Saint Thomas Aquinas. Biographical Documents.* London: Longmans, Green, 1950.

Geenen, G. "Saint Thomas et les Pères." *Dictionnaire de théologie catholique*, vol. 15, pt. 1 (1946), coll. 738-761.

Geiselmann, J. R. "Christus und die Kirche nach Thomas von Aquin." *Theologische Quartalschrift*, 107 (1926), 198-222; 108 (1927), 233-255.

Gilson, Etienne. *Introduction à l'étude de Saint Augustin.* 4th ed. Paris: J. Vrin, 1969.

——. *The Philosopher and Theology.* New York: Random House, 1962.

——. "Pourquoi saint Thomas a critiqué saint Augustin." *Archives d'histoire doctrinale et littéraire du moyen âge*, 1 (1926-27), 5-127.

Godefridus de Sancto Victore. *Fons philosophiae.* Ed. Pierre Michaud-Quantin. Analecta mediaevalia namurcensia, 8. Namur: Godenne, 1956.

Gossman, Lionel. *Medievalism and the Ideologies of the Enlightenment: The World and Work of LaCurne de Sainte-Palaye.* Baltimore: John Hopkins Press, 1968.

Grabmann, Martin. *Die Lehre des heiligen Thomas von Aquin von der Kirche als Gotteswerk.* Regensburg: G. J. Manz, 1903.

Gui, Bernard. See Prümmer, Dominicus, et al.

Guilelmus Arvernus. *Opera omnia.* 2 vols. Paris: A. Pralard, 1674.

Guilelmus de Sancto Amore. *Opera omnia. ... de periculis novissimorum temporum agitur.* Ed. Valérien de Flavigny. Constance: Alitophilos, 1623.

Guttmann, Jacob. *Das Verhältniss des Thomas von Aquino zum Judenthum und zur judischen Litteratur.* Göttingen: Vandenhoeck u. Ruprecht's Verlag, 1891.

Hamer, Jérôme. *The Church is a Communion.* New York: Sheed and Ward, 1965.

Haskins, Charles H. *The Renaissance of the Twelfth Century.* Cambridge, Mass.: Harvard University Press, 1927.

Horst, P. Ulrich. "Das Wesen der 'potestas clavium' nach Thomas von Aquin." *Münchener theologische Zeitschrift*, 11 (1960), 191-201.

Hübner Gallo, Jorge Ivan. "Catholic Social Justice, Authoritarianism, and Class Stratification." In *The Conflict Between Church and State in Latin America*, ed. Fredrick B. Pike, pp. 197-207. New York: Knopf, 1964.

Ibn Gabirol, Solomon ben Judah. *Avencebrolis (Ibn Gebirol) Fons Vitae*. Ed. C. Baeumker. Beiträge zur Geschichte der Philosophie des Mittelalters, Band 1, Heft 2-4. Munster: Aschendorff, 1892-1895.

Jaffa, Harry V. *Thomism and Aristotelianism*. Chicago: University of Chicago Press, 1952.

Journet, Charles. *L'église du Verbe Incarné*. 2 vols. Paris: Desclée, De Brouwer, 1951-55.

Kleutgen, Joseph. *Institutiones theologicae*. 1 Ratisbon, 1881.

Kristeller, Paul Oskar. *Le Thomisme et la pensée italienne de la Renaissance*. Montréal: Institut d'Etudes Médiévales, Paris: J. Vrin, 1967.

Lécuyer, Joseph. "Les étapes de l'enseignement thomiste sur l'épiscopat." *Revue thomiste*, 57 (1957), 29-52.

———. "Orientations présentes de la théologie de l'épiscopat." In *L'épiscopat et l'église universelle*, edd. Y. Congar and B.-D. Dupuy, pp. 781-811. Paris: Editions du Cerf, 1962.

Lewis, Ewart. *Medieval Political Ideas*. New York: Alfred Knopf, 1954.

Lubac, Henri de. *Corpus mysticum*. Paris: Aubier, 1944.

Macpherson, Crawford B. *Democratic Theory*. Oxford: Clarendon Press, 1973.

———. *The Political Theory of Possessive Individualism: Hobbes to Locke*. Oxford: Clarendon Press, 1962.

Mahoney, John. "'The Church of the Holy Spirit' in Aquinas." *Heythrop Journal*, 15 (1974), 18-36.

Malmberg, Felix. *Ein Leib—Ein Geist*. Freiburg: Herder, 1960.

Mansi, Giovanni Domenico. *Sacrorum conciliorum nova et amplissima collectio....* 31 vols. Venice: A. Zatta, 1759-1798.

Maritain, Jacques. *De Bergson à Thomas d'Aquin*. Paris: Paul Hartmann, 1947.

———. *Man and the State*. Chicago: University of Chicago Press, 1951.

———. *The Rights of Man and Natural Law*. New York: C. Scribner's Sons, 1943.

Marx, Karl. *Early Texts*. Ed. David McLellan. Oxford: Blackwell, 1971.

Mascall, Eric L. *The Openness of Being: Natural Theology Today*. London: Darton, Longman and Todd, 1971.

Maurer, Armand A. "Boethius of Dacia and the Double Truth." *Mediaeval Studies*, 17 (1955), 233-239.

Mayer, Hans E. *The Crusades*. Trans. by J. Gillingham. London: Oxford University Press, 1972.

McGuigan, Mark Randolph. "The Best Form of Government in the Philosophy of St. Thomas Aquinas." Ph.D. dissertation, University of Toronto, 1957.

Ménard, Etienne. *La tradition: révélation, écriture, église selon Saint Thomas d'Aquin*. Bruges, Paris: Desclée, 1964.

Mitterer, Albert. *Geheimnisvoller Leib Christi nach St. Thomas von Aquin und nach Papst Pius XII*. Vienna: Herold, 1950.

Moses ben Maimon. *The Guide of the Perplexed.* Trans. by Shlomo Pines. Chicago: University of Chicago Press, 1963.

Mühlen, Heribert. *Una mystica Persona.* 3rd ed. Paderborn: Schöningh, 1968.

Muratori, Lodovico A. *Rerum Italicarum Scriptores.* 25 vols. Milan: Societas palatina, 1723-1751.

Murray, John Courtney. *The Problem of God Yesterday and Today.* New Haven: Yale University Press, 1964.

———. *We Hold These Truths: Catholic Reflections on the American Proposition.* New York: Sheed and Ward, 1960.

Niebuhr, Reinhold. *Christian Realism and Political Problems.* New York: Scribner, 1953.

———. *The Nature and Destiny of Man,* 1: *Human Nature.* New York: C. Scribners Sons, 1941.

Noonan, John T. *Contraception.* Cambridge, Mass.: Harvard University Press, 1965.

Novak, Michael. *A Time to Build.* New York: Macmillan, 1967.

O'Malley, John W. "Some Renaissance Panegyrics of Aquinas." *Renaissance Quarterly,* 27 (1974), 174-192.

O'Neill, Colman E. "St. Thomas on the Membership of the Church." In *Vatican II: The Theological Dimension,* ed. Anthony D. Lee, pp. 88-140. Washington, D.C.: Thomist Press, 1963. [Originally published as *Thomist,* 27 (1963).]

Papadopoulos, Stylianos G. Ἑλληνικαὶ μεταφράσεις Θωμιστικῶν ἔργων, φιλοθωμισταὶ καὶ ἀντιθωμισταὶ ἐν βυζαντίῳ. (Βιβλιοθήκη τῆς ἐν Ἀθήναις Φιλεκπαιδευτικῆς Ἑταιρείας, 47). Ἀθῆναι, 1967.

Pascal, Blaise. *Pensées.* Trans., notes by H. F. Stewart. New York: Pantheon, 1950.

Pegis, Anton C. "Between Immortality and Death: Some Further Reflections on the *Summa Contra Gentiles.*" *The Monist,* 58 (1974), 1-15.

———. "The Separated Soul and Its Nature in St. Thomas." In *St. Thomas Aquinas, 1274-1974: Commemorative Studies,* 1: 131-158. Toronto: Pontifical Institute of Mediaeval Studies, 1974.

Persson, Per Erik. *Sacra Doctrina: Reason and Revelation in Aquinas.* Philadelphia: Fortress Press, 1970.

Pieper, Josef. *Guide to Thomas Aquinas.* New York: New American Library, 1962.

———. *The Silence of St. Thomas.* New York: Pantheon, 1957; Chicago: Henry Regnery Co., 1965.

Popper, Karl. "On Reason and the Open Society: A Conversation." *Encounter,* 38, no. 5 (May 1972), 13-18.

———. *The Open Society and Its Enemies.* 5th rev. ed. Princeton: Princeton University Press, 1966.

Potvin, Th. R. "Authority in the Church as a Participation in the Authority of Christ According to St. Thomas." *Eglise et théologie,* 5 (1974), 227-251.

Prümmer, Dominicus; and M.-H. Laurent, edd. *Fontes vitae sancti Thomae.* Supplements to *Revue thomiste* (Toulouse), 1911-1934; *Documenta* (fasc. 6; St. Maximin: *Revue thomiste,* 1937).

Rackl, Michael. "Demetrios Kydones als Verteidiger und Uebersetzer des heiligen Thomas von Aquin." *Der Katholik*, 1 (1915), 21-40.

——. "Die ungedruckte Verteidigungsschrift des Demetrios Kydones für Thomas von Aquin gegen Neilos Kabasilas." *Divus Thomas* (Wien-Berlin), 7 (1920), 303-317.

Rawls, John. *A Theory of Justice.* Cambridge, Mass.: Harvard University Press, 1971.

Rikhof, H. "Corpus Christi Mysticum: An Inquiry into Thomas Aquinas' Use of a Term." *Bijdragen*, 37 (1976), 149-171.

Robinson, Carol Jackson. "Dis-Honoring St. Thomas." *The Wanderer*, 23 May 1974.

Sauras, Emilio. "The Members of the Church." *Thomist*, 27 (1963), 78-87.

Scandone, F. "La vita, la famiglia e la patria dei S. Tommaso." In *S. Tommaso d'Aquino. Miscellanea storico-artistica*, pp. 1-110. Rome: Manuzio, 1924.

Schenk, Max. *Die Unfehlbarkeit des Papstes in der Heiligsprechung.* Freiburg, Switz.: Paulusverlag, 1965.

Schindler, Alfred. *Wort und Analogie in Augustins Trinitätslehre.* Tübingen, J. C. B. Mohre, 1965.

Schmaus, Michael. *Die psychologische Trinitätslehre des heiligen Augustinus.* Munster: Aschendorff, 1927.

Seckler, Max. *Das Heil in der Geschichte.* Munich: Kösel-Verlag, 1964.

Sigmund, Paul E. *The Ideologies of the Developing Nations.* 2nd rev. ed. New York: Praeger, 1972.

——, ed. *Models of Political Change in Latin America.* New York: Praeger, 1970.

——. *Natural Law in Political Thought.* Cambridge, Mass.: Winthrop Publishers, 1971.

Simon, Yves. *Philosophy of Democratic Government.* Chicago: University of Chicago Press, 1951.

Stark, Werner. *The Contained Economy; An Interpretation of Medieval Economic Thought.* Aquinas Society of London, Papers, 26. London: Blackfriars, 1956.

Synan, Edward A. "Cardinal Virtues in the Cosmos of Saint Bonaventure." In *S[an] Bonaventura 1274-1974*, 3: 21-38. Grottaferrata, Rome: Collegio S. Bonaventura, 1973.

——. *The Popes and the Jews in the Middle Ages.* New York: Macmillan, 1965.

Tavard, George H. "The Bull Unam Sanctam of Boniface viii." In *Papal Primacy and the Universal Church*, ed. Paul C. Empie and T. A. Murphy, pp. 105-119. Lutherans and Catholics in Dialogue 5. Minneapolis: Augsburg Publishing House, 1974.

Thomas Aquinas. *Commentary on Nicomachean Ethics.* Trans. by C. I. Litzinger. 2 vols. Chicago: Henry Regnery Co., 1964.

——. *In Aristotelis librum de anima commentarium.* Ed. A. M. Pirotta. Turin: Marietti, 1925.

——. *On Kingship to the King of Cyprus.* Trans. by G. B. Phelan, rev. intro., notes by I. Th. Eschman. Toronto: Pontifical Institute of Mediaeval Studies, 1949.

——. *Opera omnia.* 25 vols. Parma, 1852-1873.

——. *Opera omnia iussu impensaque Leonis xiii. P. M.* Vols. 1—. Rome, 1882—.

——. *Selected Political Writings.* Ed. A. P. D'Entrèves. Oxford: Blackwell, 1948.

——. *Summa theologiae.* Blackfriars ed. 60 vols. New York: McGraw-Hill, London: Eyre and Spottiswoode, 1964—.

——. *Tractatus de unitate intellectus contra Averroistas.* Ed. by Leo W. Keeler. Textus et documenta, series philosophica 12. Rome: Pontificia universitas Gregoriana, 1936.

Thomas de Cantimpré. *Bonum universale de apibus.* 2 vols. Douai: B. Belleri, 1627.

Tierney, Brian. *Origins of Papal Infallibility, 1150-1350.* Leiden: E. J. Brill, 1972.

Touquédec, Joseph de. "Le contenu des 'Deus Sources'." *Etudes,* 214 (20 March 1933), 641-668; 215 (5 April 1933), 26-54.

Troeltsch, Ernst. *The Social Teaching of the Christian Churches.* 2 vols. New York: Macmillan, 1931.

[Vatican ii, Council of]. "Justice in the World." *Catholic Mind,* March 1972, pp. 52-64.

——. See also Abbott, W. M.

Vauthier, E. "Le Saint-Esprit principe d'unité de l'Eglise d'après saint Thomas d'Aquin." *Mélanges de science religieuse,* 5 (1948), 175-196; 6 (1949), 57-80.

Vodopivec, Giovanni. "Membri *in re* ed appartenenza *in voto* alla Chiesa di Cristo." *Euntes Docete,* 10 (1957), 65-104.

Voegelin, Eric. *Anamnesis: zur Theorie der Geschichte und Politik.* Munich: Piper, 1966.

——. "Equivalences of Experience and Symbolization in History." In *Eternità a Storia,* pp. 349-362. Rome: Istituto accademico di Roma, 1969.

——. *Order and History,* 4. *The Ecumenic Age.* Baton Rouge: Louisiana State University Press, 1975.

Walsh, James J. *The Thirteenth, Greatest of Centuries.* New York: Catholic Summer School Press, 1907.

Walz, Angelus; and Paul Novarina. *Saint Thomas d'Aquin.* Philosophes médiévaux 5. Louvain: Publications universitaires, Paris: Béatrice-Nauwelaerts, 1962.

Weisheipl, James A. *Friar Thomas d'Aquino. His Life, Thought, and Work.* New York: Doubleday, 1974.

White, Morton. *Religion, Politics and the Higher Learning.* Cambridge, Mass.: Harvard University Press, 1959.

Wiarda, Howard J. "Toward a Framework for the Study of Political Change in the Iberic-Latin Tradition: the Corporative Model." *World Politics,* 25 (1972-1973), 206-250.

William of Auvergne. See Guilelmus Arvernus.

William of Saint-Amore. See Guilelmus de Sancto Amore.

William of Tocco. See Prümmer, Dominicus, et al.

Index

Abelard, 7
abstraction, 56-57
Acton, Lord, 105
Adam of Marsh, 5
Adelesa (sister of Thomas Aquinas), 13
Adler, Mortimer, 73
adultery, 70
agent intellect, 5
Aimone (brother of Thomas Aquinas), 19
Alan of Lille, 2
Albertus Magnus, 17, 23
Alexander of Hales, 17n
Aleyde/Alix of Brabant, 17n
Alfarabi, 20
Ambrose, Saint, 32, 151n
angels, 37; knowledge of God, 28
apocalypticism in the 13th century, 130
Apostles, 139-140, 148
apostolicity of the church, 128
Aquino, 12, 13
Arabic learning, 4, 8-19
aristocracy, 116-117
Aristotle, 5, 8, 9, 9n, 11n, 19, 21, 22, 24,
   30, 50, 51, 52, 53, 54, 57, 58, 59, 60,
   61, 62, 68, 69, 71, 77, 78, 80, 82, 84,
   93, 96, 97, 106, 108, 112, 112n, 113,
   115, 132; *Categories*, 30; *Metaphysics*,
   21, 21n, 25n, 30; *Nicomachean Ethics*,
   59, 69, 98, 112; *Physics*, 21, 21n;
   Politics, 69; *Posterior Analytics*, 21n;
   astronomy, 21; biology, 21; cosmology,
   21; epistēmē/science, 21, 22; god/gods,
   21, 59; physics, 21.
Pseudo-Aristotle, 9
Athanasius, 31, 37
attributes predicated to God, 19
Augustine of Hippo, 10, 16, 24, 29, 32, 33,
   36-37, 39, 41, 43-46, 52, 83, 108, 126,
   131, 147; *City of God*, 67; *On Eighty-
   Three Questions*, 34; and reason, 29; and
   soul, 29; and Trinity, 29
Austria, politics of, 72
autarky, *see* self-sufficiency
authentica, 2
authoritarianism, 72
avarice, 98-100

Averroës, 5, 8-9, 20, 24, 59
Avicebron, *see* Ibn Gebirol
Avicenna, 20, 151

Bacon, Roger, 5
Bañez, Domingo, 3
baptism, 135-137, 138, 147, 150
Barth, Karl, 109
Bartholomew of Lucca, *see* Tolomeo of
   Lucca
beatitudo, 80, 81, 85, 86
being, 25; *see also* existence
Bellarmine, Robert (1542-1621), 146
Benedict, Saint, 130
Bergson, Henri, 106, 119-123
Bible in 13th-century theology, 22-24; *see
   also* Index of Scriptural Citations
binarium famosissimum, 18
bishops, 139-141, 148, 149n
Bishops, Roman Synod of (1971), 152
body, 51, 52, 62, 134; *see also* soul and
   body
Body, Mystical, *see* Mystical Body
Boethius, *De consolatione philosophiae*, 30-
   32
Boethius of Dacia, 8n
Bonaventure, Saint, 8n, 129, 142
Bonhoeffer, Thomas, 151
Boniface VIII, pope, 6, 142, 142n
Brabant, duchess of, 17
Brecht, Arnold, 123
Bruno, Giordano, 18

capitalism, 71
causality, 58
charity, 70-71
Chenu, Marie-Dominique, 2-3, 4, 11n, 15,
   38, 111
Christ, 152; and the Church, 133-135, 147
Chile, politics of, 72, 73, 75
Church, 11, 125-153; as community, 127;
   in the 13th century, 3
church and state, 85, 117-118, 144, 146,
   152
Cicero, 34, 83
civic virtue, 103

Index of Scriptural Citations

Index of Citations of the Works
of Saint Thomas Aquinas